Improving Business Performance with Lean

Improving Business Performance with Lean

Second Edition

James R. Bradley

 BUSINESS EXPERT PRESS

First published in 2012 by
Business Expert Press, LLC
222 East 46th Street, New York, NY 10017
www.businessexpertpress.com

ISBN-13: 978-1-63157-051-3 (paperback)
ISBN-13: 978-1-63157-052-0 (e-book)

Business Expert Press Supply and Operations Management Collection

Collection ISSN: 2156-8189 (print)
Collection ISSN: 2156-8200 (electronic)

Cover and interior design by Exeter Premedia Services Private Ltd., Chennai, India

First edition: 2012
Second edition: 2015

10 9 8 7 6 5 4 3 2 1

Printed in the United States of America.

Abstract

This book is a concise introduction to the essential concepts and tools used in the *Lean* method for improving business processes. It constitutes a sufficient toolkit to enable practitioners to quickly start using Lean to improve business processes in their workplace. Alternatively, it can also serve as a textbook in undergraduate or master's programs. This book succinctly describes the benefits of Lean in manufacturing, sales, administration, distribution, health care, and other industries, as well as providing a step-by-step description of how Lean is applied.

Keywords

continuous improvement, efficiency, lead time reduction, Lean, Lean manufacturing, Lean Six Sigma, process analysis, process improvement, process management, process mapping, value stream mapping

Contents

Acknowledgments

I am grateful to the many opportunities that I have been provided to observe and study processes, which has allowed me to learn which process improvement practices are most effective and which attributes of culture are necessary to foster behaviors that support continuous improvement. I am especially grateful to Lord Corporation, where I was given my first opportunity to experience Lean in action, and to my colleague A. Paul Blossom: Our continual dialog has greatly deepened my understanding of Lean.

About This Book

This book is structured to succinctly describe how to apply the tools associated with Lean to improve business processes. It can be thought of as a quick-start manual that covers the essential tools, philosophies, and implementation strategies of Lean. The tools covered herein are those, in the author's experience, most frequently applied and generally applicable to processes in all contexts. Descriptions of other, less frequently used tools can be found in the citations included in this book. There are many soft issues with implementing Lean, such as how to organize a companywide effort, how to provide proper incentives, and how to build a culture conducive to Lean. Although this book addresses these important issues, more comprehensive coverage is available in other resources. This book does contain all the philosophical underpinnings related to Lean in general and, in particular, to the tools that are described. In summary, this book has attempted to include the most vital information for a reader whose goal is to effectively practice Lean as soon as possible. Including any additional materials that would not likely be immediately needed and would have unnecessarily delayed the reader from getting started with Lean. Therefore, this book can be thought of as a lean presentation of Lean.

The main text in each chapter is presented as simply and clearly as possible to communicate the essence of Lean and its tools. The finer details of Lean that are necessary, but that might sidetrack a reader, are presented in sidebars throughout the book. A reader who ignores these frames upon the first reading will still be presented with a comprehensive description of the main concepts. The reader might, however, want to return to these finer points in subsequent passes through the material after he or she understands the basics and begins to apply Lean.

Readers will find that the techniques encompassed by Lean are very intuitive and quickly learned. However, as with any topic, the lessons of Lean cannot be fully absorbed until they are practiced. Therefore, practical exercises are included at the end of chapters that suggest how a reader can further his or her understanding by applying Lean in real settings. In addition, questions are provided in association with these exercises where appropriate to help readers reflect on their experience with the exercises to maximize the learning benefit. Spending some time quietly and thoughtfully entertaining these questions will greatly enhance the benefit of the exercises. Other exercises are also presented at the end of the chapters where concepts can be explored in the format of a typical homework problem.

This book can be used in many modes. It can be used as a self-study reference, or it can be used in a course. In either case, case studies are provided in the appendix to this book that offer the opportunity to exercise all the concepts in the book and might serve as a final examination in a course. Ideally, this book can be used as a text in a course where students are applying Lean in real companies while simultaneously studying this book and using it as a reference.

This book is divided into three parts. Part I, *Basics of Lean*, describes the motivation for why companies and organizations should want to do Lean, basic process analysis and mapping skills, and the discipline that a company must demonstrate in order to make Lean successful. Part II, *Lean Tools*, discusses tools used in Lean to improve processes. This part of the book does not contain an exhaustive reference to all the tools used in Lean but rather the most frequently used tools in manufacturing, service, and administrative processes. Part III, *Implementing Lean*, discusses how to implement Lean, as well as some of the more frequently encountered roadblocks. Mastering Lean requires practice and Part IV offers opportunities for practice.

CHAPTER 1

A Brief Introduction to Lean

Have you ever been frustrated because you needed to wait a long time for a good or service to be delivered to you? Do you sometimes feel that companies do not value your time and decrease your personal productivity because they cause you to wait idly while they take their time to serve you? Have you ever had experiences similar to any of the following?

1. You arrived at the doctor's office on time; you were even a few minutes early. Then, you waited in the waiting room, well past your appointment time, before being called into an examination room. Then, you waited again in the exam room until the doctor finally arrived.

2. You ordered furniture, maybe a sofa or a chair, from a company that makes furniture to order because they could not possibly stock all the upholstery and wood finish alternatives that they offer. Upon purchase, you were informed that delivery would be in 6 to 10 weeks. You were excited about getting the new furniture but were frustrated that you needed to wait so long before receiving it.

3. You needed to order some equipment or repair parts for your company that were vitally needed to keep your operation moving. You waited a long time to receive the parts, and in the meantime, your operation's performance suffered because you needed to implement workarounds like having employees work extra hours or produce goods of inferior quality.

4. You traveled by air, your plane arrived at its destination, and the pilot taxied the plane to its gate. For two and one-half hours, you looked at the Jetway as you waited for the ground personnel to move the Jetway up to the aircraft. You either missed your next flight or returned home later than otherwise necessary.

5. You traveled by air and arrived at your destination on time, but your bags did not. You wondered how your bags could not have made your connection, which allowed for two hours between flights.

6. You contacted a landscaping or construction company to discuss the possibility of undertaking a home improvement project but found that the contractor took a very long time to return your call. Perhaps your call was never returned. You found yourself wondering how you could trust a company to finish a job on time if they had difficulty simply returning your call.

You are the customer in all these situations, and you might well be upset and frustrated, possibly so much so that you would consider changing doctors, furniture companies, equipment suppliers, airlines, or contractors. The inability of the companies in the preceding examples to provide you with the goods and services you desire in a timely manner is due to these organizations' inability to execute steps of a procedure in a timely manner. You may wait in the doctor's office, for one of many reasons, because serving previous patients took a long time. You waited for your furniture because it takes the furniture manufacturer a long time to build the wood frame, apply finish, and then upholster it. Your order for equipment took a long time because it must be manufactured first or because the equipment distributor's supply is slow or unreliable.

The purpose of the methodology called *Lean* is to remedy situations like these by reducing the time that it takes to provide customers with what they desire and, therefore, improve customers' satisfaction with a company's goods or services. One benefit, among many, of this improved satisfaction is continued and, perhaps, increased patronage from those who are served. We will give examples in Chapter 2 of how making an effort to reduce lead time also improves business performance in other ways, including improved quality, less investment in inventory, less rework, and less warranty expense.

You might have noticed that the previous scenarios were written from the perspective of a customer, and similarly, many authors emphasize that the focus of Lean projects is to enhance customers' experiences. We will see, however, that while many Lean projects have this external focus on the customers, Lean projects can be focused on providing internal benefit to the company by reducing cost, investment in inventory, and the cost of poor quality.

The History of Lean

Lean was first applied in manufacturing and was called *Lean Manufacturing*, but more recently, its principles are being applied in healthcare, administrative offices, food service, and other business contexts. To reflect its applicability to these other contexts, Lean Manufacturing is often referred to now as simply *Lean*. Arguably, Lean grew out of the Toyota Production System (TPS). TPS was developed in post–World War II Japan as the Toyoda family transitioned from manufacturing automatic looms to cars. A lack of resources in postwar Japan required *lean* operations with the minimum of parts inventory, factory, space, equipment, and labor. While the primary genesis of TPS was the need to maximize the production of automobiles with the minimum possible resources, TPS also contributed to Toyota's continued quality improvement, which in turn led to the improved competitive position of Toyota vis-à-vis the former Big Three automakers of the United States.

Business Processes

An essential concept that we will use in this book is that of a *process*. A process is a series of sequential steps that are executed in order to accomplish some goal. For example, if the goal is to build an end table, the steps employed in a furniture factory might be the following:

1. Cut wood parts to appropriate length and width.
2. Cut mortises and tenons in the wood parts that enable the parts to be joined.
3. Glue pieces together.
4. Sand assembled parts.
5. Apply stain and finish.

It is frequently helpful to display a process graphically using rectangles to indicate each process step, as in Figure 1.1. This process can be associated with the pictorial representation of an end table in Figure 1.2.

Figure 1.1 Process map for furniture manufacture

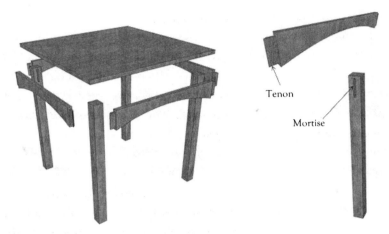

Figure 1.2 End table construction

Everything accomplished in business can be described as a process as we have done in Figure 1.1 for a furniture-manufacturing process. Whether you work in manufacturing, an administrative process (e.g., human resources, procurement, supplier management, business strategy, business development, accounting), or a service process (e.g., health care, food service, call center), what it takes to accomplish anything can be described as a series of steps, or a process. Processes are often more complex than the one in Figure 1.1 in the sense that they have many more steps, but we will postpone discussion of those situations until later in the book.

Lean can be thought of as a set of tools to improve a process, where the type of improvement we will focus on is to reduce the elapsed time required to execute the process from start to finish, which is called process *lead time*. Thus Lean is a *process improvement methodology*. Other process improvement processes exist, most notably Six Sigma. In contrast to Lean, the primary goal of using Six Sigma is to improve quality, to reduce manufacturing defects, or to reduce service and administrative errors.

Lean and Six Sigma are currently the two dominant process improvement methodologies, and they are often implemented simultaneously; when that is the case, the approach is called Lean Six Sigma.

Lean and Six Sigma can be further contrasted by comparing the tools used in each of these methodologies. Many of the tools used in Six Sigma rely on the application of statistics to processes to determine what defects are most important to address and what the root causes of the defects are and testing to see if a proposed remedy actually resolves the root causes. Learning the statistics can be difficult for many, and furthermore, collecting the data on which to use the statistical tools can be painstaking. In contrast, people who learn Lean find its tools almost without exception to be simple, intuitive, and easily learned. This is one argument for using Lean before Six Sigma: The tools are more easily learned and applied, thus accelerating the benefit achieved in improving business processes. Another argument for applying Lean first is that it generally results in a simpler process that is more readily evaluated with Six Sigma—indeed, many of the possible root causes of quality errors are likely to be resolved by streamlining the process with Lean before quality issues are explicitly addressed with Six Sigma. The more painstaking and time-consuming Six Sigma tools, then, do not have to be used to find more obvious root causes of defects that have already been sorted out.

While Lean will most frequently be the best set of tools to use first, the ultimate test is to determine which measure of performance is the most important to improve first. If quality improvement is the most important goal, then perhaps Six Sigma should be used first. Conversely, if reducing the time required to execute a process is most important (or one of the many accompanying benefits that we will discuss), then Lean should be used first. Which metrics are most important are determined at the outset of a project, and this is the first step in determining whether Lean or Six Sigma tools are most appropriate. Often, it is appropriate to apply tools from both Lean and Six Sigma. The bottom line is this: Use whatever tools are most appropriate. This book focuses on Lean, however, since it is frequently the methodology that gives the biggest process improvement bang for the buck—that is, the greatest benefit compared with the effort expended.

Returning to our discussion of Lean and TPS, one will find that virtually all of the tools associated with TPS are used in Lean. There is one tool used in Lean, however, that might never be observed in an application of TPS (at least this is the author's experience). That tool is called *value stream mapping*, which we describe in Chapter 2.

PART I

Basics of Lean

CHAPTER 2

The Motivation for Implementing Lean

We begin this chapter by establishing the link between process lead time and work-in-process inventory. Specifically, we explain how reducing process lead time also reduces work-in-process inventory. While reducing work-in-process is a fundamental goal of some Lean projects, it is not the main goal of all projects. So in the remainder of the chapter we document how reducing lead time improves many other important business metrics in various industries.

Lead Time and Work-in-Process

We begin with an intuitive example that serves as an analogy to the business contexts that we will subsequently discuss. This analogy considers a pipe that carries water, which might be the water that fills a swimming pool or water used in making paper or another manufactured material. Specifically, consider two such pipes as shown in Figure 2.1. Both pipes have identical diameters and carry water at the same flow rate (gallons per minute). Since they have the same diameters and flow rates, we know that a drop of water flowing down the center of the pipe would have the same average velocity in both pipes. Thus the time to traverse the longer pipe, intuitively, takes a greater amount of time than a drop flowing down the shorter pipe.

Long pipe

Short pipe

Figure 2.1 Two pipes for carrying water

Now, we ask the question, which pipe has more water in it? (No, this is not a trick question.) Of course, the longer pipe has more water in it than the shorter pipe: Although both pipes do the same work (gallons per minute delivered), the longer pipe has a greater volume. Therefore, the longer pipe holds more water and requires more time to traverse, whereas, conversely, the shorter pipe holds less water and takes less time to traverse. The correlation between amount of water in the pipe and the time to get through the pipe is not accidental and carries over generally to the business processes that we consider in the remainder of this chapter and, indeed, to all processes.

For those who prefer to think in mathematical terms, we can describe the situation with the long and short water pipes, and the relationship between lead time and work-in-process, with a mathematical formula. Little's Law is a mathematical law of physical processes (named after John Little, who proved this law) that states that the average work-in-process inventory (I) is equal to the product of the average processing rate (R) and the average process lead time (T)

$$I = R \times T$$

I is measured in units of whatever entity flows through a process, T is measured in time, and R is measured in units per time increment (e.g., units per minute, units per hour, units per year).

The only practically relevant requirements for this formula to be true are the following:

1. The quantities I, R, and T must be averages.
2. The flow into the process over the long run must equal the flow out of the process.

Averages must be calculated over many observations. For example, one can estimate the average inventory by observing inventory on many different occasions and then averaging those values. Similarly, the average lead time might be computed by observing the lead time of many units that flow through a process and then averaging those values. An average rate can be calculated by dividing the number of units completed by the process over some duration by the length of time over which the observations were made. We cannot expect Little's Law to hold when our measurement of I is a single observation, when R is computed over a short time duration, or T is based on a single or a small number of observations.

Issues arise if the flow into and out of the process are not the same, as stated in one of our assumptions. First, we observe that it would be difficult to apply Little's Law in this case because it requires one value of R: Should the inflow or outflow rate be used for R? The confusion that arises when the inflow rate differs from the outflow rate of the process is a sign that Little's Law cannot be applied in this case. Indeed, if more goods flow into a manufacturing operation than are completed, we should expect to see an ever-increasing inventory level within the plant. In that case, no value of R used in Little's Law could predict I.

The main point of discussing water pipes and Little's Law is to demonstrate that in-process inventory and lead time are inextricably linked. If the processing rate R is held constant over time, then Little's Law demonstrates that the average lead time (T) is proportional to the average inventory level (I). Thus although Lean focuses on reducing lead time, we can clearly see how another benefit is derived: Reducing lead time T reduces inventory I. In manufacturing processes, the benefits of reduced inventory are clear: Reduced investment and improved quality are two such benefits. In processes where entities other than manufactured goods flow through the process, the work-in-process that is reduced might be invoices that are being issued, medical patients, or project proposals. We will see in the examples that follow how reducing inventory in these cases improves business performance.

The Value of Lead Time Reduction in Various Industries

Metrics are numerical measures that answer the question *How well is our company performing?* Companies use many metrics to judge their performance. Examples include the following:

1. Profit
2. Cost

3. Sales levels
4. Return on investment and assets
5. Working capital level
6. Product or service quality
7. Cost of rework and warranty repair
8. On-time delivery
9. Fulfillment accuracy (shipping the right quantities of the right products)
10. Inventory levels or inventory turns
11. Labor efficiency and productivity
12. Cases processed per person per hour
13. Order to delivery time
14. Time required to develop and introduce new products and services

The appropriate metrics vary with the industry, the type of process, and managerial goals. For example, while measures of efficiency and productivity are ubiquitous, the specific measure used in distribution center operations (cases per hour) is different than you would find in manufacturing operations (e.g., cars per labor hour). In addition, we would expect that the portfolio of metrics used in a manufacturing operation would be tailored to a particular company's strategy, which differs from company to company.

In Chapter 1 we described Lean as a methodology for reducing the lead time required to execute the steps of a process. Of the metrics listed previously, only two describe the lead time of a process (the last two metrics in the list). A reader might wonder at this point, therefore, how effective Lean would be when most metrics of interest to companies are not time-based metrics. One of the goals of this chapter is to show that although Lean focuses on reducing lead time, it indirectly influences most, if not all, of a company's important metrics. Exposing the connection between lead time and other metrics in the examples that follow helps managers see the value of Lean for their business and might, perhaps, motivate them to adopt it. The examples come from a variety of industries that use different metrics, and we will describe how reducing lead time also improves the relevant metrics in each context.

Manufacturing

Consider, for example, the manufacture of automobiles in an assembly plant. The processing steps in the assembly plant can be thought of as a pipeline through which cars flow. Just as in the pipelines that carried water, the longer the automobile pipeline, the greater the number of cars in the pipeline. Thus, in manufacturing, longer processing lead times also imply a higher level of work-in-process inventory.

Higher levels of inventory increase costs in a number of ways:

1. An investment in inventory for which customers have not yet paid causes a financial carrying cost: Either interest payments are required for money borrowed to finance the inventory, coupon payments must be made on bonds, stock dividends must be paid on stock, or, if inventory is self-financed, the financial return on alternative investments is foregone.

2. As inventory levels increase, quality decreases. A good rule of thumb is the longer goods stay in process, the greater the opportunity for them to be damaged through mishandling, being misplaced, or being stolen. People who have worked in manufacturing have many tales about work-in-process, or finished goods, being hit by forklifts, dropped, or damaged in any number of ways.

3. Damage during storage is one way increased inventory levels increase rework and scrap costs. In addition, the greater the quantity of work-in-process inventory between two workstations, the greater the number of units that need to be repaired when a manufacturing defect is discovered.

4. In-process inventory also exposes a company to other potential costs, such as obsolescence or the cost of engineering changes. When a product's design changes parts, in-process inventory must either be reworked or scrapped, and the cost of either rework or scrap increases with the number of units in process that are not yet finished.

5. Other costs are borne in industries where component costs decline rapidly. For example, some high-value electronic components have decreased historically at a rate of 1 percent per week, while the selling prices of finished products decline. Therefore, the longer the inventory stays in process, the higher the cost of material and

the lower the price that the customer will pay for finished products made with more expensive parts: Margin is squeezed on both sides of the profit equation.

6. Labor efficiency decreases with increased inventory: Although the output and revenue of a company are not enhanced, the added operations to move, rework, and remanufacture goods add unnecessary cost.

A case study from Harvard Publishing about LanTech, which makes stretch wrap machines[1] for manufacturing and distribution companies, gives a good illustration of the causes of excess inventory in manufacturing.[2] More to the point of this chapter, it clearly demonstrates the link between reduced inventory and improved quality. While LanTech sought to reduce their process lead time, which they did by over 90 percent, they found that the number of defects per unit decreased from 8 defects per unit to 0.8 defects per unit. This may be surprising to some, since process improvement did not focus on quality at all. Quality improvement was a natural by-product of the lead time reduction for some of the reasons mentioned previously.

Distribution

Once manufactured, products need to be made available to customers. *Distribution* is the name given to this function. Large retailers, for example, often manage their own networks of facilities for distribution composed of regional distribution centers (RDCs) that supply stores, central distribution centers (CDCs) that supply RDCs, and import distribution centers (IDCs) that receive imported goods and then ship them to either CDCs or RDCs. Other supply chain facilities might include cross-docking facilities that receive containers from overseas, each with large quantities of a few items, and transfer those goods onto many trailers, each with small quantities of many goods destined for retail stores or RDCs. One example of such a global supply chain is shown in Figure 2.2. Companies that sell a range of products with different characteristics and handling needs might have separate supply chains for different types of goods. For example, grocery items, especially those that must be refrigerated, might be distributed through a different set of facilities than dry

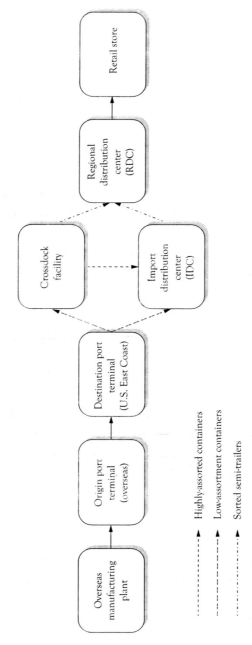

Figure 2.2 Global retail distribution supply chain

goods, such as hardware, electronics, toys, and furniture, as would be handled by the supply chain in Figure 2.2.

Distribution might be described as a necessary evil. Getting goods from the point of manufacture to the market is necessary to get the goods to the customers, although the goods in distribution serve no useful business purpose until they get to the retail stores—you can't sell goods to customers from a distribution center's shelves. Any excess goods in transit, therefore, cause unnecessary costs, many of the same type described previously for manufacturing processes. In distribution networks where reducing unproductive inventory is a focus, it is clear that focusing on reducing lead time is effective given the prior discussion in this chapter. Consequently, one finds in distribution many metrics called *level of service* metrics, which specify the maximum time allowed to complete any one step of the distribution process. While one might not immediately guess what these metrics are from the name, they explicitly motivate people to quickly move goods along their way. Thus these distribution metrics are perfectly aligned with Lean.

In addition, a shorter replenishment lead time, which is a term used to describe how much time passes from the time an order is placed by a retail store until the order is delivered from the RDC, implies greater responsiveness. Quick replenishment of the retail store in response to unusually high sales volumes helps the retail store reduce how much inventory it needs to carry for demand spikes while still satisfying a high percentage of customers with a product they want, when they want it. Furthermore, greater responsiveness can also imply that the retail store will run out of goods less often, which increases revenue.

Service Industries

In contrast to manufacturing processes, the term *service process* is often used to describe a series of steps executed to provide a customer with something other than a physical product. Some examples include a call center to respond to software problems, food service, grounds maintenance, home repair services, credit card services, and governmental services such as providing building permits. In manufacturing and distribution, what physical entities flow through the process—that is, manufactured goods.

In service industries, one might envision the customer themselves flowing through the process when they need to be physically present or, perhaps, the customer's request flowing through the system, which eventually results in something being done for the customer. In a movie theater line, it is the customer who waits until it is his or her time to be served. In other cases, what flows through the system is either paperwork or some electronic representation of the customer's request: A heating and air conditioning repair service would have a written or electronic list of customers awaiting service and information about what their problems were. The longer either customers or some manifestation of their need waits in the pipeline, the longer any one customer waits to be served, and we would expect in most cases that customer satisfaction and the prospects for future business would decrease.

Also, as implied by Little's Law, the number of customers who are waiting for service at any one time increases as the average customer wait time increases. Thus reducing the average waiting time of customers also reduces the average number of customers who are waiting. Are there any benefits in reducing the number of customers who are waiting? Sometimes waiting customers increase operation cost just as inventory that is waiting increases manufacturing cost. For example, where customers are inclined to use the telephone or send e-mail messages to ask *when will I be served*, more people in the queue implies greater costs for call centers or whatever process might handle these requests. In another context, a customer's call to an auto parts store to inquire about the status of a special order causes sales associates to perform work. The longer the delivery time for the part, the greater the number of calls the customer is likely to make and the greater will be the workload on the sales associates.

Administrative Processes

Administrative processes might be defined as processes that businesses must execute even though they generate no revenue. For example, companies must hire employees, submit tax documents, file environmental reports, and train employees on technical, health, and safety issues. These activities, however, do not contribute to sales; rather, they add to cost. When Lean is used to address such processes, it reduces not only the length of time required to accomplish a task, such as the time required to hire a new employee, but also the effort required on the part of employees and the concomitant cost. In addition, opportunities to reduce the number of errors are routinely exposed in administrative processes when Lean is applied such that quality and customer satisfaction can be improved and the costs associated with mitigating errors can be eliminated.

Benefits of applying Lean to administrative processes are likely to vary with the process, but they can be significant. For example, consider the process used to prepare invoices to send to customers. Keeping our short and long pipes in mind, an invoice preparation process that takes a longer time will have more unfinished invoices in it. Since a customer's payment clock starts ticking only when they receive the invoice, the greater the number of unfinished invoices, the greater the requirements are for funding the cost of products and services provided for which no cash has yet been received—in other words, cash flow suffers. Thus a company is in a revenue-deficit position that is directly proportional to how long it takes to issue invoices. This causes the financial structure of a company to be weakened and more working capital to be financed through loans, bonds, or stock or more of the company's own cash to be invested in the business. Each of those financing instruments has its costs that the company must bear.

Sales

We have already mentioned how reducing lead time in distribution networks can increase sales because goods can be available on retail shelves a higher percentage of time while the retailer needs to carry less inventory. In some industries, companies play a more active role in generating sales than to merely reliably stock the shelves so that customers can find what they are looking for as they peruse the shelves at their convenience. In other industries, sales are garnered only when a company successfully completes an application for a new sale. Companies that are building new manufacturing sites, for example, would issue a request for quotation (RFQ) that invites general contractors to specify the price that they would charge for completing the project. A bidder would also typically specify quality attributes of the completed project, a construction timeline, and other data requested in the RFQ. When issued, an RFQ specifies the date by which bidders must submit these responses.

Successfully submitting a response to an RFQ and eventually being awarded the job requires, at a minimum, that the response be filed on time and that all required information is specified in the response. From the bidder's perspective, the information they provide must also be accurate: Too high a price will cause the opportunity to be lost, too low a price will possibly win the contract but cause a financial loss, and promising delivery dates and quality levels that are not met will jeopardize later business.

The requirement to file RFQ responses on time is directly in line with Lean's objective of reducing lead time. An ancillary benefit of reducing the lead time for responding to an RFQ is that a company would submit more responses on time and, subsequently, win a greater percentage of the possible contract opportunities, thus increasing revenues. The author's experience in applying Lean to RFQ processes is that reduced lead time of preparation also leads to fewer errors that cause companies not to successfully generate new business or that are costly to resolve.

Health Care Processes

The health care system is currently a focus of much attention as health care costs continue to increase. Recently, Lean has increasingly been applied to health care processes to both increase efficiency and to reduce errors, which in this field can result in death. Focusing on reducing the lead times of these critical health care processes leads to improved health care outcomes due to more prompt and more appropriate treatment through:

1. Reduced lead time for diagnosed patients to start appropriate treatment;[3]
2. Patient's reduced lead time through their treatment process;
3. Reduced lead time to process and administer prescription medications in the hospital or on an outpatient basis;
4. Improved nursing processes in hospitals.

In addition, the effectiveness of Lean in reducing errors in health care has been documented.[4] Because Lean also reduces the cost of operations in hospitals and other health care facilities, patient care improves while cost is reduced. Costs are reduced or, alternatively, revenue is increased in these ways:

1. Reducing the lead time to change an operating room over from one surgery to another reduces hospital costs, increases revenue generation from facilities, and improves patient outcomes by reducing errors.
2. A more efficient and timely replenishment system for medical supplies increases the availability of supplies when they are needed while reducing the number of supplies purchased.[5]

Conclusions

We have shown in this chapter that, regardless of the industry, reducing process lead time improves business performance. If the types of benefits we have described are valuable for the company where you work or a company that you own, then implementing Lean may be an important tool to help improve your business processes.

Before the 1950s, it was commonly thought that increasing quality required higher cost. Similarly, our intuition might lead us to think that reducing lead time must make other business metrics worse. However, Philip Crosby argued in his famous book, *Quality Is Free*,[6] that contrary to the popular belief at the time, quality can most often be improved at the same time cost is reduced. That is, improving quality does not increase manufacturing cost. Similarly, the examples we have given show that there is most often not a trade-off between lead time and other business metrics: If we reduce lead time with Lean, then other business metrics improve as well. Moreover, the upfront investment to implement improvements found through Lean is often small, making the return on investment of Lean high. We have discussed the benefits of Lean in this chapter, but we have not discussed the costs of Lean or the barriers to implementing Lean, which will be discussed in Chapter 5, Chapter 7, and Chapter 13. The three most frequently encountered barriers to implementing Lean are the following:

1. Lean relies on the standardization of processes, which people often resist.

2. Many companies operate perpetually with an overwhelming number of imminent or past due deadlines or continually having a barrage of disasters needing attention. Operating in firefighting mode makes it difficult to devote resources to efforts with long-term benefits, such as Lean.

3. Applying Lean naturally leads to greater efficiencies. If workers fear that improving greater output per worker will cause the workforce to be reduced, it is difficult to get them to participate in improving processes. This is unfortunate because it is the workers who primarily need to be involved in Lean.

Exercises

1. Select something that is done in your workplace or in your personal life and map the process by doing the following:

    a. Discover and document the steps that are required to accomplish this task.

    b. List the metrics (numerical measures) that would enable you to determine how well this process is being done. Is the process currently being measured by these metrics?

    c. Is reducing lead time important to this process? By reducing lead time, what other metrics might be improved?

    d. While you were performing the previous steps, did you discover anything about how the process is performed that you did not know before? Were some of the steps difficult to research?

    e. As you were listing the sequential steps of the process, did you have any immediate ideas on ways to improve the process?

    In your workplace, you might analyze a process in which your company creates and delivers a good or service, or you can analyze an administrative process in which you take part, such as hiring employees, creating or processing invoices, or updating drawings. Alternatively, if you are a student and you neither are currently employed nor have held a job in the past on which to base this exercise, think about something that you do every day or every week, such as getting up every morning and coming to school, making dinner, or getting lunch in a café.

2. Cars traveling from Richmond to Williamsburg, Virginia, take one hour on average to make the trip. Over the course of a day, 15,000 cars per hour on average pass by a checkpoint that is set up between those two points. How many cars are on the road between Richmond and Williamsburg on average?

3. An automobile plant produces cars at a rate of 60 cars per hour on average. It takes one day (24 hours) on average for a car to make it from the start of the assembly line to the end. How many cars are in process in the plant on average?

4. A wildlife scientist measures the number of fish swimming upstream to spawn. During the spawning season, 1,200 fish per hour on average pass the scientist's checkpoint. It is estimated that 20,000 fish on average are in a certain patch of water. How long does it take for a fish, on average, to swim through that patch of water?

5. A manufacturing manager presented his goals for the next year to the division vice president of manufacturing, which included a 25 percent reduction in average work-in-process inventory level and a 25 percent reduction in average lead time. The vice president chastised the manufacturing manager for his lack of aggressiveness: Certainly 25 percent reduction in average lead time was satisfactory, but a much greater reduction in average inventory was needed to meet cost reduction targets. The vice president unilaterally changed the manufacturing manager's average inventory reduction target to 50 percent. There were no substantial changes in sales and production volumes planned for the next year and, thus, no planned changes in the production rate. Are the manufacturing manager's cost and inventory improvement goals consistent with one another? Why or why not? Are the vice president's inventory and cost reduction targets consistent with one another? Why or why not?

6. A manufacturing plant manager is in her annual personnel review meeting with her boss, the division vice president. The vice president asks about the details of the plant manager's process and performance. The plant manager mentions that it takes her plant six months, on

average, to build a piece of heavy excavating equipment used in strip mining. In addition, over the past 10 years, the average number of excavators that were built was 12.2 units per year. In addition, she said that the number of units made per year varied from year to year, but the volume did not necessarily seem to be trending either up or down. Currently, the plant manager said that she had 15 units in various stages of production. If you were the division vice president, and you knew Little's Law, would you have any basis to take issue with the consistency of the plant manager's statements? Why or why not?

Lessons from the Exercises

Besides getting experience thinking about how things are accomplished in terms of processes, here are common observations that people make as they discover a process using the steps outlined in problem 1:

1. Just taking the time to do the steps as outlined in this exercise leads to new discoveries about how things get done. Until you take time to study a process, there is a lot you do not know about it. If you analyzed a process in your workplace, you might have found that you did not know everything about the process and that you needed to talk with other people who are involved. With most business processes, there is no one who knows everything about every step in the process. This is one reason why Lean projects are usually accomplished by teams rather than individuals.

2. While documenting a process, it is most often the case that opportunities for improving the process are immediately recognized, even though the immediate goal is just to study and document the process. Lean forces us to slow down and ask how we get things done. If we can separate ourselves from the daily crises, which consume much of our time, and thoughtfully evaluate what we do, improvement ideas come easily.

CHAPTER 3

A Framework for Applying Lean

Many structured approaches exist for improving processes and solving problems. The Plan, Do, Check, and Act (PDCA) approach has existed for a long time and provides one well-known framework as does Define, Measure, Analyze, Improve, and Control (DMAIC) which is used in the Six Sigma process improvement methodology:

1. Map the process: This is called the value stream map (VSM).
2. Analyze the current state VSM looking for unnecessary lead time and possible ways to reduce that wasted lead time using Lean tools.
3. Draw a new process map that reflects ideas for improving the process and reducing its lead time: This is called the future state VSM.
4. Determine from the revised process map how much lead time can be reduced.
5. Create a priority list that reflects the order in which the planned improvements will be made.
6. Implement the improvements and check how much the process lead time (and other metrics) has improved and whether the improvement met expectations.
7. Institute the improved process by standardizing on it and expecting adherence to the new process definition.
8. Repeat the steps above indefinitely.

Parallels can be drawn, however, between the steps of Lean improvement and both PDCA and DMAIC. Companies that use Lean most often also use Six Sigma, and so describing the Lean improvement process in the context of Six Sigma is most appropriate. This is done in Table 3.1,

Table 3.1 *Analogy between Six Sigma and Lean activities*

Improvement phase	Six Sigma activities	Lean activities
Define	• Define product or service attributes most important to customers upon which to focus improvement. These are critical to quality (CTQs) • Construct charter which establishes the importance of improving the quality attributes that are selected	• Establish metrics upon which improvement efforts are focused, one of which is usually lead time • Construct charter which establishes the importance of the project either to customers or internal customers if project is for internal efficiencies
Measure	• Measure process capability • Assess the measurement system competency • Collect data about the selected CTQs and process inputs most likely to be affecting them	• Collect data to define the process steps • Draw VSM • Measure lead time and value-added ratio (VAR)
Analyze	• Analyze data to determine process inputs that most often cause defects or variation of the CTQs	• Find nonvalue-added time (waste or muda) from the customers' perspectives • Determine root causes of waste
Improve	• Design process changes to mitigate the effects of the most critical process variables identified in the Analyze phase • Conduct trials and do hypothesis tests to verify that the proposed process changes improve quality • If successful, institute the changes in a revised process description	• Design process changes that will remove nonvalue-added time while not sacrificing quality • Implement changes, possibly using Kaizen events • Perform hypothesis test to confirm that lead time is reduced by the forecasted amount • Change process description documents to institute changes
Control	• Monitor quality using control charts to ensure improvements are sustained	• Periodically audit process to ensure that it is being carried out according to the process descriptions

which demonstrates that DMAIC accurately describes the activities that are undertaken when the Lean methodology is used to improve processes.

Many types of maps can be used to map processes. The type of map used in Lean is called a VSM, and we will describe how to create one in the next chapter. We will also describe in that chapter how to analyze the process, via its map, to measure lead time and other process metrics. Part II of this book surveys some of the tools that are used within the Lean framework and how they reduce lead time and improve other business metrics. In Chapter 5, we also discuss the necessity of standardizing processes if process performance is to be improved. The last step in the list indicates that Lean is a continuous improvement process: Addressing a process just once with Lean does not reveal all the possible improvements. Processes can be analyzed and improved many times with Lean. The initial application of Lean addresses gross inefficiencies, and only after they are resolved can the minor inefficiencies be noticed and addressed. Even if lead time is reduced 70 to 90 percent in the initial application of Lean, improvements of the same order of magnitude can be made in the second and third applications.

The Lean framework outlined previously is similar to PDCA and DMAIC in that, first, the effort begins by measuring the process. Lean, like Six Sigma, is a data-driven methodology: Improvements are not based on hunches about how the process is executed, and it is not assumed that prospective changes in the process will actually result in improvement. Rather, time is spent to understand the process, map it, and analyze it, resulting in a high degree of confidence that the improvements identified will be successful. Thus both Lean and Six Sigma have an analysis component. All the process improvement frameworks end with the fix being institutionalized: If it cannot be guaranteed that the fix will continually be applied, then it cannot be guaranteed that the process will be improved.

Lean borrows a vast majority of its tools and terminology from the Toyota Production System (TPS). One tool that is used in Lean that is not part of the TPS repertoire is value stream mapping. Value stream mapping is an essential tool, however, because it is the mechanism that is employed to gain an overall understanding of the process and to point out where Lean tools can be implemented to the greatest advantage. On the contrary, process improvement in TPS is usually discussed in terms of its tools directly applied to problem areas rather than employing this overarching guiding mechanism. Value stream mapping is also advantageous because it brings about a great amount of awareness about how the process is really executed. Until such a map is created, no one person in a company is cognizant of how things are accomplished: Each person might know what role he or she plays in the process, but nobody knows the whole process or how the process steps interact. Furthermore, it is also often true that individuals cannot recite the sequence of tasks they follow to play their role in a process without thoughtful reflection, which can be motivated by value stream mapping.

Value stream mapping as mentioned in the Lean framework will probably suggest multiple actions that can be taken to reduce lead time. Therefore, some time might elapse between episodes of value stream mapping to allow for all those improvements to be implemented. Some of the improvements might be implemented through what are sometimes called *kaizen* events. The structure of *kaizen* events recognizes that some improvements can be made only if a sufficient amount of time is dedicated to the task. *Kaizen* events allow workers to be relieved of their everyday duties for multiple days (three to five days) in order to plan and implement an improvement. For example, a value stream mapping analysis might have identified that changeover time could be reduced at a particular machine. It is usually outside the scope of value stream mapping to make such an improvement, which would be implemented later via a follow-up *kaizen* project. During the time away from their jobs, a team would collect data about the changeover, find opportunities for improvements, and implement some of the improvements. Even with three to five days to work on the project, some of the improvements might need to be implemented over time if new equipment needs to be purchased or fabricated. Nonetheless, this discussion points out that making improvements using Lean does require an investment of time and resources. The inability to devote such resources because of the importance of daily deliverables and the resolution of ongoing crises is one of the most frequent barriers to implementing Lean and improving processes.

CHAPTER 4

How to Map and Analyze a Process

Measuring Processes: Lead Time and Cycle Time

Lean focuses on reducing process lead time, and so the first step in Lean is to measure the lead time of the process as it is currently executed. For the process described in Figure 1.1 (see Chapter 1), we need to measure the average amount of time that elapses from the time the raw wood is cut in the first step until the time an end table is completed. Determining total process lead time is conceptually straightforward: We need to measure the average lead time required for each process step and then add all those times together. For the first step, where raw wood is cut to length and width, the elapsed time through this step is the time from when a particular piece of raw wood is delivered to this cutting step until that piece is moved from the cutting workstation to the next step in the process. The time that a piece of wood stays at a workstation will vary from piece to piece, and we represent that varying lead time using its average value. In particular, the average could be calculated by taking several measurements and averaging them. Tagging multiple pieces of wood in some manner and tracking them through the process so that lead time can be tracked is tedious, and so we will offer an alternative method for measuring lead time (see the box titled *Alternative Method for Determining the Lead Time of a Process Step*). For now, however, think of the average process step lead time as the average of many measurements.

Note that raw materials are often delivered in batches in manufacturing processes, which, for the cutting process step, would be the case when more than one piece of wood is delivered at one time. Deliveries of a batch of wood would be expected in a furniture-manufacturing process in which transporting wood by the pallet-load would reduce material

Alternative Method for Determining the Lead Time of a Process Step

Tagging many units of work to determine each piece's lead time is a tedious endeavor. A simpler way to determine the average lead time of a process step is to employ Little's law. It is easier to count the inventory at a step on multiple occasions than to measure the lead time of multiple items going through a process. Therefore, lead time is more conveniently estimated by measuring the average inventory level at a process step and then determining lead time by rearranging Little's law: $T = I/R$.

handling time in comparison with delivering wood one piece at a time. Processing can occur in batches in service and administrative processes as well, examples of which are given in the box titled *Batch Processing in Service and Administrative Processes*. Computing the lead time through a process step might be confusing when goods are processed in batches. For example, should the lead time of one piece be measured or the lead time of the entire batch? The answer is that we want to track the lead time for each individual piece of wood. To do so, we must take into consideration all time that a piece spends at a workstation, including the processing time, the time that a piece waits for its turn to be processed, and the time it waits after processing until it is transported to the next process step. When the entire batch is completed before being transported to the next step, one piece must wait for its turn to be processed and it must wait for the completion of the remaining pieces in the batch after it has been processed. There might also be some wait time for the entire batch if other batches are processed before it.

The foregoing discussion makes clear that the lead time of a process step is not necessarily the time it takes for the actual processing of one unit of work at a particular process step. Actual processing time might be only one minute, but a piece of wood might spend two hours waiting at a workstation, including the waiting time before it is processed and the waiting time after it is processed. The terminology that describes the amount of time that one particular piece of work is actively being worked

Batch Processing in Service and Administrative Processes

Batch processing often occurs in administrative processes where people have multiple responsibilities. For example, an engineer in a manufacturing plant might be responsible for estimating the time and cost of work orders that will be completed by the in-house maintenance department, making drawings for the installation of new production equipment, and inspecting existing equipment periodically. It is natural, it seems, for people to wait to switch to one of these tasks only after some amount of work has built up. An engineer, for example, might wait for some number of work orders to accumulate before turning to that task. Perhaps it takes some time to start another computer application, which the engineer does not want to do for just one work order. Or it may take effort to turn one's attention to a new task, and sufficient motivation to do so does not exist until multiple work orders pile up. This story holds true for possibly any administrative worker with multiple responsibilities. Another example is a procurement worker who is responsible for evaluating requests for quotations from new suppliers, evaluating and developing existing suppliers, dealing with supply problems, and many other tasks.

In service processes, credit card bills are processed and mailed in batches, prescriptions are processed in hospitals in batches, tours are given to randomly arriving customers in batches, movies are shown to batches of people, tests are most often given to batches of students, professors grade tests in batches, and amusement parks process customers through rides in batches, to name a few examples.

on at a station is called *cycle time* (one minute in this case). Lead time is the total amount of time a piece of wood stays at the cutting step (two hours in this case). *Cycle time and process step lead time are not necessarily equal.* Processing work in batches causes the two times to be different, as does waiting for batches that arrived previously to be processed, workstation downtime, and workstations that are not continuously staffed. The only circumstance when process step lead time and cycle time are equal is

Possible Confusion Between Lead Time and Cycle Time

The meanings of *lead time* and *cycle time* as defined here are common among virtually all companies that practice Lean. However, in other companies the term *cycle time* is sometimes used to connote what would be called lead time in Lean. It is, therefore, always wise to ask what somebody means by cycle time or lead time. Not doing so can lead to misunderstandings.

when raw materials are delivered one unit at a time, the processing step can always immediately start processing the item and is never interrupted by a breakdown, and then the item is immediately taken to the next process step. However, this is an unlikely circumstance.

Notice that if we had measured the lead time of the batch rather than a single part in this example, the lead time for the cutting step would have been the same. However, thinking about the lead time in terms of a single part allowed us to clearly identify the various components contributing to that part's dwell time, and doing so is important because it is important to distinguish between waiting time and actual processing time.

Having measured the lead time of each process step, it might be apparent that we have not comprehended all of the lead time in the furniture-making process in Figure 1.1. Materials must be transported from one step to the next, which is not reflected in Figure 1.1. In addition, inventory is sometimes stored between steps in staging areas, warehouses, or somewhere near the next processing station. Our goal is to quantify all the time that work spends in a process, and so we must account for these waiting times as well. Triangles are typically used to denote transportation and storage operations between steps, as shown in the updated diagram in Figure 4.1. It is also perfectly acceptable to reflect transportation, alternatively, as a process step. To measure the lead time of the entire process, we must also measure the lead time of these intervening steps, which we could do in the manner previously described. Now we can add up the lead times for all the process steps to arrive at the lead time for the entire process as shown in Figure 4.1. The lead time for this entire process is 33,355 minutes.

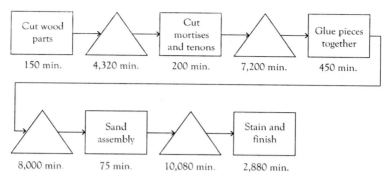

Total process lead time = 33,355 min.

Figure 4.1 End table process with lead times

In studying Figure 4.1, one might notice that most of the lead time is composed of waiting—that is, periods in which unfinished parts wait in inventory. This observation is made almost without exception. It is a rude awakening when a manager finds that most of the time a product spends in their factory, it is not being actively worked on but rather it is waiting to be transported or waiting for the next processing step. Lead time is most often noted in minutes or even in seconds rather than in hours or in days. The rationale for this is, perhaps, that a larger number gives the impression that more improvement is possible and provides the motivation for making that improvement.

Work Units, External Versus Internal Orientation of Projects, and Process Scope

This book will use the terminology *work units* to describe what is flowing through a process. In the case of Figure 4.1, the entities that are flowing through the process can be thought of as the tables or, in the beginning of the process, the parts that will eventually be assembled into a table. Thus, in Figure 4.1, the work units are tables.

Mapping the process in Figure 4.1 and applying Lean might likely be for the purpose of reducing lead time so that customers can receive their tables as soon as possible, thereby increasing customer satisfaction and, perhaps, positively influencing repeat business. Such a goal could be considered an *externally oriented project* because the primary benefits of the project are intended to benefit parties external to the company: the customers. Some references on Lean advocate that projects always should be pursued with the external customers' benefit in mind. However, Lean can also be employed for the benefit of the company itself: Such a project would be *internally oriented*. To distinguish between externally and internally oriented projects, we will discuss the process depicted in Figure 4.2, which is a simplification of the process for getting a jet aircraft to the terminal gate and unloaded once it has landed. Improving the process for this process flow might likely focus on reducing the lead time and, in particular, the time it takes to get customers off the plane and on their way once the plane has landed. This goal would be externally focused on the customers, who will either get to their destination sooner or have an increased probability of getting to their next flight on time. This implies that the work units flowing through the process are the customers. The process is typical in that the actions that materially help the customers get closer to getting off the plane take a relatively small amount of time, and the most significant lead time components are constituted by waiting.

Alternative work units might be viewed as flowing through the process steps in Figure 4.2 as well. For example, the plane also carries luggage, which also needs to get off the plane and be sent either to the baggage carousel or to the next plane. Reducing the lead time of getting the luggage off the plane would also be an externally oriented goal because the primary benefits are likely to accrue to the customer. One might also view the plane as being the work unit flowing through this process. What benefits derive from reducing the time that the aircraft spends getting to the gate and discharging passengers? As Southwest Airlines has demonstrated, reducing the amount of time an aircraft spends on the ground maximizes the time the aircraft is in the air generating revenue.[1] Drawing

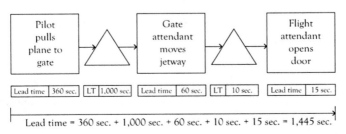

Figure 4.2 Airport process example

the process map to support an effort to reduce the time an aircraft spends on the ground therefore can be viewed as an internally oriented goal: The primary benefits accrue to the airline.

Considering the possibility of using Figure 4.2 for reducing the lead time of getting luggage processed or getting the plane into the air again raises a question: Would considering the process steps in Figure 4.2 be sufficient to help us uncover all the possible improvements that would increase the time an aircraft spends generating revenue or reduce the amount of time required to transfer baggage? Focusing on the latter objective, the answer is likely that we would need to consider more process steps in addition to those shown in Figure 4.2. Other important steps to consider are the unloading of the bags from the aircraft, transportation from the aircraft to the baggage handling system, and the induction of the bags into that system. Of course, we must consider all the waiting time between those steps, which also adds to lead time. If we do not consider these additional steps, then we would likely miss some important opportunities to reduce lead time. If the goal is to reduce the time a plane spends on the ground, then considering the time to get to the gate after landing might be important, as would including other steps like cleaning and restocking the aircraft. Including more steps in the definition of a process is said to increase the scope of the improvement project.

Considering an appropriate process scope is an important part of defining a Lean project. If the process scope is too narrow, then process steps that affect lead time significantly might be ignored. Considering too large a scope makes it difficult to complete a project in a reasonable amount of time and to focus on critical process steps. Thus defining an appropriate scope for a Lean improvement project requires good judgment to negotiate this trade-off.

Waste and How to Find It

Having mapped the process as in Figure 4.1, we must now analyze it in order to find the best opportunities for reducing lead time. To do this, we adopt the perspective of the customer who will purchase the product or use the service created by executing the process. It is the customer who decides if our product or service is worth the price we are charging: If a customer finds a company's offering to be worth the cost, he or she will buy it. We do not want to reduce lead time in any step of the process if it is going to reduce the value of an offering to customers. Note that this is true regardless of whether process improvement is pursued for external or internal benefit: If the value of a product or service to customers is reduced for the sake of better internal business performance, then a company's existence might be jeopardized. If, however, in executing a process step nothing is done to enhance the attractiveness of the product to customers, then perhaps that step can be shortened or eliminated altogether in order to reduce the overall lead time of the process. To determine which steps provide value from the customers' perspectives, we ask the following questions for each process step and intervening wait time:

Good intro to idea of VA vs NVA

1. Would the customer pay more because this step is performed?
2. Would the customer's satisfaction be increased because this step is performed?
3. Would the customer choose the product or service generated by this process over a competitor's product or service because this step is performed?
4. Does performing this step increase the probability of repeat business?

For a step where the answer to such questions is yes, then we say that the step is a *value-added* (VA) step. When the answer to these questions is no, then we have identified what is called a *nonvalue-added* (NVA) step. The lead time involved in executing NVA steps is also called *waste*. Many companies when implementing Lean also borrow a term from the Toyota Production System (TPS) to describe NVA activity: *muda*. The waste thus identified becomes the target of opportunity for reducing lead time.

VA and NVA time is recorded in Lean process maps using a zigzag line below the process steps as shown in Figure 4.3. NVA time is noted on the peaks of the zigzag line whereas VA time is listed in the troughs. This makes it convenient to add up all the NVA times because those data are all aligned on the same vertical level on the zigzag: The total NVA time is noted at the right end of the zigzag. Similarly, the VA time is summed and noted at the right end of the zigzag below the total NVA time.

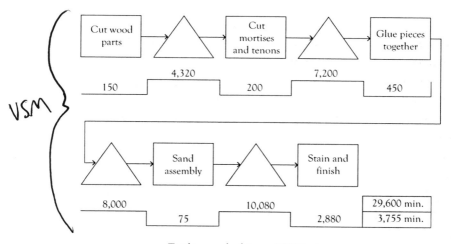

VSM

Total process lead time = 33,355 min.
Value added ratio (VAR) = 11.3%

Figure 4.3 Furniture process with VA, NVA, and VAR

Note that although we have already computed total lead time for the process, it can be computed by adding the total NVA time and total VA time from the figures computed on the right-hand side of the map. Another use of these sums is to compute the percentage of lead time where something productive is being done to the product or service from the customer's perspective. Intuitively, we calculate this quantity by dividing the total VA time by the total lead time:

$$\frac{VA}{Process\ Lead\ Time} = \frac{VA}{VA + NVA}$$

This is called the value-added ratio (VAR), and together with total process lead time, these are the two most important metrics that describe the performance of the overall process.

The VAR for the process in Figure 4.3 is approximately 11.3 percent (3,755/33,355). A statistic in this range usually strikes people as being an astonishingly small number. However, many processes, before Lean is applied, have a VAR on the order of 1 percent or even less. Some manufacturing processes where, for example, large batches are used and a large variety of products are manufactured might have a VAR of much less than 1 percent. The author, for example, has observed VARs as low as 0.001 percent. So it is important to map, analyze, and improve a process, or a majority of processing time is likely to contribute nothing to the desirability of a product or service to the customer. Rather, the extra unproductive time adds cost (multiple handling steps and added inventory), reduces quality (more opportunities for damage), and reduces customer satisfaction (because of delayed gratification). Perhaps the most significant value of computing the VAR is to emphasize how much time in a process is wasted. Upon calculating a VAR of 1 percent or less, it is difficult for any participant in an improvement effort to argue that the process does not need attention. As an exercise, the VAR can be computed for the process in Figure 4.2: It is approximately 30.1 percent.

Notice that the peaks of the zigzag line, where NVA time is noted, are aligned with the waiting steps that are between the processing steps. This is indicative that waiting, a vast majority of the time, is NVA, and customers will not pay a company more money for its product or service or choose its product because it spends more time gathering dust in the process. The rare exception to this rule are things such as wine, where aging is an essential part of the process. Still, if these essential waiting times can be reduced, the performance (lead time and VAR) of the process would be increased.

Disagreement can arise in the midst of determining whether a particular process step or component thereof is VA or NVA. Prolonged conversations of this type serve little purpose and are, in a way of speaking, NVA. One way to resume constructive discussion in a team discussion is to agree on the ground rule that all process steps where such disagreement arises shall be considered NVA. This approach has the advantage that it considers by default more steps to be NVA than would otherwise be the case and therefore targets a greater number of process steps for scrutiny.

In some circumstances, some portions of a process step might be VA whereas other components are not. In that case, these components can be segregated. Specifically, the zigzag line below the process maps can have two entries for any process step: The VA portion of lead time can be entered on the lower level, and the NVA component can be added at the upper level, as shown in Figure 4.4. Figure 4.4 shows the circumstance where 30 of the total 75 minutes in the sanding step were NVA, such as changing sandpaper on random orbital sanders. This example also shows that waste is found not only when goods and customers wait between

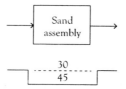

Figure 4.4 Accounting for lead time in steps with VA and NVA time

process steps but also within processing steps. Intuition leads some to believe falsely that all activities in a processing step are VA time.

Thus far, we have referred to the representations we have drawn of processes simply as process maps. In Lean, however, process maps using the special notation as shown in Figure 4.3 are referred to as *value stream maps* (VSMs). Figure 4.3 is a fairly complete rendition of a VSM, although more detail could be added. The name reflects that our goal is to identify where value is added from the customers' perspectives and then to eliminate other contributors to lead time. There are many types of process maps, but the value stream mapping format is fairly universal among those who practice Lean.

Categories of NVA Time

The TPS identifies categories of activities that are generally NVA, and acknowledgment of these is usually included in Lean training. These categories are often referred to as the *seven deadly wastes*, and the titles of the categories can vary from one Lean program to another. Indeed, we have included an eighth category of waste (the last one on the list) that is sometimes included. If you find activities in a process that fit these descriptions, then they are likely to be NVA:

1. *Waiting.* The time when the work unit is waiting for the next VA process, usually between process steps.
2. *Overproduction.* When the first of two sequential steps processes work units faster than the subsequent step, even for a relatively short period, this is called overproduction, and an inventory buildup results.
3. *Inventory.* Inventory can be at the end of a process (finished-goods inventory) or between processing steps (work-in-process inventory).

Inventory connotes that goods are waiting, either for subsequent processing or for sale to a customer. Overproduction also leads to inventory accumulation.

4. *Defects*. Defects in goods and services cause excess cost because defective products must either be discarded or reworked if the defect is caught prior to the receipt by the customer. If the customer receives defective goods or services, then they may become dissatisfied and the company will incur a cost if the customer brings this to the attention of the company, possibly in the form of warranty cost. Alternatively, the customer may penalize the company by not purchasing additional goods.

5. *Transportation*. Transportation between processing steps within a factory or between links of a supply chain is NVA. Certainly, transportation between steps is required, but the degree to which it is excessive constitutes waste. Deeming all transportation time to be waste focuses attention on finding ways to reduce transportation. Within a factory, this is often the impetus for moving workstations closer together.

6. *Overprocessing*. Overprocessing is when processing imparts characteristics to work units that are not valued by customers. These are types of activities that are likely to be thought of as VA within the organization that produces a good, but researching customer expectations, needs, and desires would reveal that the customer would not pay more for a good or service with these characteristics.

7. *Wasted motion*. Just because a person is in motion and working hard does not mean that anything of value is being done for the customer. Reducing wasted motion increases efficiency and helps companies reduce the costs of serving customers.

8. *Underutilized worker and equipment resources*.[2] The time a worker or a piece of production equipment (or any process resource) is idle represents the time that could be spent on activities that generate value for customers. Reorganizing process flows can sometimes utilize employees and equipment to fuller advantage.

One might notice the close relationship among waiting, overproduction, and inventory: Both waiting and overproduction result in a buildup of inventory, or whatever work unit is flowing through the process.

The last waste, underutilized resources, which is not always listed as a category of waste, deserves more discussion. Certainly resources that are not fully used represent financial costs that are not being fully leveraged. This cannot be completely avoided because there will always be at least one bottleneck in a process, which is the slowest step that governs the rate (e.g., units per hour) at which the process can produce goods or services. This implies that other steps of the process must sometimes be idled (i.e., underutilized resources) possibly through a kanban system or, otherwise, overproduction and inventory will result. Bottlenecks are not often discussed in Lean, but when operating practices exacerbate bottlenecks, then the increased restraint on the production rate implies that the idle time in other process resources will increase, thus increasing waste. Furthermore, a bottleneck that imposes a greater restriction on output either restricts revenue (another type of waste) or causes greater investment in the bottleneck resources. An effective practice in Lean is, therefore, to identify the bottleneck and ensure that management practices do not cause undue restriction on that step and the process in total. Upon observing that a bottleneck is being unnecessarily restricted, a plan should be put in place to resolve that situation.

These categories of waste were originally developed with manufacturing processes in mind. However, they can easily be applied to administrative and service processes. For example, transportation can be thought of as the exchange of data between the parties at different steps of a process when services are being provided (e.g., processing applications, processing invoices, or processing insurance claims). Overprocessing can be thought of as providing some aspect of a service that is not valued by a client, such as providing a redundant hard copy of a document when an electronic version would have sufficed. Defects, rather than being mistakes made in producing physical goods, are errors made in the execution of administrative processes and the delivery of services. Overproduction in administrative and service processes results in a backlog of work at one processing step, just as in manufacturing, but the work backlog in administrative processes and services is often in the form of an electronic representation of the work that needs to be done rather than a physical pile of work-in-process (inventory). The translation of waiting, wasted motion, and underutilized resources from manufacturing processes to other processes is fairly apparent.

Accuracy in VSMs

We have discussed the role of VSMs in the Lean improvement process. One main purpose they serve is to identify the biggest and most feasible lead time reduction opportunities. Lead time accuracy is needed only to the degree that the most significant contributors to NVA time can be accurately identified. Since we have observed that the magnitude of NVA components of lead time is most often significantly larger than that of the VA components, a reasonable amount of error in measuring lead time of process steps would still result in the same NVA tasks being identified as the main contributors to lead time. Estimates of average lead time at process steps can easily be 25 percent in error, and even more, and the large NVA times (e.g., waiting) will still be the largest components of lead time and at the top of the list of opportunities.

Drawing VSMs

VSMs can be constructed using a variety of methods, each with its own advantages and disadvantages:

1. *By hand.* This is easy to do and makes maps easy to change. Flip charts can be utilized for larger scale drawings and for involving team members. Alternatively, representing each step on its own piece of paper and pinning them to the wall allows for easy rearrangement of steps when a team member remembers a step that has not yet been included in the map. There is nothing wrong with this approach at all, except that if the VSM needs to be presented, it will most likely need to be rendered electronically so that it is compatible with a PowerPoint presentation.
2. *Excel.* Excel is widely available and offers the advantage of accumulating VA time, NVA time, and total lead time using a simple formula. The graphics capability of Excel to draw rectangles and triangles is convenient. Other icons require the user to construct templates.[3] Excel generates a reasonably aesthetic map, although other approaches (PowerPoint and Visio) would be considered by many to be more aesthetic.

3. *PowerPoint.* It is easier to do graphics with PowerPoint than with Excel and the resulting VSM is already in the format needed for presentation. One disadvantage is that VA time, NVA time, and lead time need to be computed manually, but this is not a large amount of work. It is convenient to have an Excel spreadsheet in the background to store process step lead times and recompute the total lead time when data change.[4]

4. *Visio.* Visio creates perhaps the most aesthetic VSM. In addition, recent versions of Visio come with a template with the shapes needed for VSMs. Data can be specified for process steps, such as cycle time, changeover time, number of workers, percentage yield, and so forth, which can automatically appear on data graphics that are associated with the rectangles for process steps. Disadvantages include the fact that fewer people are familiar with Visio than those with either Excel or PowerPoint, and there is a bit of a learning curve to use Visio to its full advantage in generating VSMs. In addition, Visio is not included with the Microsoft Office suite and therefore represents an additional investment.

5. *Electronic value stream mapping (eVSM).* This is an add-in to Visio and it provides additional functionality not included with Visio. For example, it allows data about process steps to be specified and tabulated more easily, which facilitates the summing up of the total lead time of a process by downloading process data to Excel or entering formulas directly in Visio. It includes other functionality, such as creating spaghetti diagrams. The disadvantage of eVSM is that it represents an additional cost (see http://www.evsm.com).

Careful Observation of the Process

Taiichi Ohno is credited with encouraging a method of waste identification called *standing in a circle,* in which managers would literally stand in a circle drawn on the floor of a factory for hours on end.[5] This exercise has many potential lessons.

First, concentrating on a process intently for a prolonged period allows many instances of waste to be observed. Once the mission of a process is established in terms of the value it provides to customers, then any action or inaction that does not accrue value to customers is waste. Of course, the found waste can be categorized according to the seven deadly wastes. The list that one might generate from observing a process for six hours, and the subsequent categorization, can impress upon an organization that significant improvement is possible. This exercise can, therefore, help to convince an organization not familiar with Lean that it might be a good method to adopt. An example of an activity similar to standing in a circle is described in a case about the Deaconess-Glover Hospital in Needham, Massachusetts.[6] In that case, a researcher followed a nurse, observing her activities for one hour. A review of the activities revealed that approximately two-thirds of the time the nurse was not contributing to their core mission of helping their patients to become healthier. That is, two-thirds of their activities were nonvalue-adding. Such a figure should grab a manager's attention and cause them to ask why. In this case, much time was spent searching for items that did not have a standardized location, asking questions about patient status when information should have been readily available, and wasting effort with needless travel between patient rooms and other locations in the ward.

Standing in one place, if it is done at only one step of a process, is the antithesis of how a Lean project is prototypically approached, which normally follows a process from start to finish in order to draw a VSM. It is likely that an entire process cannot be viewed from one vantage point. It is more likely that portions of many processes might be observed from one spot. While the VSM allows waste reduction opportunities to be prioritized in light of the entire process, observing waste from one vantage point might still unearth fruitful opportunities. If done from many vantage points, however, intently observing a process could result in a complete VSM and a good understanding of the process.

One Lean practitioner learned about another benefit of standing in a circle: It can teach one to question whether every action is value-adding or not.[7] Learning to instinctively ask questions like the following activates a healthy skepticism that does not take for granted that any activity is inherently VA:

1. What is this person doing now?
2. Why is this person doing that?
3. Where is this person going?

4. Why is this person going there?

5. What is this person waiting for?

Workers and managers can fall into the trap of thinking that the activities required by the current process are value-adding, when they are, in fact, not value-adding. Questions that start with *why, where, how,* and *what* challenge that complacency.

Remember, Lean is a data-driven methodology. Whether the standing in a circle is used or not, somehow a process must be observed or the experience of people involved in the process tapped in order to discover how a process is executed. This knowledge is the basis for improvement and allows for the identification of waste.

The 5 Whys Method

The 5 Whys method is closely associated with the TPS and the resolution of quality defects in Six Sigma. Its purpose in Six Sigma is to aid in identifying the root cause of errors and defects. The procedure is simple:

1. First, ask *Why did the error occur?*

2. Take the answer to the previous question and ask: *Why did these circumstances occur?*

3. Repeat the step above asking *Why?* about each successive answer until a root cause is identified that is actionable and can be resolved with a high degree of reliability.

The technique gets its name because it often takes asking *Why?* about five times to get to the root cause, although *Why?* is usually asked more or fewer than five times. The practice is effective because it does not allow actions to be taken in response to the first answer, which are often knee-jerk, superficial remedies. Instead, insisting on asking *Why* multiple times gets at the core cause of the problem. The 5 Whys is most often used with quality problems or equipment failure as illustrated in Figure 4.5.

The example in Figure 4.5 is different from many that one might find in other references, which are most often *linear* in that each *Why?* question has only one possible response. Ultimately, a linear structure might appropriately reflect the results of a 5 Whys investigation.

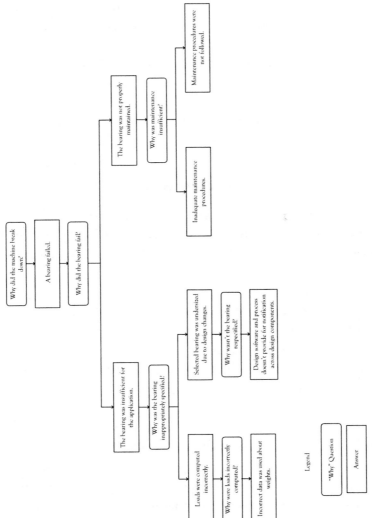

Figure 4.5 5 Whys analysis for a machine failure

However, there are often several possible failure modes, or answers for each *Why?* question at each stage of the analysis for real problems with any complexity whatever, and investigation is necessary in that case to determine which is the appropriate answer to each *Why?* question. In the end, after the correct answers have been determined and the irrelevant questions and responses are removed from the diagram, then the analysis will look linear rather than like a tree. The *tree* of possible root causes in many cases is likely to branch out much more quickly than the previous example. Moreover, in some cases multiple root causes can conspire to cause a defect or a problem because none of the factors alone would cause the problem. This is usually the failure mode for catastrophic disasters such as the British Petroleum (BP) oil platform explosion in 2010 and the Challenger Space Shuttle explosion in 1986. The Challenger disaster was caused by mechanical and organization failures: o-rings that sealed two stages of the solid rocket motor were not qualified to operate in cold temperatures and organizational communication and incentives prevented recognition of that information by those who could have delayed the launch. In the BP Deepwater Horizon explosion, a BP accident report document characterized the root causes:

> [...]a complex and interlinked series of mechanical failures, human judgments, engineering design, operational implementation and team interfaces came together to allow the initiation and escalation of the accident. Multiple companies, work teams and circumstances were involved over time.[8]

Specific root causes included using an insufficient number of centralizers, using insufficient spacer material between the wellbore and the casing, using substandard concrete, and inoperative redundant safety systems.

The 5 Whys can be applied also in Lean, in which case it might be used to resolve an error or a defect just as it is in Six Sigma. It might be used more often in Lean, however, to ask *Why does this lead time exist?* or *Why does this inventory exist?* Figure 4.6 shows such an example.

The actions to resolve the terminal root cause of excessive lead time are sometimes obvious. For example, if the root cause of spending too much time searching for an empty pallet is that a standard location has not been specified, then a prudent first step is to establish a single location

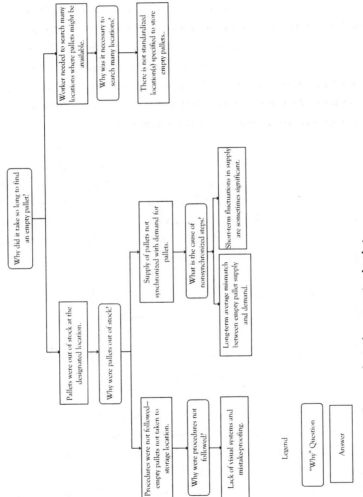

Figure 4.6 5 Whys analysis for excessive lead time

where the pallets are to be found. Whether obvious or not, resolving these root causes of waste involves implementing various types of Lean tools, which are the subject of Part II of this book.

What Next?

Having found waste, or NVA time, with a VSM, we must next eliminate it. Many tools exist within the Lean tool kit for that purpose. We describe some of those tools in Part II. Applying Lean tools to eliminate some of the NVA time allows the process to be remapped as it will be executed after the improvements have been implemented. This rendition of the process map is called the *future state value stream map.*

Exercises

1. Return to the process that you documented in Chapter 1, or select a new process, and do the following:
   a. Draw a VSM indicating the average lead time for each step or reasonable estimates of each step's lead time. Also note the lead time for the waiting steps.
   b. Classify all lead time in the process as VA or NVA, and display it on a zigzag line.
   c. Compute the total process lead time and the VAR.
2. Analyze the Harvard Business School Publishing case titled *Deaconess-Glover Hospital (A)*[9] by drawing the VSM for the medication-delivery process beginning at the point in time when a doctor issues a prescription. Make a list of all the waste that you find in that process and potential areas for mistakes to be made.
3. Pick a process or work area in your workplace to observe, or get permission to observe processes in a doctor's or dentist's office, a retail store, a fast-food restaurant, or other venues where the process is visually apparent. Watch the operation for one hour or more and make a list of wastes that you observe. Then, construct a list of questions you could ask a manager that would determine if there was a purpose to an apparently wasteful practice or would help to uncover the root cause of the waste.

CHAPTER 5

The Need for Reduced Variation in Processes

This chapter discusses the need for predictable outcomes of processes and how the predictability of outcomes can be controlled by reducing the variation in how a process is executed. The importance of reducing process variation in Lean is twofold. First, reducing variation in how a process is executed reduces the variation in the characteristics of the product or service being created, which reduces defects and errors that, in turn, improves quality. Besides improving customer satisfaction, improving quality reduces waste due to defects. Second, reducing variation in process execution reduces the variation in how long the process steps take to perform. Although the explanation is beyond the scope of this book, reducing the variation in process step lead times reduces overall average process lead time, even if the average lead times of the steps are left unchanged. Thus reducing process step lead time variation reduces overall process lead time and, by Little's law, in-process inventory levels. Hence, this chapter provides the motivation for why variation in how processes are executed should be reduced and, in turn, an argument for standardizing processes at a detailed level. We return to the topic of how processes can be standardized in Chapter 7 where we will discuss Standard Work.

An Experiment in Variation

In this section, an exercise is described that can be used in a Lean course to illustrate how variation in process execution causes variation in the attributes of products or services created by the process and, hence, how it reduces quality. The exercise also shows how more precise process descriptions and standardization of process execution reduce variation in the execution of a process and thus how process standardization improves quality. Furthermore, the exercise provokes discussion on how processes should best be improved, how reacting to the quality of output with insufficient data can cause quality to degrade, how simpler processes often result in better quality, and the importance of product and service specifications. It also provides an introduction to the topic of measurement system analysis.

The Penny-Dropping Exercise

The exercise described in this section is inspired by a game conceived by Donald G. Sluti, which is contained in a compilation of exercises edited by Heineke and Meile.[1] The title of that exercise is *Common Cause or Special Cause?* and the game focuses on identifying special versus common causes of variation in dropping pennies on a target. The exercise here also involves identifying common and special causes of process variation, but this game is constructed differently from Sluti's to focus on one particular special cause of variation: not adhering to process descriptions. The game here is, in addition, more comprehensive in that many additional topics can be discussed that Sluti's game does not apparently address. Sluti suggests that his game be played independently by students in teams of three, whereas the most effective method for this exercise in the author's opinion is to have two people perform the exercise in front of a class, which provides a shared experience for the entire class. The author's version of the exercise makes use of the instructions shown in Figure 5.1.

The exercise begins by introducing the general directions to the entire class using the first slide in Figure 5.1. (These slides can be downloaded from http://mason.wm.edu/faculty/bradley_j/LeanBook.) Next, two volunteers are recruited from the class, one to be a fixture and one to be an operator, and called to the front of the room. Then, the volunteers receive more detailed instructions with the aid of the second slide in Figure 5.1. The participants are instructed that the goal of the game is to repeatedly drop a penny through a cardboard tube such that it falls as close as possible to the crosshairs on the third slide of Figure 5.1. The quality of penny-dropping is defined by the distance of the penny's landing position from the crosshairs: The closer to the crosshairs, the better the quality. The slide with the crosshairs can be printed on a transparency

- Goal
  - Achieve quality placement of pennies
- Definition of quality
  - Perfect quality = penny landed with its center on the crosshairs
  - Quality degrades with increasing distance from crosshairs
- Equipment
  - Paper towel cardboard tube
  - Penny (U.S.)
  - Ruler
  - Target

- Directions
  1. Hold the official tube upright at a 90° angle to target, aimed at crosshairs, with the bottom of the tube 1.5 inches above target.
  2. Hold a penny above tube and parallel to target surface.
  3. Droppenny.
  4. Mark position of the center of the penny with an "X."

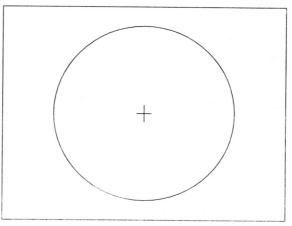

Figure 5.1 Penny-dropping exercise instructions

and placed on an overhead projector or, with more recent technology, it can be placed on a document camera platform; either approach allows the entire class to observe the process. The exercise setup involves placing multiple cardboard tubes among the other game materials—which

include a ruler, transparency pen, and penny—on a table near the target.
The tubes are as follows:

1. A paper towel tube (1.75 inches diameter; 11 inches long)
2. A toilet paper tube (1.75 inches diameter; 4.5 inches long)
3. A plastic wrap tube (1 inch diameter; 12.25 inches long)
4. A gift wrap tube (1.625 inches diameter; 18 inches long)
5. Another gift wrap tube (1.625 inches diameter; 26 inches long)
6. A larger tube (3.25 inches diameter; 24 inches long)

The instructions to the participants on the second slide include directions
to the participant who plays the fixture to hold the cardboard tube at 90°
to the target with the bottom of the tube 1.5 inches above the target.
The second participant, the operator, is instructed to drop the penny and,
subsequently, mark the location of the center of the penny with an X.
A penny is dropped approximately 10 times.

Some key lessons from the exercise are facilitated by the instructions
being less specific than they should be and the process equipment not
being up to the task at hand. For example, while the first slide of instructions references a paper towel tube, the participants in the exercise are not
yet identified when that slide is covered. Thus, perhaps, because nobody
with specific responsibility for carrying out the instructions has been
identified, the specification of a paper towel tube is uniformly missed by
the class members. The availability of many tubes laid on a table requires
that the participants make a decision, which is always made based on the
expectation of which tube will perform better. Also, although a ruler is
available to the participants and listed as a piece of equipment for this
exercise on the first slide, no specific mention is made about using a ruler
to maintain the 1.5-inch height on the second slide, and it is left to the
participants to infer that the ruler's purpose is to ensure the proper height
of the tube from the target. Also, participants are told to use the transparency pen to mark the X, although the pen is not referenced in the instructions. Finally, although it is a requirement that the tube be perpendicular
to the target, no means is provided to the participants to adhere to that
requirement, nor is any means provided to reliably or steadily maintain
the 1.5-inch height.

The most frequently asked question before the operator and fixture begin their task is *Which tube should we use?* The faculty facilitator, posing as the worker's supervisor, best leaves this point ambiguous (to supply content for follow-up discussion) by reiterating that the participants should use the official tube, claiming ignorance on which tube that is. Without variance, subjects have taken this opportunity to hypothesize and use whichever tube they feel will give the most accurate results. Almost uniformly, subjects have selected the narrow plastic wrap tube, at least to start the exercise. When questioned about the reasons for this choice, it is always that the participants hypothesize that the smaller diameter will help direct the penny toward the target more accurately. The results using this tube are unsatisfactory for many participants, who sometimes switch to another tube partway through the exercise. Some participants have switched tubes multiple times.

The Results

The results of the penny-dropping game are characterized by a large variation in the locations where the penny lands on the various attempts. Very rarely does the penny land on the crosshairs, or even near it. Not infrequently, pennies bounce completely off the target when the target is placed on a hard surface. The varying landing position of many pennies is analogous to widely varying quality in a product or service. Those subjects who have selected the narrow, long plastic wrap tube are universally dissatisfied with their choice and often change mid-process to a shorter tube. Some participants change tubes frequently, sometimes with every penny that is dropped. Other observations that are routinely made over the course of the exercise include the following:

1. Operators often forget the instructions about how high to hold the tube above the landing surface and the orientation of the tube relative to the target.
2. Besides switching tubes, subjects also purposefully vary other parameters of the process in an attempt to improve accuracy. Most often these are small variations from the directions that were given, although some participants' deviations from the stated directions are quite

severe. The constant process revisions most often do not improve accuracy significantly and many times make the results worse.

3. It is necessary for the operator to move the penny to mark its location, which reduces the accuracy of the marks.

The Lessons

The follow-up discussion to the exercise starts with the instructor asking the students about what conditions of the exercise varied from attempt to attempt or what could vary trial by trial in how the subjects executed the experiment, which caused variation in the location of the X that indicates the center of the penny's landing position. These are relevant responses:

1. Varying height of the tube above the target
2. Varying angle of the tube
3. Varying aim of the tube
4. Steadiness of the tube
5. Steadiness of the operator's arm and hand when dropping the penny
6. Varying angle of the penny relative to landing surface as it is held and dropped
7. Varying height of the penny above the tube
8. Location of the penny relative to the centerline of the tube as it is released
9. Varying dynamics of the penny's release (whether it stuck to the operator's fingers, which edge of the penny stuck to the fingers, and what rotation was caused)
10. Angle of the penny's impact on landing surface
11. Using different pennies on different trials
12. Not following the defined operation description
13. Changing from one tube to another (varying length and diameter of the tubes)
14. Varying and changing location of the document camera and interference with the tube
15. Variation in where the mark was made relative to the actual location of the penny's center

16. Variation in the direction of ventilation breezes
17. Somebody suddenly opening a door and causing a draft

Brainstorming this list allows identification of common versus special causes of variation. As defined in statistical process control, common causes are the frequent but small variations in how a process is performed that are not tightly controlled. These causes should have a small effect on the output variation of a process relative to the effect of special causes. Likely examples of common causes from the list are ventilation air currents in the room and people entering or leaving the room causing sudden drafts. Special causes, conversely, are infrequent, unexpected variations in the process that cause a more substantial degradation in quality. Although it can be difficult to identify and resolve special causes of variation, they can in general be found and mitigated more easily than common causes of variation. One example of a special cause of variation is changing which tube is used: The effect of using different tubes on the penny's landing position can be significant, and one should not expect a variety of tubes to be used (if directions were sufficiently specific). This raises the more general discussion about how not following the operation description should be considered a special cause of variation. The most important lessons of this exercise focus around this point and the role that process descriptions play:

1. Deviating from the process instructions is a special cause of variation and quality degradation. Although participants are well intentioned in making these deviations and, in fact, quality improvement is their motive, deviation from the crosshairs increases and quality suffers due to these deviations.

2. Deviation from the process description is not solely the fault of the participants. The process definition offered in the PowerPoint slides is insufficient. Much more detail is required if the subjects are expected to carry out the process in the same way every time. The definition leaves a lot of room for interpretation and thus in and of itself is a cause of variation.

3. The process is poor in that many of the causes of significant quality degradation should be expected because the tooling and penny-dropping instructions do not allow the operators a good way

to control the aim of the tube, hold the tube at the correct height and angle, and so forth. A better process would make it easier for the participants to execute the process as defined.

The main point of this exercise in terms of the topic of this chapter is that if the way a process is performed changes, then the results change. Thus it can be argued that process descriptions must be specific to control variation, and they must be followed consistently for consistent quality and processing times. The last point in the list facilitates the observation that management, not the worker, is responsible for ensuring that the process and the process description are sufficient. Even in organizations where the workers contribute to defining process descriptions, management must permit them to participate in that process. W. Edwards Deming and Joseph Juran maintained that a vast majority of quality problems (80 to 85 percent) are not the fault of the operators but rather management's fault because management is responsible for defining the process or supporting the operators in defining the process, as well as for providing appropriate equipment and otherwise ensuring a satisfactory system of product manufacturing or service delivery.[2]

Other important lessons that can emerge from this exercise besides this key point are the following:

- *Intuition about process improvement can be incorrect.* When operators switch tools in an attempt to improve quality, the choice is based on intuition. Intuition or, in other words, hypothesis, is often wrong because our intuition might focus on a single factor affecting quality that we believe is the most significant. For example, participants use the plastic wrap tube because of its small diameter and its promise for better aim. However, our intuition might not comprehend other process factors that are more consequential than those we focused on. For example, the plastic wrap tube is longer, thus creating a higher velocity at impact, and velocity seems to be a more significant factor in this process than aim.
- *Frequent changes in process execution exacerbate process variation.* Frequent changes in tube selection cause variation to increase and quality to degrade. Furthermore, the tube that led to a

particular outcome is not identifiable from the data on the observations, which would hinder problem-solving efforts.

- *Process improvements should be based on sufficient data.* The two previous points suggest the need for collecting data to validate hypothesized process improvements in a controlled fashion. Because hypothesized improvements do not always succeed, hypotheses need to be verified with data. Ideally, sufficient data can be collected to ensure a statistically significant difference in the process results. Changing tubes after each penny is dropped not only fails to give sufficient data upon which to base a decision about how to execute the process but also often causes quality to degrade by increasing variation. This suggests the need for a controlled environment in which deviations from the defined process are sanctioned as experiments to collect data, which determine whether they are indeed improvements. This underscores the importance of process improvement methodologies such as Lean and Six Sigma being data driven.

- *Simpler processes often produce better quality.* The procedure of using a tube, at a certain height, at a certain angle, and so forth is a very complex setup. One can envision much simpler and much more accurate processes, such as simply placing the penny by hand on the crosshairs. Thus the point can be made that complex processes are not inherently better. In fact, the simpler the process—with fewer steps, less equipment, less complex fixtures and procedures—the greater the accuracy and quality. Furthermore, there are fewer factors that affect the process, which can vary and cause quality to decline.

- *Specifications.* No specifications were given to the participants to define acceptable quality, and so quality performance cannot be measured. This can be taken as an opportunity to define tolerances on product dimensions and to discuss the Taguchi loss function.

- *Measurement system analysis.* The penny must be moved before an X can mark its center. We would expect variation in the location of where the penny landed and where the mark was made. This motivates the discussion of whether a measurement system can be trusted to measure the quality of a product or service and how we might ensure that measurements were sufficiently accurate.

Standardization and Its Difficulties

Arguments Against Standardization and Their Rebuttals

The following are the most frequent and instinctive responses as to why managers do not think that Lean will work for their business:

1. "The customers we serve or the products we manufacture have so much variety that we cannot apply Lean, which depends on a large degree of standardization."
2. "Our industry is more art than science: We need to rely on the experience and expertise of our employees to determine how to resolve issues that arise. You cannot apply Lean's formulaic management tools to these situations because the resolution is always different depending on the circumstances."
3. "Our business offering relies on creativity, and standardizing the way that we did things would make our product or service less innovative."

The author, prior to writing this text, had cataloged various arguments against Lean, which he thought to be fundamentally different points. However, thinking through this issue more carefully and distilling the long list of arguments revealed that, at heart, an overwhelming majority of people's objections to Lean take issue with standardization. Moreover, the bases of their arguments are not significantly different: standardization (a) cannot be applied to complex processes, (b) impedes the operators' need to apply their intelligence, or (c) stifles creativity that is needed to address substantially varying clients or instances. The author has found that although circumstances can be complex and varied and intelligence and creativity are sometimes necessary to cope with these circumstances, there are always aspects of processes that can be standardized such that customers and clients are better off.

Health care is one venue where one might hear all of the previous arguments. Dr. Atul Gawande, in his book titled *The Checklist Manifesto*,[3] describes the vast variety of diseases that a doctor might face on any one day, let alone in any one year. Gawande also describes the complexity in health care in terms of the volume of knowledge that doctors must possess. So this is a likely venue where doctors and other health care professionals might argue for the importance of reliance on experts and their knowledge. Still, Dr. Gawande shows that checklists, which are a standardization tool that might be used in a Lean implementation, effectively reduce accidental deaths in health care and improve patient outcomes.

Another example of using a tool akin to a checklist is provided by a company in the business of delivering customized transportation services, which acquires business by responding to requests for quotation (RFQs) as described in Chapter 2. Its managers argued that each RFQ had its own peculiarities and no standardized process could address each RFQ's idiosyncrasies. At the conclusion of a Lean project the company found, to the contrary, that approximately 80% to 90% of the data fields required to reply to an RFQ were common among all RFQs. By creating a form (much like Dr. Gawande's checklist), the company was able to reduce the number of data omissions, errors, and rework steps significantly, resulting in reduced lead time for completing the response. Reduced lead time in this case implies more responses to RFQs are completed on time, and presumably, a higher percentage of bids are successful.

In an automotive part-stamping operation, the author observed a plant that routinely took six hours or longer to change stamping dies, whereas Toyota plants routinely changed dies in minutes. Each time a die was inserted into a press, a lengthy calibration process was required to remove creases in the metal parts or other defects before production could be started. One part of the calibration process to remove creases was to insert shims, which raised the height of the die in certain areas. The skill and expertise of the skilled tradespeople who shimmed the dies was revered: These were experienced and knowledgeable people who could do what few others could. A different number of shims needed to be placed in different locations each time. They might describe their job as being more of an art than a science, one implication being that art cannot be codified. This process, however, could have benefitted from some standardization. One fundamental tenet of the single-minute exchange of dies (SMED) technique used at Toyota is to ensure the repeatable placement of a die in a press. Less erratic placement of dies implies less time calibrating to compensate for varying placement. Ironically, the techniques for consistent die placement also help dies to be installed and to become productive more quickly.

The need for the die setters' expertise and art bears an eerie resemblance to that of artisans in the American Industrial Revolution before mass production. In that era, *puddlers* mixed small batches of steel according to their own recipes before large mass-production furnaces were invented, and gunsmiths hand fit each part on a musket because the dimensions of manufactured parts varied so much. A key enabler of mass production was, indeed, reducing dimensional variation in parts. It is ironic that a century later erratic die placement is overlooked and die setters are revered for their ability to cope with dimensional uncertainty.

As much difference as a company might think it has among customers and jobs, and as much expertise as one might claim is needed to adapt to continually varying circumstances, many parts of processes can often be codified. One example is the explicit definition of how a die should be placed in a press. This leaves more time to focus on the remaining portion of the job that does require expertise, creativity, or innovation. The author has come to believe that the statement "Our business is more art than science, so we cannot standardize" should most often be interpreted as the following:

1. We have not taken the time to understand our business processes, and so we do not know how the execution of the process is related to the outcome of the process.
2. We do not understand our processes sufficiently to know which parts of the process can be standardized such that the process could actually be improved.

If the inputs to a process and the manner in which it is executed are not formally studied in terms of how they affect the quantity and quality of the process output, then executing the process relies on intuitive relationships between process inputs and outputs that have been informed by experience. This is a reasonable definition of art. All too often, however, an intuitive approach is neither efficient nor effective because the intuitive connections between efforts and results may in fact be invalid. In that case, applying expert knowledge is closer to trial and error than we might like to believe and is therefore not an efficient way of getting a job done. Such is the job of a die setter fiddling with shims and a puddler spitting on his pool of molten steel. Taking time to understand the process, and taking time to collect and analyze data, would more definitively establish the connections between what people do in processes and the results. When these connections are clear, then standardizing on the actions that produce the desired results is possible and desirable.

It is interesting and ironic to note that even though the arguments previously mentioned against Lean are often arguments for why a particular industry is different from normal processes where Lean can be used, the same arguments against Lean are heard in all industries. There seems to be a tendency to think that one's own industry is special and immune from standard techniques that are generally applicable elsewhere. Is this a manifestation that processes are generally interpreted as art rather than science? The motivations to resist standardization might be many. Some rebel against notions associated with Henry Ford and mass production. Perhaps the notion of being an expert and work being an art rather than a routine promotes self-esteem. Maybe doing an expert's work increases the intellectual challenge of work and thus satisfaction of doing work, even if it is inefficient. Possibly, being more familiar with our own industries, being less familiar with other industries, and perhaps being a bit egocentric might lead us to believe that our industry is truly different. Or being unfamiliar with the value of Lean and having the current mind-sets about experts challenged is threatening. Nonetheless, even where experts, variety, and complexity exist, managers who seriously consider Lean are likely to find some value in it for their operations.

Arguments for Standardization

In a previous chapter, we outlined the steps of Lean, which begin with mapping the process to identify waste. The tools of Lean are then applied to reduce unnecessary lead time. Then, the future state value stream map (VSM) is created that shows the process as it will be executed once the planned improvements are made. One might ask two questions:

1. Will the process improvements that we have identified today be valid if the process is being executed another way tomorrow?
2. Of what value is the future state VSM if we cannot execute it as planned?

To the first question, the future state VSM reflects solutions to waste as it was observed in the process initially. Surely, if the process is being executed differently tomorrow, the waste we observe in the process on another day may be different and the solutions as originally conceived may not be effective for the new current state of the process. This hypothetical question suggests the importance of executing a process in a consistent way. You cannot fix problems if they are always changing. Also, any metrics taken over the long term for such a situation do not measure one consistent execution mode for the process but rather an amalgam of processes, which has little meaning if one were to numerically compare before and after a change.

The second question offers an even more powerful argument for the importance of standardizing how processes are executed. Clearly, if we cannot practice the future state VSM as it is planned, then the solutions to waste cannot be implemented. The process must be reorganized around this new definition and practiced consistently for improvement to be realized. We will talk later in this book about process definitions more detailed than VSMs, and the lesson applies to that level of process description as well: If the process definition cannot be executed reliably, then the waste intended to be eliminated by the definition will likely persist.

Thus consistent process execution is a requirement of process improvement. Any efforts put into improving the process without standardization are a waste of time because they will not be implemented. Furthermore, with no standardization, the varying execution of a process creates process metrics that likely will wander from higher to lower levels and back again, with no apparent improvement trend: Even if a good process unknowingly was practiced long enough to be recognized via process metrics, it soon will be replaced by another set of process steps.

Spear and Bowen analyzed the Toyota Production System (TPS) and identified the critical aspects of how Toyota executes and improves processes.[4] They identified these practices, which contributed to Toyota's surpassing the Big Three American automakers in quality and productivity in the 1980s:

1. Highly specified work sequence and content
2. Standardized connections between process steps
3. Simple, specified, unique path
4. The scientific method as an underlying principle of process improvement

Standardization is a common element of all of these practices. To be effective, highly specified work sequences need to be executed in the specified way every time. Standardized connections between process steps ensure that a specific person is responsible for receiving items for further processing and that the items are always put in a specified location; otherwise, work dumped off at the next step at varying locations can wait a long time before it is noticed, and there may be confusion over who is responsible for handling it. Simple, specified, and unique paths for each type of item manufactured ensure that every unit is produced in the same (standardized) manner. This minimizes variation in processing and makes identifying root causes of quality problems easier.

Most importantly, Toyota follows what Spear and Bowen call the scientific method. The scientific method can be described with an illustration that those who have had high school or college physics courses will readily understand. Physics courses typically begin by introducing Newtonian physics. Those sets of principles and equations that describe how physical bodies act with respect to one another and gravity were used for 250 years before Albert Einstein developed new theories for bodies that are moving very fast or that are very heavy. Engineering and scientific endeavors in the intervening years did just fine using Newton's theories in all but the most extreme situations. Einstein's theories of relativity refined Newton's ideas for those extreme environments. The important point is that Einstein's theories were not accepted in place of Newton's until experimental physicists carried out experiments to validate those theories. Thus, in science, theories precede experimentation, but both are required to establish a new belief.

The scientific method, then, requires that we operate under the current, proven hypotheses until better theories are developed and validated experimentally. This is a data-driven approach; we do not change our beliefs when new theories come about but only when experimental data validate those ideas. Similarly, the current process definition is our validated hypothesis for the best known way to operate the system, and as such we standardize on it. We are open, however, to better ways to execute the process, and we will adopt those new methods, but only when we have tried them out and validated with data that they are indeed better. Ideas about improving processes are merely hypotheses until proven. Unlike the penny-dropping exercise, hypotheses should not be implemented unless the results are going to be studied and verified with data.

It is appropriate at this point to make a few more comments about why tasks should be defined and executed in fine detail. First, one of the main lessons of the penny-dropping exercise described earlier in this chapter is that unless a process is defined in detail, the considerable latitude allowed in the execution of the task allows deviations that could have catastrophic effects. In that vein, the paragraphs that follow offer three more arguments for process specificity from real-world processes.

To illustrate, we will use an experience that many readers have likely had. Specifically, we will talk about how to change a wheel and tire on a car and, more specifically, the order in which you should tighten the lug nuts. When tightening the lug nuts on a wheel, one should first install all the lug nuts finger tight before fully tightening any of the nuts. When tightening the lug nuts, one should tighten in two passes, using the sequence indicated in Figure 5.2 (for a five-lug wheel). (The starting lug, which is indicated with a 1 in Figure 5.2, can be any lug.) If either a lug nut is fully tightened before the other lug nuts are put on finger tight or the pattern shown in Figure 5.2 is not used, it is possible that the wheel might not be seated flatly on the wheel hub. This can result in vibration and even loosening of the wheel. Thus for safety it is extremely important that these steps be followed. Spear and Bowen discuss a similar example in which Toyota has specified the sequence for tightening seat bolts. Does deviating from this specified sequence cause the seat to not be placed properly or restrict the bolts from attaining proper torque, as is the case when we mount a wheel onto a car? We do not know, and Toyota may

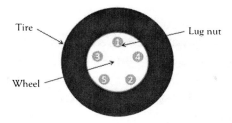

Tire

Lug nut

Wheel

Figure 5.2 Lug nut tightening sequence

not know whether there is such a link between cause and effect. But why take a chance and leave the sequence and quality at risk on such a critical operation? Toyota should know the quality they have attained with a certain bolt-tightening sequence, and maintaining that same sequence guarantees that same performance.

An example of a standardized, consistent process from food service is the process for preparing McDonald's French fries. It is one of the hallmarks of McDonald's, and possibly a strategic advantage, that customers can expect French fries to have the same characteristics regardless of which McDonald's location they visit.[5] Leaving details about the process up to individual discretion invites not only differences in taste from location to location but also process variation that could cause customers to experience poor quality. Customers who are dissatisfied by such a critical facet of McDonald's business threaten McDonald's strategic positioning, so why take a chance on variation?

An example from an administrative process was observed by the author in which it was left to individual discretion how to gather data and write it up in response to an RFQ, where the company responding to the RFQ was doing so to secure new business in the form of a contract with another company. Although it was indeed true that *some* aspects of the data required for each RFQ were different, a great many of the data items were consistently required for each RFQ response. Leaving it up to individuals to catalog the requirements of each RFQ afresh created a situation where some requested data items were missed. Creating a standard form that required the most frequent data items to be included in each RFQ response eliminated the possibility that those items would be forgotten because it was obvious when fields on the form were left blank.

Conclusions

This chapter has presented arguments for the necessity of performing a process consistently every time if its performance is to be improved, or even maintained. Standardization is required at two levels: First, at a macro level, each of the specified steps of a process must be executed in the same sequence every time. For example, the steps in a VSM must be followed in every instance. Additionally, at a detailed level, the minute steps of a process must be performed as specified and in the sequence specified; for example, failing to tighten the lug nuts in the proper order could cause damage to the vehicle, an unstable ride, and injury. The mechanism in Lean to specify the macro process is the VSM. The tool used to specify the details of how tasks are to be executed when Lean and the TPS are used is most often *Standard Work*, which connotes a standardized way to do an operation. We will describe how to use Standard Work in Chapter 7.

PART II

Lean Tools

Once a process is revealed through its map and its lead time and value-added times, nonvalue-added times, and value-added ratio are computed, opportunities for reducing lead time can be brainstormed. One approach to generating improvement ideas is to, first, convene the improvement team for a brainstorming session to solicit team members' ideas for reducing lead time. A brainstorming session is effective because one team member's idea can spark additional ideas from other members. Of course, the typical rules of brainstorming apply—most importantly, that no idea is critiqued or vetted for feasibility during this stage. Criticism can stifle the input of more timid team members, and what is needed at this point is a constructive atmosphere that invites participation. Vetting ideas for feasibility can be done later, and sometimes ideas that seem crazy and infeasible actually turn out to be feasible ideas that nobody ever tried because they thought they were infeasible, so it is important that these ideas are not killed early on. At the least, wild ideas, even if infeasible, can induce other feasible improvements. Subsequent to brainstorming, more structured input can be generated by focusing on the process steps and waiting steps that have the longest lead time or, in other words, the process steps that present the greatest opportunity. If no ideas were spontaneously generated during brainstorming for these critical steps, then this is an opportunity to address the main culprits of long lead time.

Even without formal exposure to tools used in Lean to reduce lead time, people often intuitively have good ideas for reducing lead time. Still, familiarity with a broader tool kit provides greater opportunity for improvement, and enlarging your tool kit is the focus of Part II of this book.

The goal is to identify and eliminate the seven types of waste that were previously mentioned. The tactics for doing so and reducing lead time fall into these categories:

1. Simplify
2. Streamline
3. Standardize
4. Use visual systems
5. Mistake-proof processes and product designs
6. Synchronize
7. Collocate
8. Reduce changeover time

These tactics are not aligned with the seven types of waste in a one-to-one fashion. Rather any action falling into one of the preceding categories often reduces multiple types of waste. The best way to describe which types of waste are reduced is to describe each of these tactics in the context of real situations where they have been applied. In this part of the book, we do just that for each of the eight improvement tactics previously listed.

We will also observe that the categories do not separate improvements made in Lean projects in a mutually exclusive manner; some actions might fairly be put into multiple categories. That observation motivates us to say that a main purpose of the category labels is not only to neatly classify Lean tools but also to remind us of the different ways that we can improve processes. The category labels are purposefully stated as directives, which if followed will reduce lead time and improve processes.

CHAPTER 6

Simplify and Streamline

There are many ways to simplify or streamline a process and many tools that can be used, including these:

1. Eliminating a process step
2. Creating and analyzing a spaghetti diagram
3. Applying the 5S methodology
4. Simplifying tools, equipment, jigs, fixtures, and procedures

We will discuss each of these methods in this chapter. The simplifying and streamlining categories are related, and so we present them here in the same chapter. In fact, some of the tools we discuss might fit under simplification just as well as under streamlining. Thus although it may seem that these two categories should be combined, there may be a good reason for maintaining an extra category, as its moniker might provoke additional ideas for improving processes.

Eliminating Process Steps

The quickest way to reduce wasteful lead time is to eliminate an entire step from a process. Reducing big chunks of lead time in this way is powerful motivation for creating a value stream map (VSM) that shows a process at the macro level: Without a VSM to point out these opportunities for process improvement, effort might otherwise be spent on steps where improvements were more modest.

One scenario in which steps can be eliminated is when it is discovered that a process step does not add value. Sometimes operations are thought to be value-added, but if you asked customers whether the work done in a step motivated them to pay more for the product, the answer would be no. The work performed in these steps is the type of waste we call *overprocessing*. One example of overprocessing is options added to automobiles that customers pay for even though they do not want them. These are options that cannot be purchased separately but rather come bundled together in option packages. One vehicle, for example, is sold with a 110-volt outlet bundled together with a rear-window sunscreen. Even though some owners do not want the rear sunscreen, they are forced to pay for it anyway. This overprocessing is motivated by automakers' desire to smooth the workload of operators along the assembly line, but it results in extra content that some consumers do not want.

Sometimes multiple process steps can be combined into one step. While this does not always eliminate the work performed in the combined steps, it has much the same effect. One example of where combining steps has a beneficial effect is in a hiring process where a job applicant was required to travel to the company three times to interview with three different individuals, one trip per interview, as shown in Figure 6.1. This company reduced the lead time of this process by having all three people interview job candidates simultaneously, which required only one trip. The improvement eliminated 15 minutes of interview time but, more significantly, the delay between interviews and transportation to and from interviews was eliminated. It might not always be the case, but in this instance, the wait time between interviews was thought not to improve hiring decisions and, therefore, was nonvalue-added. The cost of this process rearrangement was an additional five minutes for one manager per interview and the effort to coordinate managers' schedules. In addition, the lead time was reduced further by making a hiring decision immediately while the applicant was still in the store. This eliminated another waiting period and another trip back to the store for the applicant. In total, lead time is reduced from 8,282 minutes to 27 minutes in this example. Although lead time might not be reduced in some processes if this tactic is exercised, combining steps invariably eliminates intervening transportation and waiting periods. For example, moving two sequential manufacturing steps next to one another on the production floor would not reduce the total processing time (each machine would still require the same cycle time), but the transportation between the two steps is virtually eliminated.

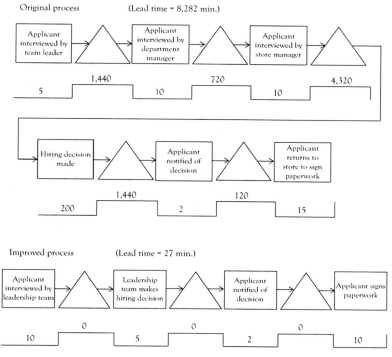

Figure 6.1 Hiring process VSM

Spaghetti Diagrams

A spaghetti diagram simply shows the movement of goods or people using lines superimposed on a layout of the work area. For example, Figure 6.2 shows the movement of a person changing a die in a manufacturing operation, and Figure 6.3 shows the movement of a café worker preparing a Cobb salad, both of which are based on a real example. These diagrams can be drawn for any operation to trace the path of a worker who needs to physically move from point to point to accomplish a task or to trace the path of physical goods traveling through a process. Spaghetti diagrams can be as sophisticated as those created in Computer-Aided Design or Computer-Aided Manufacturing software, which automatically computes travel distance, or as simple as hand-drawn illustrations. Microsoft PowerPoint also provides an effective platform for spaghetti diagrams intermediate between these two alternatives.

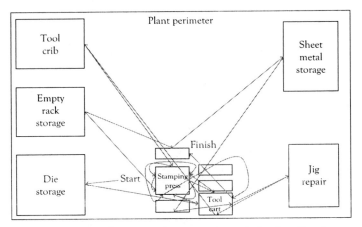

Figure 6.2 Spaghetti diagram of a person's path during die changeover

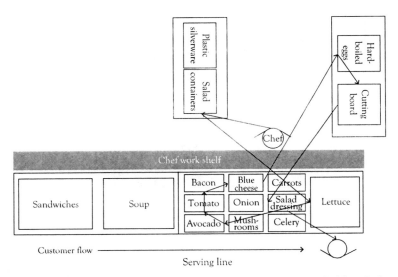

Figure 6.3 Spaghetti diagram of a café worker making a Cobb salad

The first purpose served by a spaghetti diagram is to graphically and vividly make the point that people or goods often follow a serpentine path as they move through a process, doubling back on their paths multiple times. Serpentine paths are indicative of wasted motion, either on the part of an individual or on the part of the goods being processed. In the former case, wasted motion is, indeed, one of our seven deadly categories of waste. In the latter case, extra travel distance implies excess transportation, which is another form of waste leading to excess lead time. A messy spaghetti diagram that looks like a bowlful of spaghetti provides a palpable realization, and irrefutable evidence, that the process can be rearranged to create a more direct path that reduces these types of waste. It is perfectly fine and desirable to report total travel time or total travel distance to a Lean team, but seeing a messy graphic image with lines crossing over one another that looks like spaghetti is a much more convincing argument for the presence of waste and the need to address it. Creating a less wasteful flow usually requires rearranging operations so that goods and people move in a more direct path without backtracking, which can be done on two different scales. First, at a macro level, workstations can be rearranged so that the path goods follow is more direct. This type of activity is often associated with a 5S event (discussed later in this chapter) where the layout of a process is viewed afresh and equipment is relocated to create a more amenable flow. In one such 5S exercise, a spaghetti diagram like the one shown in Figure 6.4 was created of the process before improvement. After the conclusion of the 5S event, the workstations were arranged as shown in Figure 6.5, which reduced travel distance by approximately 50 percent. At a more detailed, micro level, the layout of tools and equipment at particular workstations

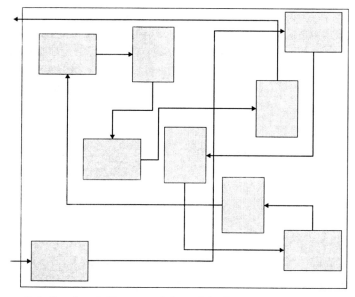

Figure 6.4 Spaghetti diagram of the original process

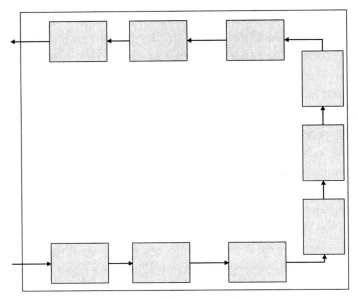

Figure 6.5 Spaghetti diagram of the improved process

can be rearranged to reduce the distance traveled by a worker, as in the example with the café worker.

The relationships between creating and resolving the convoluted flow depicted in a spaghetti diagram and other tools used in Lean are worth noting. For example, using a spaghetti diagram to help rearrange workstations is related to creating a work cell (discussed in Chapter 11) where machines are relocated next to one another to shorten and simplify the flow of goods. In addition, creating a more direct path for a worker at a workstation could involve using Standard Work (as discussed in Chapter 7), as well as a spaghetti diagram. In essence, the graphical work layout that usually accompanies Standard Work would look like a spaghetti diagram if work were arranged poorly.

Applying 5S

The 5S method is for organizing and rationalizing a work area or an entire process flow. The term 5S comes from the Toyota Production System and was originally described by the following Japanese words, each of which appears with one English translation:

Seiri	Sort
Seiton	Set in order
Seiso	Shine
Seiketsu	Standardize
Shitsuke	Sustain

Many translations of the 5Ss can be found, and some companies have expanded the 5Ss to 6 or 7Ss. Furthermore, at least one company has co-opted the term *5S* to describe their strategic planning process, which has quite a different meaning than the original one. This is just another example that suggests that not all companies use the same terminology, and it is best to look at the details of a company's practice before assuming that it conforms to standard practice. That said, what we will describe here is the traditional meaning of 5S. The most apparent benefits of 5S are that it reduces transportation time and distance and reduces wasted motion looking for goods to process, tools, and equipment, but it has other benefits that we will discover.

The first step of 5S is to *sort* out the equipment, tools, and fixtures in a work area. The main goal is to determine which items are essential to the process and which items can be disposed of. Excess equipment and materials make it difficult to find items that are needed, increase travel time and distance around these obstacles, and prohibit placing work-stations in a more efficient layout. Getting rid of excess equipment and materials eliminates these wastes. The typical sort step is to remove all equipment from the work area, and as each item is removed, its status is determined from the categories listed in Table 6.1. Red, yellow, or green tags are attached to the equipment and materials as they are removed from the work area according to whether they are essential to the operation or not. As the work area is redesigned, only the essential items with green

Table 6.1 5S Tagging protocol

Item status	Tag color
Equipment is essential to the process	Green
It is unclear if equipment is needed	Yellow
Equipment is not needed	Red

tags are returned to the work area. Conversely, the items tagged with yellow and red tags are not returned to the work area. Instead, they can be stored elsewhere for a brief period until their final disposition is determined. If, over the course of a number of weeks or months, an item with a yellow or red tag is found to be necessary, then it is returned to the work area. Conversely, all other items with yellow and red tags can be either redeployed elsewhere or disposed of.

The next step in 5S is to organize the flow of goods through the work area, or *set in order*. With all equipment removed from the work area, a new workflow can be established that requires less travel distance on this clean slate. An example of this was given when we discussed spaghetti diagrams and, in particular, the improvement from Figure 6.4 to Figure 6.5. Besides locating workstations, tools, and equipment, setting a process in order also requires that locations be specified for materials being processed (i.e., in processes with physical goods flowing through them). Maximum inventory quantities are normally specified, which reduces lead time (think of Little's law) and minimizes clutter.

Before the essential equipment and materials are moved back into the work area, the work area is cleaned. This is the *shine* step of 5S. Floors are typically swept, washed, and, perhaps, waxed. Equipment is cleaned before being placed back in the work area. Clean equipment has more than an aesthetic advantage: Clean equipment also makes maintenance issues like leaking oil readily apparent.

Embedded in the process redesign, which is constituted by the *set in order* step of 5S, is a detailed specification for where everything goes in the work area. These and other facets of how the process is performed must be standardized. The expectation expressed in the *standardize* step is that the process will be practiced according to the new design from now into the foreseeable future until such time as data proves that a different process design is better. This requires discipline on the part of workers and, perhaps, surveillance and audits by managers.

Finally, the *sustain* step requires that the order and cleanliness of the work area are maintained and possibly, again, verified by occasional audits. However, the author has been told by native Japanese that *sustain* is not the best translation of *shitsuke*. *Shitsuke* has a connotation of continuous improvement, whereas sustain, obviously, has a connotation more in line with maintaining the status quo. Thus the original Japanese connotation is more aspirational than the translation presented here. One can imagine that in a quest to translate five Japanese words starting with S into five English words starting with S, meaning may have been compromised in favor of starting a word with S to retain the 5S slogan.

From the foregoing discussion, 5S clearly offers the prospect of reduced lead time because travel distances are reduced and locations for equipment and materials are defined, which reduces searching time. Less obvious benefits are, in manufacturing operations, reduced safety issues due to a less cluttered workspace (e.g., fewer tripping hazards) and an opportunity to resolve ergonomic issues that can lead to repetitive stress injuries or back strains (two of the most frequent injuries in industry). In addition, a less cluttered workspace where the flow of product is more apparent and in-process inventory is limited offers the possibility of readily observing the process status. When the sequence of operations is visually apparent and uncluttered, it is easy to see where inventory might be piling up, for example, and it is apparent to workers and managers where a problem exists in the process that is restricting flow. Inventory piling up might be a symptom of a machine that is broken down, an absent worker, or some sort of manufacturing problem that is slowing down a particular operation. The work area shown in the spaghetti diagram in Figure 6.5 has these characteristics. A manager can look into this 40 × 40 inches work area and see the whole process without moving, including symptoms of process problems.

Simplifying Tools, Equipment, Jigs, Fixtures, and Procedures

The discussion following the penny-dropping exercise in Chapter 5 often highlights the unnecessarily complicated nature of fixtures and procedures one finds in many operations and how simplified equipment can yield better results. The author's anecdotal observations of many plants in the automobile industry corroborate this observation. Often, simpler, less expensive equipment can generate better quality products. Furthermore, cost of repair and downtime are reduced because equipment has fewer parts that can fail. So, while 5S can simplify the process flow, better equipment simplifies the tasks at each workstation.

Exercise

1. Select a task that you perform at work. Alternatively, select some task that you perform around your house or apartment. Draw a spaghetti diagram of the path that you follow to complete that task. Measure the travel distance. Can you see any opportunities to reduce the travel distance by redesigning the process or the layout of the workspace?

CHAPTER 7

Standardize

Standardizing a process means to define a set of steps that are followed every time the process is executed. We argued in Chapter 5 that it is important these definitions be as detailed and comprehensive as possible. In particular, these aspects of processes can be defined and standardized:

1. Order of process steps
2. Order of tasks within each process step
3. Tools, equipment, jigs, and fixtures used
4. Workstations where particular tasks are performed
5. Materials used
6. The environment in which the process is executed
7. Specifications that define when a task is completed successfully
8. Locations where materials, tools, and equipment can be found
9. How materials are presented to workers (e.g., location and orientation)

A value stream map (VSM) most often defines a process at a very high level—that is, it does not contain the detailed description about how each processing step is accomplished. Thus although VSMs identify a standard sequence of process steps, which is the first point in the list, each step in the value stream can be defined in more detail. Sometimes the details of process steps in a value stream can be shown in a more detailed rendition of the VSM by creating a VSM that defines individual steps in the original map in greater detail. In this case, the resulting VSMs have a hierarchical relationship. As a process is defined in greater and greater detail, at some point a list of very specific instructions can be constructed that give people explicit details on how to do a task within the process. Such detailed documents are the topic of this section.

In particular, we describe in this section an example of work definition that closely follows Standard Work used in the Toyota Production System.

(The term *Standard Work* may be interpreted as standardized work.) Examples of the two documents that typically compose Standard Work are shown in Figure 7.1 and 7.2.[1] These figures show details for an operation that the author performed for students at the end of each semester—namely, to provide a CD-ROM containing the course web page along with all its content. (Recent technology allows for easy downloading of compressed files over the Internet, making the CD-ROM obsolete.) Although obsolete, this process has characteristics that provide for an informative discussion on the advantages of Standard Work, and so the author still uses it in his courses as an illustration. Figure 7.3 shows the physical layout used for recording CD-ROMs. The document in Figure 7.1 shows a representation of the physical layout of the CD-ROM recording process, specifying the number of workers, the sequence of locations where each worker performs his or her tasks, and the standard inventory allowed in the process and its location. (The standard inventory can be interpreted as the maximum inventory that can be in the process at any one time.) In this process, there is one operator, who is depicted as a circle with an attached semicircle that represents arms. The numbers in the circles on Figure 7.1 represent the task numbers from Figure 7.2, which lists the sequence of tasks that the operator must perform, as well as detailed instructions. Thus Figure 7.1 indicates the sequence of locations that the worker visits in order to perform all the tasks required to record a CD-ROM. The combination of the two documents in Figure 7.1 and 7.2 specifies a majority of the items detailed in the previous list or could specify all those items if the task descriptions in Figure 7.2 were expanded.

The amount of time required for each step is recorded both numerically and graphically on each line of the second form (Figure 7.2). The data columns allow for operator time, machine time, and walk time between steps to be recorded. Manual time is the time that the operator spends physically doing work. Sometimes an operator is required only to initiate the work, such as when they click on a graphic user interface icon to cause a computer to execute a task or hit palm buttons to cause a manufacturing machine to execute an operation. The automatic or machine time indicated in Figure 7.2 is the time required for a machine to execute its work when the operator need not be present. Walk time in manufacturing is the time required for a worker to relocate himself or herself

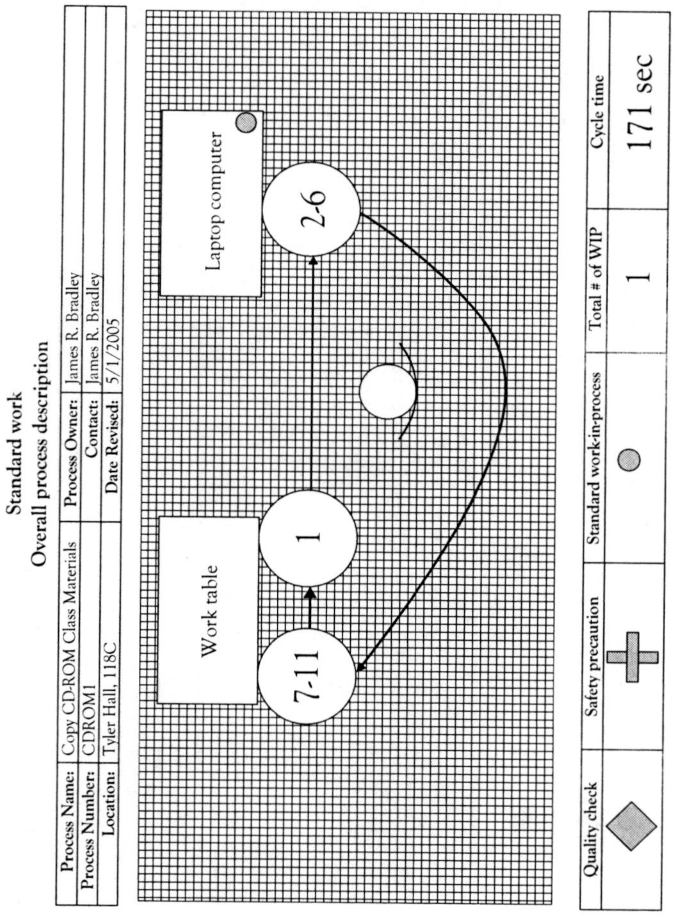
Standard work
Overall process description
Process Name: Copy CD-ROM Class Materials
Process Number: CDROM1
Location: Tyler Hall, 118C
Process Owner: James R. Bradley
Contact: James R. Bradley
Date Revised: 5/1/2005
Work table
Laptop computer
7-11
1
2-6
Quality check
Safety precaution
Standard work-in-process
Total # of WIP
1
Cycle time
171 sec

Figure 7.1 Graphical process description

Standard work
operation detail

Process Name:	Copy CD-ROM Class Materials	Operator Number:	1
Process Number:	CDROM1	Date Revised:	5/1/2005
Location:	Tyler Hall, 118C		

Legend: Manual ■ Automatic/Machine ▬ Walking ∿

Step #	Description of operation	Time (seconds)			Operation time diagram (in seconds) 10" 20" 30" 40" 50" 60" 70" 80" 90" 100" 120" 140" 160" 180"
		Manual	Auto	Walk	
1	Get CD	2	0	2	
2	Insert CD (including closing the disc drive)	6	3	1	
3	Click button to start	1	3	1	
4	Rename file (Click "Continue")	1	98	1	
5	Click "Done" in recording software	1	3	1	
6	Remove finished CD from computer	5	0	2	
7	Get label	18	0	1	
8	Put label into Machine	2	0	1	
9	Affix label to CD	5	0	1	
10	Put CD into envelope	7	0	1	
11	Put CD in FGI	2	0	2	
	Totals	50	107	14	

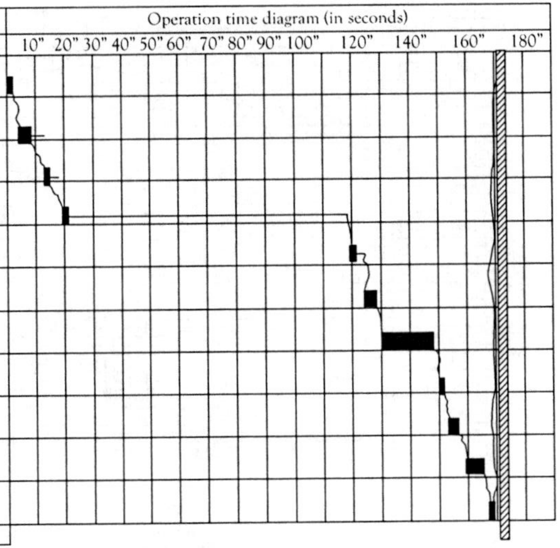

Figure 7.2 Task detail and timing

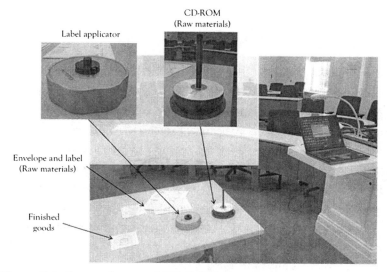

Figure 7.3 Process layout of CD-ROM recording process

in order to perform the next operation. In a broader sense, especially in administrative and service processes, walk time can instead be thought of as transition time from one task to the next. In these types of processes, workers may not need to physically relocate themselves, but they may need time to make a mental switch between tasks. Figure 7.2 also allows for these times to be shown graphically using bars or lines for operator time, machine time, and transition time. For example, in Figure 7.2 we can see both graphically and in written form that removing the finished CD-ROM from the computer requires only manual effort and takes five seconds. Step 4, where recording of the CD-ROM is initiated, requires one second for the operator to initiate the recording, while the computer takes 98 seconds to complete the recording task. In summary, the graphical display in Figure 7.2 effectively communicates the overall timing of each task and the overall operation.

The total time required for an operator to do one cycle of his or her job, before repeating the cycle multiple times, is easily calculated with the Standard Work form: It is the amount of time required for the operator to do all the tasks and then reposition himself or herself to start the sequence again. This duration of time is called *cycle time*. In Figure 7.2, cycle time is 171 seconds, which is graphically indicated by a vertical bar. Note that

Creating Standard Work Documents as an In-Class Exercise

The Standard Work documents for the CD copying process can be constructed in class with students as an exercise. Alternatively, any process that requires relatively little space and can be set up quickly in a classroom can similarly be used as an exercise. The experiment is divided into two phases, as is construction of Standard Work documents in practice. In the first stage, every student in class is responsible for identifying the sequence of tasks carried out by the operator (the instructor), and in the second stage, one student is assigned to measure the manual time, machine time, or walk and transitional time for every task. This allows all the timing data to be collected by executing the sequence of tasks one time. It is advantageous to include some obvious inefficiency in the process, as has been done in the case of the sequence of tasks documented in Figure 7.2, which facilitates discussion of one of the values of documenting a process. Specifically, this helps students to realize that by merely documenting a process, opportunities for improving the efficiency of the process are immediately apparent.

these documents are intended to document standards for repetitive work in which sequences of tasks are executed over and over. Nonetheless, we will describe later how documenting processes in this manner has benefits even if processes are executed only occasionally.

In constructing a Standard Work document, the following observations can be made:

1. Taking time to observe and document a process allows for easy identification of inefficiencies, which leads to ideas for immediate improvement.

2. The timing established with the as-is process provides task timing data that can be used for estimating cycle time if ideas for improvement were implemented. Specifically, rearranging the tasks and using the current timing (which may need to be estimated in some cases) gives good estimates of cycle times with different task sequences.

In some cases, transition times might need to be adjusted if a change in task sequence causes longer or shorter transitions. Similarly, if improvements are possible to reduce either manual or machine time, then those new values can be estimated subject to verification.

3. If the output rate of the operation needs to be increased, then the current task times often give sufficient information to determine how best to increase the production rate (i.e., reduce the cycle time). For example, a paper-based analysis can be conducted to see how the task sequence needs to be revised if output is increased by adding equipment, increasing the number of operators, or both, and to determine which is the best approach.

The CD-ROM recording process as defined thus far contains a noticeable inefficiency, which is easily observed in Figure 7.2. Specifically, the operator waits idly for 98 seconds as the computer finishes recording the CD-ROM. (This occurs starting at 20 seconds into the cycle and finishing at 118 seconds into the cycle.) This observed inefficiency should motivate discussion about how to resequence the tasks in order to eliminate such waiting time (one of the seven deadly wastes).

This issue can be resolved by rearranging the task sequence as shown in Figure 7.4 by having more than one CD-ROM in process at any time. The sequence in Figure 7.4 and work layout in Figure 7.5 indicate that while the computer is recording one CD-ROM, the operator moves on to the next step and applies the label to a CD-ROM that has already been recorded. These work documents for the revised process have been constructed by using the manual and auto task times from the original documents while adjusting the transition time where a greater distance between tasks has been introduced. This process change reduces the idle time of the worker, thus reducing the cycle time to 130 seconds—a 24 percent improvement. Additional opportunities are apparent from the new work description. First, an additional transition from the table to the computer location has been added. While this does not affect cycle time with the present task sequence, moving the table and, in particular, the stack of blank CDs next to the computer would reduce transition time between the two work locations. The reason why the extra transition time does not affect cycle time with the current setup is that it

Operations with Multiple Workers

If multiple operators were required to work together, then the diagram equivalent to Figure 7.1 might look like Figure 7.6, which shows a process layout with four workers. The sequence of stations in each worker's path is shown with circles with operation numbers in them, as in the prior example. Each worker would then have a document such as Figure 7.2 that describes specific task instructions corresponding with those numbers.

Finer Details of Standard Work

The process with reduced cycle time in Figure 7.4 and 7.5 demonstrates some finer details of documenting Standard Work. For example, in Figure 7.5 the circle icons indicate where inventory resides in the system. In this case, one CD-ROM will always be in the computer and at most one CD will be at the applicator tool. Thus maximum work-in-process inventory is two units, which is also indicated at the bottom of the form. Safety hazards for manufacturing work can also be highlighted using the cross icon.

is absorbed in the time that the operator would otherwise be idle waiting for the computer to finish recording the CD. Idle time remains with the revised process that presents a possible opportunity for reducing the cycle time further or an opportunity to increase the production rate by adding another computer so two CD-ROMs can be recorded at one time, allowing the operator to remain busy.

The information in the two Standard Work forms previously discussed is a valuable resource when new operators are trained. Workers often undergo on-the-job training (OJT), where the current operator simply trains the new operator to do the job as it is currently performed. OJT based on a verbal description of the operation allows the operation to change over time. Even if current operators can accurately communicate how they perform a job, operators performing a job without concrete standards are free to innovate and find what they think to be better

Standard work
Operation detail

Process Name:	Copy CD-ROM Class Materials	Operator Number:	1		Manual	▬
Process Number:	CDROM1	Date Revised:	5/1/2005		Automatic/Machine	▬
Location:	Tyler Hall, 118C				Walking	∿∿

		Time (seconds)			Operation time diagram (in seconds)
Step #	Description of operation	Manual	Auto	Walk	10" 20" 30" 40" 50" 60" 70" 80" 90" 100" 120" 140" 160" 180"
1	Get CD	2	0	2	
2	Insert CD (including closing the disc drive)	6	3	1	
3	Click button to start	1	3	1	
4	Rename file (Click "Continue")	1	98	2	
5	Affix label to CD	5	0	1	
6	Put CD into envelope	7	0	1	
7	Put CD in FGI	2	0	1	
8	Get label	18	0	1	
9	Put label into Machine	2	0	2	
10	Click "Done" in recording software	1	3	1	
11	Remove finished CD from computer	5	0	2	
	Totals	50	107	15	

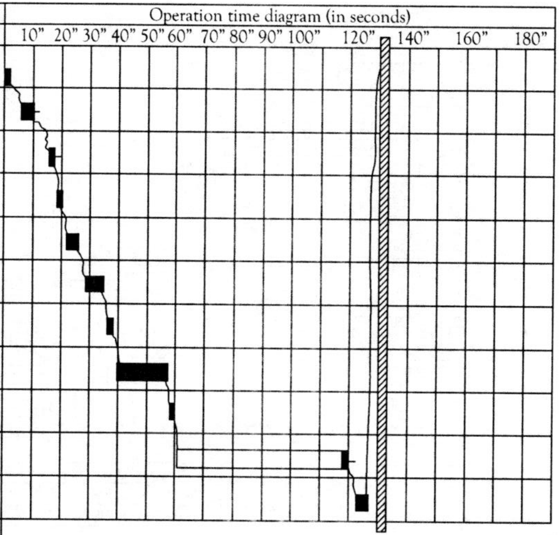

Figure 7.4 *Task detail and timing of improved process*

Standard work
Overall process description

Process Name:	Copy CD-ROM Class Materials	Process Owner:	James R. Bradley
Process Number:	CDROM1	Contact:	James R. Bradley
Location:	Tyler Hall, 118C	Date Revised:	5/1/2005

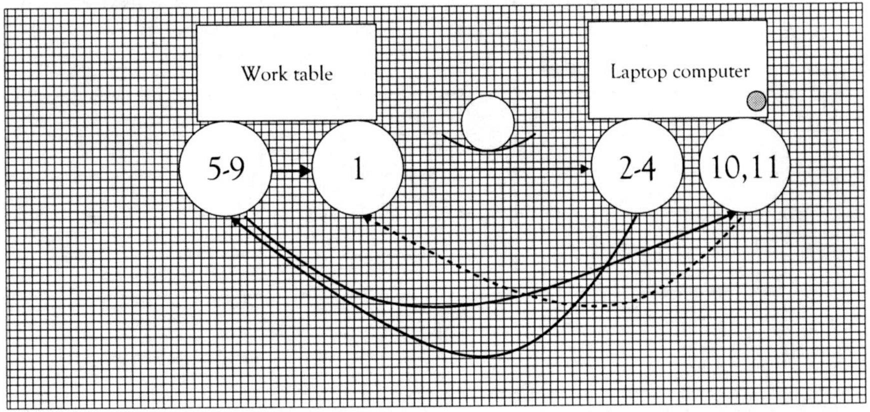

Quality check	Safety precaution	Standard work-in-process	Total # of WIP	Cycle time
			2	130 sec

Figure 7.5 Graphical representation of improved process

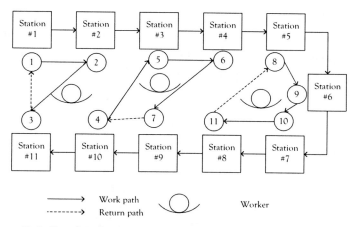

Figure 7.6 Graphical representation of a process with multiple workers

methods of work. Without data to confirm that a hypothesized improvement is indeed an improvement, the evolving job changes, sometimes for the better and sometimes for worse. The evolution of the job execution due to poor communication can be likened to the game of *telephone*. In this game, one person would start by whispering a phrase into the next person's ear. Sequentially, every person would whisper their interpretation of the message to the next person until the message was transmitted all the way around a circle of players. When the last person received the message, they would announce it out loud. Invariably, this result would always be far from the original message, which the person who started the process would then announce. Written and detailed job instructions (Standard Work forms) help to accurately communicate the job requirements during training and serve as an ongoing benchmark against which the current execution of a job can be compared. They inhibit the reinterpretation that occurs in a game of telephone.

While Standard Work forms are associated most often with repetitive work, they are also a valuable resource for work performed infrequently. When tasks are performed intermittently, such as the CD-ROM recording process, which was executed every six months, it can be easy to forget the details of how the process was set up and executed previously. Without documentation to remind us of the process details, it is necessary to reinvent the process from scratch, and we may forget about innovations used in the past to improve efficiency or quality of the operation. The Standard Work documentation allows us to recall the process that has delivered the greatest efficiency to date and prevent back-sliding in efficiency and quality performance.

Exercise

1. Prepare a Standard Work document for an operation using the method described in this chapter. Did documenting the task steps allow you to think of any opportunities to reduce cycle time by rearranging the steps or by rearranging the workspace?

CHAPTER 8

Visual Systems

Visual systems, or visual tools, are devices that make apparent what should be, and is, going on in a process. Depending on how they are employed, visual tools can make the following apparent:

1. When something in the process is going wrong, where it is going wrong, and what is going wrong. For example, a visual device might signal when a step in the process has broken down or is running slow. Thus the need for attention is visually apparent.
2. When the process is being executed according to plan.
3. What employees need to do next, lessening the burden on supervisors to direct employees' every move. This facilitates a more worker-directed process with less management intervention.
4. Where a piece of equipment or a unit of work-in-process should be placed. This can eliminate wasted time looking for material whose whereabouts is uncertain.
5. When errors have been made. They can also prevent errors and defects from occurring. Many devices that serve this purpose are called *mistake-proofing devices*, and Chapter 9 is devoted to these mechanisms.

One hallmark of an effective visual device is that its intended meaning is apparent even to someone who is not familiar with the process. One example is the picture of an airport tarmac with a Jetway with wheels parked in the center of a segment of concrete painted with diagonal lines (see Figure 8.1). Given that only one of many segments of concrete is painted, a reasonable conclusion is that the paint strips indicate where the Jetway wheels should be located when it is not in service. In this case, observing the scene in Figure 8.1 would lead you to believe that everything was in order and there is nothing to worry about. Conversely, Figure 8.2

Figure 8.1 Markings indicating proper positioning of Jetway wheels

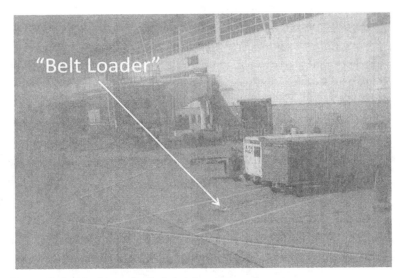

Figure 8.2 Markings for belt loader storage location

shows an airport tarmac that is clearly out of order. The picture indicates where the (illegible) words "Belt Loader" appear. One would guess that the square surrounding these words is where the belt loader should be parked. Hence, one would conclude that the belt loader is mislocated because it is parked elsewhere. Is this a significant problem? In some cases, the rationale for the belt loader's location might be to provide for a more efficient process, as would result from a Lean implementation. Specifically, the specified belt loader location might reduce wasted motion when a plane arrives and bags need to be unloaded. Alternatively, equipment locations might be specified for safety reasons: Keeping equipment at a safe distance from the plane prevents damage to the plane and the equipment. For example, a piece of equipment kept in the path of an aircraft could damage a wing or fuselage if it were too tall. Regardless of what rationale might be behind the specified belt loader location, Figure 8.2 shows that the process is not being practiced as defined and any intended safety or efficiency benefits are not being realized. To return to the question of the significance of the mislocation of the belt loader, it represents a loss of efficiency at a minimum. At its worst, it could present a safety hazard and the possibility for equipment damage. While many may agree that the latter effect is significant, some may say that the former effect is minor—certainly less significant than potential equipment damage. However, if a company wants to improve its processes using Lean, not properly and consistently locating the belt loader is a sign that the company will not be able to implement productivity improvements found through Lean. Recall the in-depth discussion of this topic in Chapter 5.

Tape, paint, or other floor markings can be used in other contexts. Markings on a factory floor can indicate various work protocols. For example, tape of various colors on the floor often indicates where various items should be placed, such as trash receptacles, recycling receptacles, and other pieces of equipment. Colored lines on the floor can also help ensure compliance with safety, health, and hazardous-material procedures. A blue line on the floor, for example, might indicate an area where safety glasses or other protective equipment is required. The blue line would allow a manager or a worker to react more quickly to an unsafe situation, as recognition of the blue line is immediate, whereas looking up written documentation would take time, accurately remembering the boundaries of the safety-glass area might be difficult, and different recollections might cause debate. More importantly, the blue tape quickly communicates to people entering the area the required safety equipment and they know that everyone can easily observe them violating safety protocol if they were to enter the area unsafely. Thus a manager's time is less likely to be taken up with monitoring safety practices.

Still another use of floor markings can be observed in the Toyota Production System (TPS) along automotive assembly lines, where signal lines painted on the floor subdivide the segment of the assembly line where each worker performs his or her job. Each line might represent when 10 percent of the allotted cycle time had passed. Thus these lines allow workers to gauge the amount of time remaining to work on the current vehicle and to determine if they are likely to complete work on that car in time. If not, then managers can be signaled using an andon cord (discussed later in this chapter—*andon* is a Japanese word that means *lantern* or *lamp*).

Shadow boards are devices to visually show where equipment goes and when it is missing. Silhouettes on shadow boards specify positions for each tool or piece of equipment so that when the silhouette is visible it indicates that the tool is missing. Figure 8.3 shows an example of a shadow board used by a cabinetmaker. Specifically, Figure 8.3 shows the outlines for two bevel gauges and a mortise gauge in one image and another image where the shadow of one bevel gauge makes it apparent that it is missing. Shadow

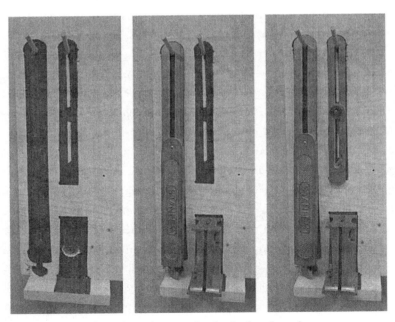

Figure 8.3 Portion of a cabinetmaker's shadow board

boards can also facilitate greater efficiency by having tools arranged in the order they are needed for specific procedures, such as medical operations, jet aircraft overhaul, and machine changeovers.

Andon devices, like markings on floors and shadow boards, visually alert management and workers when a problem exists in a process. (*Andon* is a term used in TPS.) Andon devices can take many forms in manufacturing, including a stack of green, yellow, and red lights in the bottom, middle, and top positions, respectively, as shown in Figure 8.4, which are used to indicate a machine's status. Each colored lens has a light within it and one light is illuminated at any one time. The lights sit atop a pole sufficiently high that they can be seen from a reasonable distance, and the particular color that is glowing indicates the status of a workstation:

1. Green means the machine or station is running.
2. Yellow means that a station is not running due to another machine. Yellow can indicate that either a machine is starved for material from a prior workstation or it is backed up to the next machine.
3. Red means the machine has broken down.

These lights placed on a sequence of machines or workstations that constitute sequential steps in a process allow the point of trouble to be easily identified when one exists. A maintenance or production person, whoever is responsible for responding to equipment breakdowns, would look for red lights and proceed to that machine to repair it. Machines

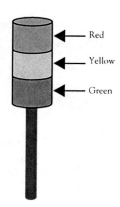

Figure 8.4 Andon light stack

that display yellow lights are not operative, but the problem is not at any of those locations. However, the yellow lights do give some indication of the severity of the problem or how long it has been going on: A greater number of yellow lights indicates that the machine breakdown has been occurring for a longer period of time.

Other types of andon systems can also be employed, such as andon boards and andon cords. Andon boards display the status of production. Figure 8.5 shows typical information that might be communicated on an andon board. At the top of that andon board the number of units produced thus far in the shift is shown, as is the target for that point in the shift. The difference between those two figures is the number of units ahead or behind schedule. In this case, production is 42 units behind where it should be, and that number is displayed in red as the status. The andon board in Figure 8.5 lists the numeric codes for work areas through which parts proceed: 10, 20, 30, and so forth. When those work area numbers are displayed in red, yellow, and green, it has the same meaning as the andon light stack. Additionally, the andon board gives a visual bar chart-style display of buffer inventory between the work areas, where red, yellow, and green bars indicate low inventory, inventory that is not quite up to desired levels, and satisfactory inventory levels, respectively.

Andon cords are used on manufacturing lines to let workers alert managers of problems. A typical andon cord setup would have a piece of rope

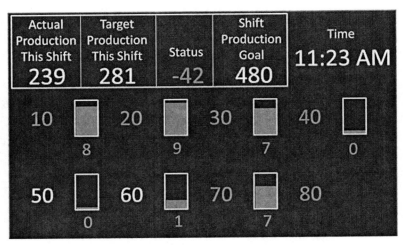

Figure 8.5 Andon board

or wire running alongside an assembly line that an operator could pull if a problem occurred, such as when parts do not fit or when a shortage of parts exists. Pulling the cord, which would be attached to an electrical switch, would cause a light or lights to be illuminated and, in some cases, music to play. The music is sometimes unique for a particular workstation so that a manager knows the location of the problem without needing to look for lights and can promptly go to that location and help to resolve the problem.

The use of visual systems is not limited to manufacturing processes. They can also be used in administrative and service processes. One example from food service is one that many readers may have observed. Some fast-food restaurants use electronic screens to display the queue of orders that have been placed but not yet delivered to customers waiting in the drive-thru lane. In some restaurants, each order will have a clock running associated with that order displaying the elapsed time since the order was placed. This allows workers to gauge progress and determine how likely it is a particular order would be delivered within the allowed time. (Restaurants such as this often have a specified lead time within which to fulfill a customer's order, which demonstrates that Lean is particularly appropriate for these operations.) An order might even start flashing in yellow or red when it is imminently or actually past due, respectively. Another example in health care services occurred when a Lean consultant improved the productivity of a dentist's office by indicating to the dentist via an andon board which examination rooms held patients who were ready for him, as shown in Figure 8.6.[1] Lights appeared on a computer screen to show the rooms in which patients resided whose service had progressed to the point where he was needed. Before the andon system, the dentist did not know when he was needed and so he was idle at the same time that a patient was waiting for him. The resulting productivity gain greatly increased the profitability of the practice.

Visual systems seem more difficult to implement in administrative processes where information, rather than a physical good, is being processed. Where physical goods are processed, the work-in-process is easily observed and can itself serve as a signal. Particularly where service and administrative work-in-process is held in digital form, it cannot be observed within a computer unless some physical manifestation of it is

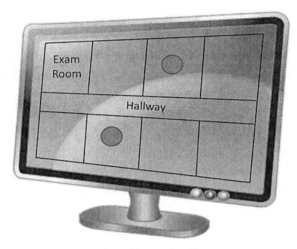

Figure 8.6 Andon screen for a dentist's office

rendered. In these situations, visual systems might be real-time displays on computer screens showing the number of units at various stages in the process and, perhaps, some color-coded signal (e.g., red, yellow, green) that indicates favorable or unfavorable circumstances. Data mining and other business-intelligence methods might also provide for visual signals when an unacceptable delay or backlog was imminent. Many, if not most, companies gather quite a bit of data about their businesses from day-to-day transactions, but few companies use this information to its full advantage. For example, one landscaping company had a transactional software system that recorded all of the work that it did for its various accounts, including the prices charged, the number of hours spent on the account, and the cost of materials used. The software system, however, did not provide a report to answer an important question that the company's owner had: Which clients are we making money on and which are costing us money? The company developed a customized piece of software to dip into the database of the transactional software and generate a report on the profitability of various accounts on a spreadsheet, including color-coded cells indicating the most and least profitable accounts. This report was useful in adjusting prices for the upcoming year. While data processing in this manner is not usually considered in the context of Lean, it is indeed taking a business situation and creating a visual representation of it that is actionable.

In summary, visual systems reduce the seven deadly wastes in these ways:

1. Motion wasted in looking for things is reduced. Shadow boards and lines on floors indicate where items can be located and where they should be returned.
2. Progress lines painted on assembly line floors indicate production problems. This could signal impending defects or a shutdown that would cause workers' time to be wasted.
3. Visual indications of equipment placement can eliminate damage (which can be interpreted as being in the defect category of wastes).
4. Supervisory direction, which can be interpreted as wasted motion or effort, is reduced. If an automatic means of communicating what needs to be done can be devised, then it can be argued that the supervisor's time giving direction is wasted.
5. There is less downtime and underutilized people and equipment. If visual systems make process problems more apparent and the problems are resolved quickly, then less machine and people time is spent idle.

We later describe a mechanism for controlling material flow called a kanban system. It will be apparent that kanban systems provide a visual signal that directs workers to either do work or move material. We will also discuss mistake-proofing devices that, by definition, provide a visual signal that a mistake has been or is about to be made. Thus making the status of a process and its steps visually apparent is a fundamental tactic used in Lean.

Exercises

1. Look for visual systems in the processes you encounter on a day-to-day basis. Are the systems effective?
2. Document the value stream map (VSM) for a process and identify waste in the process, or use the VSM for a process that you have documented as part of prior exercises in this book. Determine how visual devices might be used to reduce waste.

CHAPTER 9

Mistake-Proof Processes and Product Designs

Mistake-proofing in its most ideal form is designing a process or product so that mistakes cannot be made. W. Edwards Deming and Joseph Juran were famous for arguing that the majority of defects and mistakes were management's fault.[1] Deming argued that 85 percent of problems were due to management's actions, while Juran argued 80 percent. One might argue for management's overwhelming responsibility for errors by observing that managers are responsible for a vast majority of the factors that affect quality, such as the quality of incoming material, specification of tooling and equipment, ensuring proper maintenance, providing appropriate information and training opportunities to employees, and ensuring complete work specifications. Even in a system like the Toyota Production System (TPS), in which employees are mainly responsible for process improvement, management needs to ensure that employees have time away from their assembly line jobs to conceive and implement those improvements. Mistake-proofing therefore recognizes that a vast majority of workers are trying to do their job properly and that most mistakes occur because the process makes it easy to make mistakes or makes it difficult not to make mistakes. The TPS uses the term *poka yoke* for mistake-proofing or error-proofing.[2]

Mistake-proofing is closely related to visual systems because there is always a visual cue in every mistake-proofing tactic that signals that a mistake is about to be or has been made. However, because the goal of mistake-proofing is so important, it makes sense to create a category for these methods separate from visual systems. In the remainder of this chapter, we will present a number of examples of mistake-proofing.

The first example is a circuit board that controls the activation of an air bag in an automobile (see Figure 9.1). This is an undeniably important

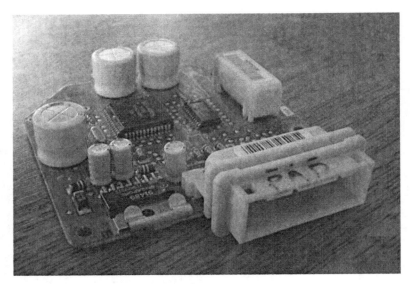

Figure 9.1 Air bag circuit board

safety component in a car. If the air bag is not activated in a crash, then it is not providing the important function for which it is intended. If the air bag goes off when it should not, it could actually cause accident and injuries. In the generation of circuit boards represented by the example in Figure 9.1, there were many different variants of these circuit boards, each one calibrated specifically for the mass of a particular vehicle. Thus installing the wrong board in a particular vehicle could have caused a catastrophic event.

Figure 9.2 shows a close-up of the circuit board's yellow connector. This connector mated with another connector on the wiring harness in the car. The first thing one might notice about the connector is a series of slots, holes, and grooves at the top of the connector. This pattern mated properly with a wiring harness connector that was intended to be installed in the same vehicle as this circuit board: It was physically impossible to mate this connector with a wiring harness connector for a different car without damaging the connectors, in which case an operator would first notice that the connector was difficult to insert and, subsequently, hear breaking plastic. If one had visited the factory that made these circuit boards, one would notice many different types of connectors in many different colors of plastic: yellow, green, blue, pink, red, and so forth.

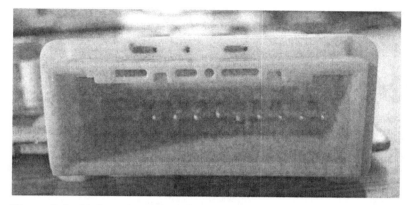

Figure 9.2 Air bag circuit board connector

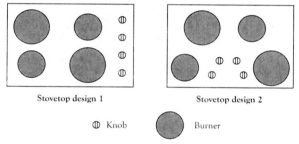

Figure 9.3 Stovetop design and mistake-proofing

The color of the connector also helped to eliminate mistakes because the wiring harness connectors were also color-coded to match the colors of the circuit board connectors: Yellow connects to yellow, red connects to red, and so forth. If an operator found himself or herself attempting to attach a yellow circuit board connector to a red wiring harness connector, that visual signal would have indicated an incorrect circuit board, an incorrect wiring harness, or both.

The next example of mistake-proofing is one that the author could have used to his advantage to prevent him from making a mistake he has made many times. In particular, the author has a stovetop of design 1, as shown in Figure 9.3, and he is embarrassed to admit that he has turned on the wrong burners many times. After telling himself upon moving into the house that he would become more acquainted with the stove and stop making that mistake at some point, the author still occasionally turns on the wrong burner from time to time after having lived in the house for seven years. This experience led the author to investigate stovetop designs, and he discovered one that he felt would significantly reduce, or totally eliminate, turning on the wrong burner. This is shown as Design 2 in Figure 9.3, where the configuration of the knobs matches the configuration of the burners giving a visual cue as to which knob controls which burner.

The third mistake-proofing example is for reducing data entry errors. It demonstrates how computer programs can be designed to remove ambiguity, to detect errors, and even to correct errors. Before taking a look at that example, ask yourself if you have ever been required to enter your phone number on a web page where it was unclear whether you should type parentheses around the area code or type a dash between the first three and last four digits of the phone number? Have you ever been aggravated when you guessed wrong and needed to reenter the phone number? Possibly, on poorly designed websites, all the data you entered in the form was cleared when the phone number was improperly entered and you were required to reenter all the data.

This third example helps to resolve these sorts of misspecification of data, errors that can occur due to erroneous data, and the rework that is required to reenter data if, indeed, the error is ever discovered. Figure 9.4 shows an Excel spreadsheet created to demonstrate various

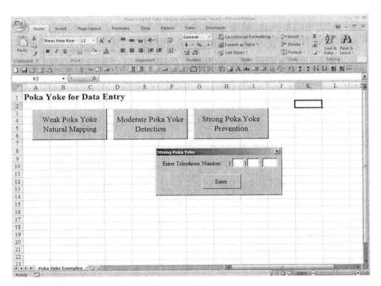

Figure 9.4 Data entry mistake-proofing

mistake-proofing devices with varying degrees of effectiveness. Upon clicking the button labeled Weak Poka Yoke, the dialog window in Figure 9.5 appears. This dialog gives visual cues about how data should be entered. For example, parentheses are displayed so the user would likely infer they need not type parentheses (resolving one error previously described). In addition, the data-entry fields for the phone number data are separated into three boxes proportionally dimensioned to indicate which boxes should contain three digits and which should contain four digits. This data entry window, however, allows many mistakes, including typing too many digits and typing letters. Typographical errors are possible even with dedicated, motivated, and conscientious workers and would be allowed by this version of the software.

An improved data entry screen is displayed when the Moderate Poka Yoke button is clicked (see Figure 9.6). This display is similar to the

Figure 9.5 *Weak poka yoke* **dialog window**

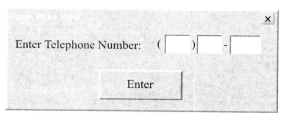

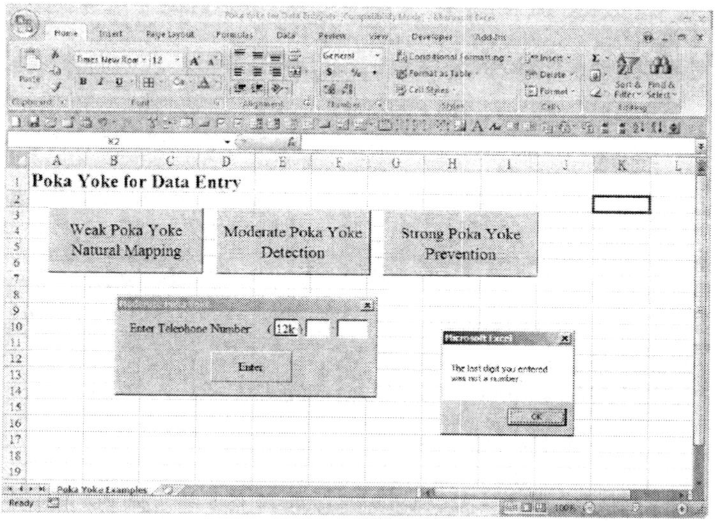

Figure 9.6 *Moderate poka yoke* **dialog window**

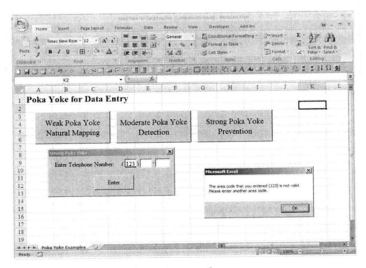

Figure 9.7 *Strong poka yoke dialog window*

previous dialog window, except its enhancements include the detection of letters and when the number of digits exceeds the allowable number for each data field. However, the program does nothing to correct mistakes or prevent erroneous data from being entered into the data system. In contrast, the final version of the data entry form (Figure 9.7), displays a message and erases those invalid alphabetic characters and, additionally, checks numeric area codes that have been entered against a list of valid area codes in a database. This strongest version of mistake-proofing also prevents more than the maximum allowable number of characters from being entered and displays a message when an attempt to enter excess characters occurs. This might signal that two keys were inadvertently struck simultaneously and allow that error to be detected and corrected. Lastly, this data entry form checks the validity of area codes once the third numeric digit has been entered into the area code field. If the area code typed is not valid, then a message is generated and the data in the area code field is cleared.

The sequence of three data entry screens demonstrates mistake-proofing schemes with varying effectiveness. At its least effective, mistake-proofing provides visual cues but no physical barriers to creating errors. At its most effective, mistake-proofing physically prevents mistakes, such as is the case with the circuit board connector and the computer program that prevents typing an area code that does not exist. Thus, although we said at the beginning of this chapter that the ideal goal of mistake-proofing devices is to prevent errors from occurring, we have seen that sometimes mistake-proofing devices only signal when errors have been or are about to be made.

While we should strive toward mistake-proofing mechanisms that physically prevent mistakes, we might ask if there is such a thing as a mistake-proofing device that is guaranteed to prevent mistakes 100 percent of the time. To contemplate this question, we will use the circuit board as an example, since it presents physical barriers to making errors and it seems to be very effective. Can it prevent errors 100 percent of the time? The answer is no for the following reasons:

1. The wrong connector might have been installed on the circuit board.
2. The wrong wiring harness could be installed in the car, which would allow the wrong circuit board to be installed in the vehicle.

In the second instance, two mistakes would need to be made to create a defect: The wrong wiring harness would need to be installed and an operator would need to select an incorrect circuit board that corresponded with the wrong wiring harness. The probability of both mistakes being made should be much less than the probability of making one mistake, which is all that is needed without any mistake-proofing.

If mistake-proofing was used with the installation of wiring harnesses, then the probability of a defect would be reduced further. But we can see that the answer to our question is likely no, mistake-proofing devices are never 100 percent effective.

Mistake-proofing is aimed at reducing defects, which clearly identifies which of the seven deadly wastes it is intended to primarily address. However, mistake-proofing also reduces cost because of less rework and scrap, reduces lead time because goods do not need to go through additional rework steps or need to be restarted into production, reduces transportation and handling due to rework, and reduces inventory of the parts going through reprocessing.

Exercises

1. Look for mistake-proofing devices in your day-to-day experience. In addition, look for situations where mistake-proofing devices could be used to an advantage. How would you design such devices? How effective would they be?

2. Look for opportunities to apply mistake-proofing in the processes you encounter on a day-to-day basis and, in particular, those in your workplace.

3. Consider the process that was mapped in response to the problem at the end of Chapter 2. Suggest how visual tools might be helpful in eliminating defects and saving time and effort.

CHAPTER 10

Synchronize

Controlling Material Replenishment with Kanban

What happens when one step of a process runs faster than the process step it feeds, even for a short period? Inventory builds up between the two steps, of course. From Little's law, we also know that the increased inventory causes increased lead time. The additional inventory also reduces quality (as was discussed in Chapter 2). Reducing inventory and unnecessary lead time requires *synchronizing* the two process steps, which requires that (a) the two process steps must operate at the same rate and (b) the two consecutive steps must process the same item at the same time where sequential process steps work on several products or services. For example, if step 1 processes product A while step 2 processes product B, then inventory of product A will accumulate between the two process steps. If steps 1 and 2 are both processing product A at the same number of units per hour, then no inventory will accumulate between the two steps.

The main technique used to synchronize the processing rates of sequential steps is called *kanban*, which originated in the Toyota Production System (TPS). Although translations of *kanban* from Japanese vary, it roughly means *signal, signboard, sign card,* or simply *sign* or *card*. The kanban is indeed often a card or metal sign that signals workers that a task should be done, either to produce or move goods in process. The rules that govern material movement and control in kanban systems are simple:

1. When a kanban card is not attached to material, this signals that action should be taken. Depending on the structure of the kanban system, the kanban might signal that production of an item should commence, material should be moved from one workstation to another, material should be moved from a storage location to a workstation, or material should be ordered from a supplier.

2. If all kanban cards are attached to material, then do nothing.

Rule 2 really follows directly from rule 1, so one could argue that there is really only one rule for kanban systems.

Kanban can be used in many different ways, and Figure 10.1 shows one example where two sequential process steps are coordinated with a kanban system. The soft drink bottling process in that figure is fed empty aluminum cans from a warehouse. Every pallet of aluminum cans that comes from the warehouse has a kanban card attached to it. When the operators insert a pallet of cans into the bottling line, they remove the kanban card and put it in the kanban card rack. A material handler occasionally checks the kanban card rack for cards, and when cards are present in the stand, they move more cans from the warehouse to the bottling operation. The quantity of pallets that are moved is determined by the number of kanban cards in the stand: One pallet is moved for each kanban card. Upon retrieving the required number of pallets, the material handler attaches the kanban cards to the newly replenished pallets of cans, one card per pallet.

When all the kanban cards in Figure 10.1 are attached to full pallets of cans at the bottling operation, then the material handler, by the rules cited previously, will not bring any additional cans out of the warehouse. Thus the maximum number of full pallets on the conveyor, in the case of Figure 10.1, assuming that the driver has no cards in his possession, is seven: Four cards are already attached to pallets of cans on the conveyor and three more cards could be attached to additional pallets of cans. This is the manner in which kanban cards limit inventory and synchronize process steps. The material handler can never get too far ahead of the bottling process because the number of pallets waiting to be used at the bottling line is limited by the number of kanban cards.

Because kanban cards establish maximum inventory levels, they can be used to control the amount of inventory in the system. Reducing the number of kanban cards reduces the maximum inventory level and also reduces the average inventory level. However, one must be careful in reducing inventory by removing kanban cards from the system because too few cards will starve downstream workstations of material, thus idling them. For example, once a particular kanban card has been detached from material, the remaining inventory at the workstation plus all the material that will be delivered in response to other kanban cards already detached

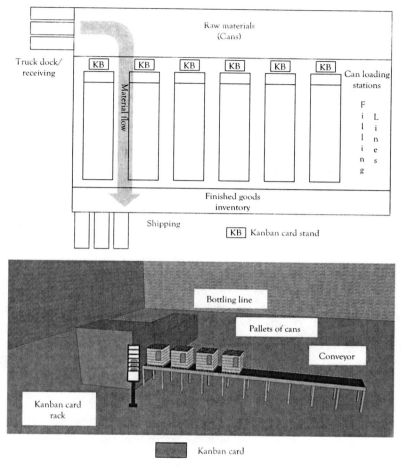

Figure 10.1 Kanban control of empty can supply

from material must sustain production until the material replenished in response to that particular card arrives. In the case of the bottling line in Figure 10.1, if the next pallet was inserted into the bottling line and its kanban card detached and placed in the kanban card rack, then there would be three remaining pallets of cans on the conveyor to sustain the line, plus the pallet just inserted into the bottling line, plus three more pallets that should be on their way due to the unattached kanban cards in the kanban card rack. Thus a total of seven pallets are available to sustain production until the material driver successfully responds to the most recent card put in the kanban card rack, which equals the total number of kanban cards in this example. Thus the number of kanban cards determines how long the driver has to respond to the kanban signal. Fewer kanban cards provides an operator at the workstation with less material over the duration required to execute replenishment in response to a particular card, and unless that replenishment can be completed within that time frame, then production will cease. The fewer the kanban cards, the faster the replenishment must be. Conversely, given a particular replenishment duration, too few cards will cause the workstation to run out of material. (This and the following analysis is based on several implicit assumptions that we will ignore for the moment, including that kanban cards are not lost, that kanban cards are picked up with a sufficient frequency, and that kanban cards are removed from containers of material when the container is put into production rather than when it is empty.)

Assuming that (a) material is consumed at a constant rate of R units per minute, (b) n kanban cards are used to replenish inventory to the bottling line in Figure 10.1, (c) each pallet of material to which a kanban is attached holds Q units of material, and (d) the average time required to replenish material once a kanban card has been detached from material is L minutes, then at least RL units of material must be available to the bottling line in the time it takes to replenish inventory in response to a kanban card being removed from a pallet of cans. Thus the minimum number of kanban cards required can be computed as follows by setting the amount of material made available by kanban equal to the required usage over the replenishment period

$$nQ = RL, \text{ and } n = \frac{RL}{Q}.$$

This is the minimum number of cards, n, required. However, additional kanban cards are required because, in general, we can expect variability in the timing of when a driver will observe an unattached kanban card, how long it will take to retrieve material, and the rate at which materials are consumed due either to the production process itself or to variability in demand. When replenishment lead time varies, we would interpret L as the average lead time. When replenishment time is longer than average, then we need some number of kanban cards greater than RL/Q to sustain production over the duration. When the consumption rates vary, the number of kanban cards must be able to sustain production in periods of high consumption of a part—that is, when consumption is at a rate in excess of the average rate R over a short period of time. Hence, to guard against stock-out on the occasions when replenishment is slow or demand is high, one must add some number of buffer cards to the quantity RL/Q for protection; how many depends on how much the replenishment time, L, and the consumption rate, R, *vary*. The greater the variability, the greater the number of cards required and the greater the inventory that will be in the system. (Thus we have found another root cause of excess inventory—variability.) In any case, the number of buffer cards in practice is found by starting with an obviously sufficient number of cards and then withdrawing them until the buffer cards sustain production without causing excess inventory. Nonetheless, a mathematical approach could be used to estimate the number of kanban cards that are required, and we have provided in the appendix a spreadsheet model that can be used to better understand the effect of variability on the number of kanban cards required or used to make such an estimate for real systems.

The need for buffer kanban cards and, hence, additional inventory due to variability highlights the importance of reducing variation in the process. The more reliably the material is replenished and more constantly the material is consumed, the less the inventory that is needed, and so the lead time through the entire production process is reduced accordingly. In the TPS, parts consumption is made as constant as possible by controlling the sequence in which products are made. For example, if an automobile assembly plant made two-door (2DR) and four-door (4DR) models of cars in a ratio of two to one, respectively, they would sequence car models on the assembly line like this:

2DR, 2DR, 4DR, 2DR, 2DR, 4DR, 2DR, 2DR, 4DR...

rather than this:

2DR, 2DR, 2DR, 2DR, 2DR, 2DR, 4DR, 4DR, 4DR...

The former sequence causes less variation in the consumption of parts for the different models. Assume for the moment that doors for two-door and four-door models come from different workstations. In that case, if too many two-door vehicles are intermittently scheduled together, those demand surges necessitate a greater number of kanban cards, and more inventory between the source of the doors and the assembly line. Sometimes the production sequence cannot be controlled so tightly due to variability in customer preferences or because of other considerations that trump parts inventory reduction. However, to the extent that parts usage is not made constant, a greater number of kanban cards will be required.

In conclusion, RL/Q kanban cards plus a suitable buffer is required to sustain raw materials supply to a production process, and the only ways to reduce the number of kanban cards required, and the associated inventory, are the following tactics:

1. Reduce replenishment lead time, L.
2. Reduce variability in replenishment lead time, L, or variability of material consumption, R.

Of course, one could argue that reducing the average consumption rate R also reduces the number of kanban cards, and this is true, but this would also decrease production and revenue and so we ignore this option. Note that reducing variability reduces the extra buffer of kanban cards, but the base number of RL/Q kanban cards will always be required. Assuming that consumption stays at the same level, the only way to reduce this base number of cards is to reduce the average replenishment lead time.

Important Observations About Kanban Systems

1. Losing a kanban card has the same effect as removing a kanban card from the system. Losing kanban cards can, thus, cause material shortages. Discipline is required to ensure that kanban cards are not lost.
2. Kanban cards, or other kanban devices, can be color-coded to denote the location of the factory where the kanban is used. The color-coding serves as a visual signal when a kanban card is inadvertently taken to the wrong part of the factory. This is

important because a misplaced kanban card has the same effect on material replenishment as a lost kanban card.

3. Kanban cards, at a minimum, should have printed on them:
   a. Part number of the material
   b. Part name
   c. Location where the material is delivered to
   d. Location where the material is delivered from
   e. Quantity of material in the container to which the kanban is attached

4. Note that when the consumption rate R increases, the number of kanban cards must be increased, unless the replenishment lead time L can be reduced sufficiently.

Other Kanban Systems

Kanban systems can be structured in many ways. In the previous example, kanban cards were used to signal replenishment from a warehouse. In some instances, kanban cards also signal goods to be produced rather than be simply replenished from a stocking point. Various methods can be used to accomplish this, and in some cases, separate sets of kanban cards are used to provide signals to the production people and to the material-movement operators. In that fashion, Figure 10.2 shows a schematic diagram of a system with triangular cards that signal the need for material to be moved and rectangular cards to signal production. This is called a *two-card kanban system* because it uses two *types* of kanban cards: One type of card signals production, and one signals material movement. Material replenishment and production could have alternatively been accomplished in the case of Figure 10.2 with one type of kanban card—for example, the triangular card could also be used to signal the need for production to commence. This would be accomplished by sending the unattached triangular kanban card directly to the camshaft fabrication operation. After camshafts are fabricated in response to the presence of an unattached triangular card, all containers of camshafts would have a triangular card attached and be taken directly to engine assembly. (For a similar example, see the first exercise at the end of this

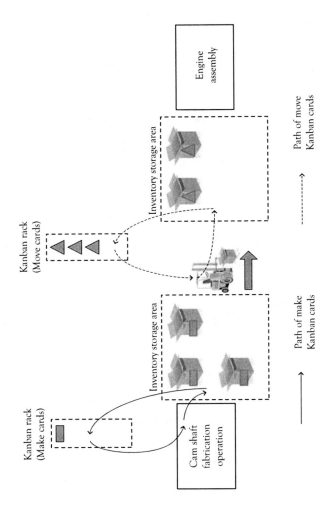

Figure 10.2 A two-card kanban system

chapter.) Discussing the comparative advantages and disadvantages of one-card and two-card systems is beyond the scope of this book. However, the reader can consult the book *Toyota Production System* by Yasuhiro Monden, which gives more details on kanban systems that inform this type of decision.[1] Additionally, since the examples included in this chapter represent only some of the ways that kanban systems can be structured, Monden's book is useful as a comprehensive reference that describes a variety of kanban mechanisms.

Kanban signals need not be cards. Kanban systems can use any device that creates a visual signal to workers about what needs to be done next. For example, squares painted on the floor or marked with tape can indicate the appropriate number of pallets of raw materials that should be available at a process step. Figure 10.3 shows a process step that assembles shafts and bearings where a maximum of four pallets of raw materials should be available to the operator. In the current state of the system as shown in Figure 10.3, the material handler should be bringing one more pallet of material because one kanban square is empty: An empty square serves the same purpose as an unattached kanban card. Reusable bins and racks can also be used as kanban signals: When the rack or bin is empty,

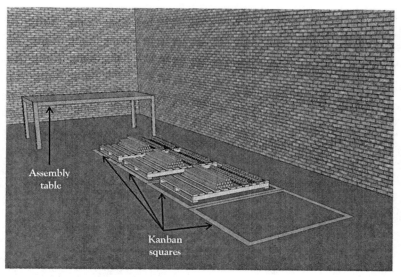

Figure 10.3 A kanban square signaling device

it is taken back to the process step or supplier where the item is produced so that the rack can be refilled.

Pull Systems

Systems of kanban cards that control material, or other analogous devices, are called *pull systems*. This label is appropriate because, for example, in Figure 10.3, the act of withdrawing material from one of the squares marked on the floor and using that material causes a material driver to bring more material to the work area—that is, use of material pulls more material into production. This is contrasted with push systems in which material might be brought to the work area even if it was not needed in the foreseeable future and work was currently piling up because incoming material was being delivered at a faster rate than it was being used. This pull effect is present between all steps of a process where replenishment is governed by kanban and, if adopted throughout the entire process, causes a chain reaction when material is consumed at the end of the process. Thus a customer who purchases goods sets in motion a chain reaction of production and material replenishment all the way back to the first step in the process.

The term *just-in-time* (JIT) *inventory replenishment* is often used to connote kanban and pull systems. However, in some cases people will use JIT to refer to all the methods that comprise the TPS. Thus whenever the phrase *just-in-time* is used, a listener should be careful to infer the intended meaning, or they should ask.

Exercises

1. In Figure 10.4, a two-station process is shown in which door panels are stamped at a stamping press and, subsequently, fabricated into doors in the next step. Kanban cards control the supply of parts from the stamping press to the fabrication step. Once the worker at the fabrication operation withdraws a pallet of door stampings from the inventory, she removes the kanban card from the pallet and places it in the kanban card rack in the inventory area. Occasionally, the forklift driver takes the unattached cards from the inventory area

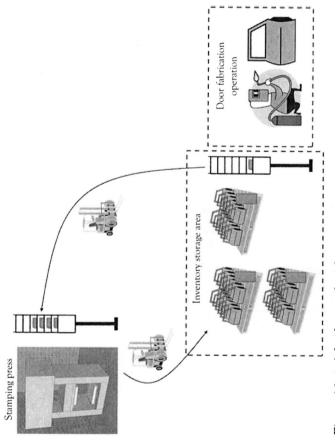

Figure 10.4 A kanban replenishment system

to the stamping press area and puts the cards in the kanban card rack there, which signals the press operator to stamp more pallets of parts. As the operator stamps parts, he removes the unattached kanban cards from the rack in his area and attaches one kanban card to each pallet of completed stampings. The forklift driver takes any completed pallets of door stampings with kanban cards attached from the stamping area to the fabrication area. Assume in the picture that there are currently no pallets of parts being transported from stamping to fabrication and that no kanban cards are currently in transit from the fabrication area to the stamping area:

   a. What is the maximum number of pallets of door stampings that can be in the inventory area awaiting processing at the fabrication station? Why?

   b. How could the maximum amount of inventory between stamping and fabrication be reduced?

   c. What problems might result if too many cards were removed from the process?

   d. Without adding cards back into the system, how might those problems referenced in the previous exercise be resolved?

2. Read the book *The Goal*.[2] Describe the components of the Drum-Buffer-Rope method that were used in that book to control the release of work onto the plant floor. Describe how the Drum-Buffer-Rope could be considered a pull system and, in that regard, is analogous to a kanban system. Describe the similarities and differences of a pull system as described in this book with the material control system in *The Goal*.

CHAPTER 11

Collocate

Job Shop Versus Work Cell Layouts

One tactic to reduce transportation time is to collocate sequential steps of a process. We will discuss this idea in the context of the traditional manufacturing setting, but later in the chapter, we will also describe how this idea can be applied to administrative processes. Although transportation time is the most apparent type of waste that collocation addresses, our discussion will identify other types of waste that are also reduced by collocation.

One way to arrange a factory is called a *job shop layout*, where similar pieces of equipment are located in their own department (see Figure 11.1). For example, all the drill presses that drill, tap, and bore holes are located in the same area, all the milling machines are in the same area, and all the heat-treat ovens are next to one another. Equipment in this type of factory is usually very flexible, which means that each piece of equipment can perform a variety of operations depending on how it is configured. For example, a drill press, with which some readers may be familiar, can drill a range of hole diameters depending on which drill bit is used. A fixture to hold a work unit in place might be required to ensure that the hole is drilled in the proper location at the proper angle. Fixtures are often suited to a particular part because each part or product is shaped differently. Setting up a drill press for a particular operation on a particular part therefore would entail installing the correct drill bit and attaching the correct fixture. The act of preparing the drill press for this operation would be called a *setup* or a *changeover*. Similarly, other general purpose, flexible equipment can be set up differently depending on the specific operations required for different parts: These machines include lathes, horizontal milling machines, vertical milling machines, and heat-treat operations.

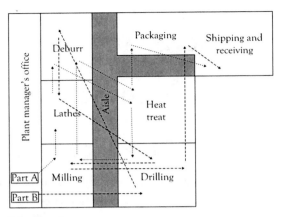

Figure 11.1 Job shop layout

The advantage of job shops is that the general-purpose equipment can be set up for many different operations and is therefore flexible to permit a wide variety of operations that might be required for a wide variety of parts produced. Further, any particular sequence of operations required to make a particular part can be accommodated by routing the part to the appropriate sequence of production departments. For example, Figure 11.1 shows the paths of two different parts, which vary due to their different processing needs. Job shops might make hundreds or thousands of parts or products and overlaying the part paths generated by all those processing paths, similar to Figure 11.1 but with many more lines, would look like an incoherent bowl full of spaghetti. This is the motivation for a term often used to describe the flow of work through a job shop: *jumbled flow.*

One downside of job shop layouts is that transportation is required to move parts from one department to another. The necessity of transportation motivates parts to be moved in batches: As long as a material handler is moving goods from one department to another, it makes sense to move more than one part at a time. If parts were not moved in these batches, then additional resources (people, forklift trucks, etc.) would be required and, at some point, would cause the profitability of the operation to suffer. Working on items in batches, in turn, causes excess inventory and additional lead time. Rather than proceeding directly to the next step after being worked on, most items in the batch must wait for the remaining items in the batch to be completed, thus causing waiting time as items await their turn for processing at the next processing step. Our knowledge of Little's law (Chapter 2) tells us that this additional waiting time must always be accompanied by additional in-process inventory. Conversely, observing the work-in-process waiting at various machines would allow us to infer from Little's law that batches must increase lead time. One further disadvantage of batch production is that if one step in the process starts to produce defective items, then many more defective items will be made before the defect is found compared to when the downstream processing steps were executed immediately and the defect was observed at the subsequent step. This increases waste due to defects, rework, and repair.

An approach to remedy these shortcomings is to construct *manufacturing cells* where the processing steps are located next to one another on the factory floor or, in other words, the process steps are *collocated*. In some cases, this means that heavy equipment must be moved from the department where similar machinery resides (we will call this the *home department* of the equipment in question) to another part of the factory. In other cases, only small hand tools might be required along with simple workbenches, and relocating equipment or purchasing additional equipment in this case is less of an issue. People, too, must be assigned to these cells from other parts of the factory. This layout, where the sequential processing steps are collocated, is also called a *product layout* because the equipment is laid out according to the products' processing needs rather than by the functionality of the equipment.

With collocated process operations, we no longer need material handlers to move goods from one step to the next. Operators can simply pass the item to the next step themselves, perhaps by pushing it along a roller table. The motivation for batch production is thus eliminated: Each station can process one item at a time and immediately pass it along to the next station. Waste due to transportation is thus significantly decreased and, with batch sizes of one, inventory and lead time are reduced.

Another advantage of cells is that they enable process steps to be coordinated and synchronized. With the process steps for any product being widely dispersed in the job shop layout, it is difficult to know which process step might be the momentary bottleneck or to know the progress status of the items in a customer's orders. At best, one needs an effective information technology system to determine status and, at worst, the entire factory would need to be scoured to determine the status of an order. With a manufacturing cell, or work cell, the entire process and all the work-in-process can be viewed in one glance. This allows a worker or a manager to see which step may be holding up the process at a given time by just looking for the inventory backup, which visually signals the need for remedial action, such as repairing a machine or replacing defective material. Additionally, if the amount of inventory between the stations is limited, then the steps of the process are better synchronized—that is, they are working on the same product at the same time, at the same rate, with little inventory buildup between. Limiting in-process inventory in this way also reduces process lead time, as we could infer from Little's law.

General Criteria for Work Cell Design

The primary difficulty in implementing a work cell is ensuring the proper utilization of equipment and people in the cell and in the remainder of the plant, with the remainder of the plant meaning the home departments where the equipment in the cell formerly resided. Specifically, the equipment and people in the work cell should not be overloaded with work. However, they should not be substantially underutilized because, as we shall see, this can cause the equipment and people in the home departments to be overloaded.

Utilization is most simply defined as the percentage of available time that equipment or people are used for productive activities.[1] Available time might be defined as all the hours that the production workforce is present at the factory. In that case, if a factory operated on one shift, the shift was scheduled for eight hours each day, and 240 working days were scheduled in each year, then 1,920 hours of production would be available each year:

$$1\frac{\text{shift}}{\text{day}} \times 8\frac{\text{hours}}{\text{shift}} \times 240\frac{\text{days}}{\text{year}} = 1,920\frac{\text{hours}}{\text{year}}$$

If the parts produced over a year caused a particular machine to be used 1,700 hours, then its utilization would be

$$\text{Utilization} = \frac{\text{hours in operation over a year}}{\text{hours available in a year}} = \frac{1,700}{1,920} \approx 0.885 = 88.5\%$$

This calculation could be made over a month, a year, or any period as long as the quantities in the numerator and denominator corresponded to the same time period.

Assume that the machine referred to in this example is a drill press and it was moved from the drill press department to a work cell. Further, assume that there were six drill presses in the drill press department before one drill press was moved to the work cell. Also assume that 11,100 hours of drill press time are required per year by a company's orders. With all the drill presses located in the home department, the utilization of the drill press department is

$$\text{Utilization} = \frac{11,100 \text{ hours}}{6 \text{ drill presses} \times 1,920 \dfrac{\text{hours}}{\text{drill press}}} \approx 96.4\%$$

Once one drill press is removed from its home department and moved to a work cell, the utilization of the machines in the home department is

$$\text{Utilization} = \frac{11,100 \text{ hours} - 1,700 \text{ hours}}{5 \text{ drill presses} \times 1,920 \dfrac{\text{hours}}{\text{drill press}}} \approx 97.9\%$$

Thus because the utilization of the drill press in the work cell (88.5 percent) would be less than the utilization if the machine had remained in its home department (96.4 percent), the utilization in the home department after reassigning the drill press would increase to 97.9 percent in this case. In the worst case, it is possible that the utilization in the home department could go above 100 percent, which would indicate that the five drill presses do not provide sufficient machining time to complete the required work. In such a case, it probably means that the work cell is infeasible, another piece of equipment must be purchased, overtime work is required, work must be outsourced, or the capacity discrepancy must otherwise be resolved. Table 11.1 illustrates that the utilization in the home department can go either up or down when a machine is relocated from a drill press department with six machines to a work cell depending on how much the machine would be used in the work cell.

Table 11.1 *Effect of cell on home department machine utilization*

Scenario	Total plant drill press hours required per year	Drill press hours required for work cell	Home department utilization before work cell	Home department utilization after reassigning one drill press	Drill press utilization in work cell
1	11,100	2,000	96.4%	94.8%	104.2%
2	11,100	1,800	96.4%	96.9%	93.8%
3	11,100	1,639	96.4%	98.6%	85.4%
4	11,100	1,400	96.4%	99.5%	80.7%
5	11,100	1,200	96.4%	101.0%	72.9%

We have thus identified these considerations for designing a work cell:

1. The products manufactured in the cell must have a common set of sequential process steps.
2. The work cell capacity utilization cannot be unacceptably high, and it should be sufficiently high to justify creating the cell.
3. Relocating machines from the home department to a work cell must not increase the utilization of the home department machines to unacceptably high levels.

Some phrases in the previous points are uncomfortably vague—for example, *sufficiently high* and *unacceptably high levels*. This is because universal rules of thumb are difficult to specify here, and precise quantification depends on many factors, some of which we will mention later in this chapter. However, capacity utilization above 100 percent qualifies as *unacceptably high*: People or machines cannot operate for more hours than are available. (Note that while overtime production is possible, if one were to include those hours as *available*, then the previous statement holds.)

These criteria must be considered when constructing a cell, which requires these tasks:

1. Identifying a group of products that share a common sequence of process steps;
2. Specifying how many machines (alternatively, other resources such as people) to relocate from the home departments to the work cell; and
3. Completing previously listed items while maintaining acceptable utilization rates in the cell and in the home departments.

To illustrate the process of designing a work cell, we will use the data for the operation described in the example titled Job Shop Inc.

Job Shop Inc.

Job Shop Inc. has seven production departments, as shown in Table 11.2 along with the abbreviations for each department.

Table 11.2 Job Shop Inc. departments and abbreviations

Department	Abbreviation
Stamping	S
Deburring	DB
Heat treating	H
Milling	M
Drilling	D
Lathe	L

The company makes 10 products, which are shown in Table 11.3 along with each product's average annual demand and the sequence of operations required for each product.

Table 11.3 Products manufactured by Job Shop Inc.

Product	Average annual demand (units)	Sequence of operations
1	1,100	S1, DB1, H1, M4, L1, D2
2	2,200	S2, DB2, H2, M4, L1, D2
3	3,300	S6, DB6, H6, M4, L1, D2
4	5,000	S3, DB3, H3, D4, L1
5	1,900	S4, DB4, H4, M1, D1
6	200	S5, DB5, H5, M4
7	500	S9, DB9, H9, D2, L2
8	10,000	S10, DB10, H10, D3
9	4,200	S11, DB11, H11, D3
10	3,200	S12, DB12, H12, L4

The leading letter in the sequence of codes for the sequence of operations in Table 11.3 indicates the production department (and the type of machine) that performs that process step using the abbreviations for each department. The number indicates a particular setup or configuration for that type of machine where a particular set of tooling is used with the machine and the machine is calibrated to perform that very specific operation. Changing a milling machine, for example, from setup 4 (M4) to setup 7 (M7) requires a different cutter and different calibration of the same machine. Furthermore, the setup takes time and requires an experienced and technically trained setup person to make that transition. Figure 11.2 graphically shows the sequence of operations or path of each of the 10 parts through the factory, where each part path is depicted by an arrow of a particular pattern.

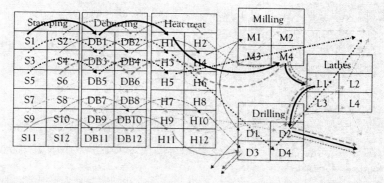

Figure 11.2 Part production sequences

The production times required for parts 1, 2, and 3 on operations M4, L1, and D2 are shown in Table 11.4.

Table 11.4 Production cycle times

		Product 1	Product 2	Product 3
Workstation	M4	15 min.	18 min.	17 min.
	L1	15 min.	16 min.	27 min.
	D2	15 min.	17 min.	10 min.
	Cell cycle time	15 min.	18 min.	27 min.

The current capacity, demand, and utilization of machines in the home departments for milling, lathes, and drilling before any machines are relocated to a work cell are shown in Table 11.5.

Table 11.5 Initial home department machine utilization

Department	Number of machines	Annual hours of work at average demand	Utilization
Milling	6	10,000	86.8%
Lathes	7	12,500	93.0%
Drilling	4	7,200	93.8%

Job Shop Inc. operates on one shift, eight hours per shift, on 240 working days each year. Thus 1,920 hours of production are available each year:

$$1\frac{\text{shift}}{\text{day}} \times 8\frac{\text{hours}}{\text{shift}} \times 240\frac{\text{days}}{\text{year}} = 1,920\frac{\text{hours}}{\text{year}}$$

An Example: Designing a Work Cell at Job Shop Inc.

The first step in designing a work cell is to determine a set of parts that share a common sequence of operations. In the data provided for Job Shop Inc., this can be done visually by finding paths for different parts, each of which requires the same sequence of process steps. The visual depiction of part paths for Job Shop Inc. is jumbled, except for three parts, parts 1, 2, and 3 that share a common sequence of process operations: M4, L1, and D2. Note that the three process steps identified do not compose the entire processing for parts 1, 2, and 3. Although a work cell might perform all the processing for all the parts it manufactures, it is not required to do so.

Having established candidate products for a cell, we now evaluate the utilization of resources within that cell if it contained one of each of the required machines: one milling machine setup for operation M4, one lathe setup for operation L1, and one drill press setup for operation D2. (We will also refer to these machines as workstations.) First, we need to determine the rate at which the cell would produce each part. The pace of production for each part is determined by the machine with the slowest cycle time, and so when the cell is producing product 1, product 2, and product 3, it will complete a part every 15 minutes, 18 minutes, and 27 minutes, respectively.

Based on the annual volumes of these parts, we can then calculate that 145,200 minutes, or 2,420 hours, of production time are required in the work cell each year.

$$\left(1,100\,\text{units}\times15\,\frac{\text{min.}}{\text{unit}}\right)+\left(2,200\,\text{units}\times18\,\frac{\text{min.}}{\text{unit}}\right)+\left(3,300\,\text{units}\times27\,\frac{\text{min.}}{\text{unit}}\right)=145,200\,\text{min.}$$

The utilization is thus

$$\text{Utilization}=\frac{\text{hours in operation over a year}}{\text{hours available in a year}}=\frac{2,420}{1,920}=1.26=126\%$$

Clearly, producing all three parts in the work cell would overload the cell: There are not enough working hours in the year.

We can determine why the cell is overloaded by looking at the required utilization of each machine as if each machine in the cell was operating independently. Based on the cycle times at each machine, we would find that workstations M4, L1, and D2 have utilizations of approximately 97 percent, 122 percent, and 75 percent, respectively. For example, the calculation for workstation M4 is

$$\text{M4 Utilization}=\frac{\left(1,100\,\text{units}\times15\,\frac{\text{min.}}{\text{unit}}\right)+\left(2,200\,\text{units}\times18\,\frac{\text{min.}}{\text{unit}}\right)+\left(3,300\,\text{units}\times17\,\frac{\text{min.}}{\text{unit}}\right)}{1,920\,\text{hours}}$$

$$=\frac{112,200\,\text{min.}}{1,920\,\text{hours}}=\frac{1,870\,\text{hours}}{1,920\,\text{hours}}\approx97.4\%$$

The utilizations of workstations L1 and D2 are calculated similarly. The utilization statistics clearly indicate that workstation L1 is the most significant contributor to the cell's utilization being greater than 100 percent. More specifically, the issue seems to be product 3, which takes a long time to produce on operation L1. The operation on L1 for product 3 takes significantly more time than on other operations at other workstations for product 3. Note also that the differences in the cycle times across the workstations for product 3 cause other operations to have idle time while L1 completes its operation. Attempts to redesign the cell to resolve this situation and, particularly, the overload on L1 and the imbalance among the operation cycle times might include the following:

1. Relocating more machinery to the cell—in this case another lathe to perform operation L1;
2. Removing product 3 from the cell;
3. Producing some of the requirements for products 1, 2, and 3 in the cell and some in the home departments using the traditional job shop routing; and
4. Increasing the number of hours available for the cell to operate, either through a second shift or overtime.

We will investigate the first two options next.

If we relieve the overload on operation L1 in the cell by relocating another lathe to the cell and setting it up to perform operation L1, then the cycle times for all products on workstation L1 are cut in half: Twice as many units can be produced in the same time. The workstation utilization results are shown in Table 11.6. We also need to compute the utilization of the machines in the home department by subtracting from their workload the number of hours of production performed by each workstation in the work cell as shown in Table 11.7. For example, the utilization of the machines that remain in the lathe department if two lathes were put in the work cell is computed as follows:

$$\text{Utilization} = \frac{12{,}500 \text{ hours} - 2{,}347 \text{ hours}}{5 \text{ lathes} \times 1{,}920 \dfrac{\text{hours}}{\text{lathes}}} \approx 105.8\%$$

In this case, while relocating a second lathe from the home department to the cell resolves the overutilization problem in the cell, it causes an overload in the home department. Thus it is not a feasible work cell design unless another lathe is purchased.

Table 11.6 Work cell utilization with two lathes

Operation	Number of machines	Annual hours of work at average demand	Utilization
M4	1	1,870	97.4%
L1	2	2,347	61.1%
D2	1	1,448	75.4%

Table 11.7 Home department utilization with two lathes in work cell

Department	Number of machines	Annual hours of work at average demand	Utilization
Milling	5	8,130	84.7%
Lathes	5	10,153	105.8%
Drilling	3	5,752	99.9%

Table 11.8 Work cell utilization without product 3

Operation	Number of machines	Annual hours of work at average demand	Utilization
M4	1	935	48.7%
L1	1	862	44.9%
D2	1	898	46.8%

Negotiating the requirements of satisfactory utilization in the work cell and the home department is therefore one of the difficulties of work cell design. One potential downside of cells is that unless an appropriate mix of products can be found for the cell, additional investment in machinery might be required. At the heart of this issue is the lumpiness of machines and other resources: We can relocate only an integer number of machines and sometimes placing one fewer machine in a work cell is too few machines and placing one additional machine in a cell is too many. And where machines are heavy and immobile, perhaps bolted to the floor with rigid connections to electricity and compressed air, they must be dedicated to the work cell on a full-time basis. Where resources required for production are people and the only tools needed are relatively inexpensive hand tools, however, the option does exist to assign people to cells on a part-time or as-needed basis, thus avoiding the integer lumpiness issue. We will explore this tactic later in this chapter.

The next alternative solution to resolving the overloading problem that we can explore is removing product 3 from the cell. The reader may verify that by doing so, the utilization of the workstations in the cell is as shown in Table 11.8. Furthermore, the utilization of the home departments is as shown in Table 11.9.

Table 11.9 Home department machine utilization without product 3

Department	Number of machines	Annual hours of work at average demand	Utilization
Milling	5	9,065	94.4%
Lathes	6	11,638	101.0%
Drilling	3	6,265	108.8%

This tactic, then, causes the machines in the cell to be underutilized while overloading the machines in the home departments. While overtime production might be a possible resolution to this problem in the home department, it increases production costs and compromises the flexibility of the home department to react to demand spikes.

If in this example we were not contemplating a cell with heavy machinery but rather a cell with people operating relatively inexpensive hand tools, then removing product 3 from the cell might be a viable solution. In that case, we might be able to staff the work cell roughly half the time, and for the remaining work time, the workers could work back in their home departments, which would relieve the overload indicated in Table 11.9.

Note also that our utilization calculations did not include the effect of changeovers. One important observation to make about work cells is that they eliminate the need for changeovers on the machines in the cell: Once the machines are set up for their specific operation, they are dedicated to that task for all working hours and will not be switched to another task. This is convenient because some unproductive changeover time is eliminated, as are the required labor hours and materials for changeovers. Setups are still required in the home departments, however, and productive time must be sacrificed in order to make the changeovers there, whereas that is not the case in a work cell. Thus the percentage of time that a workstation is in production can be closer to 100 percent for machines in work cells than for machines in the home department.

Work Cells in Service and Administrative Processes

Figure 11.3 shows the paths for two administrative processes: creating a purchase order and processing an employee grievance. Because

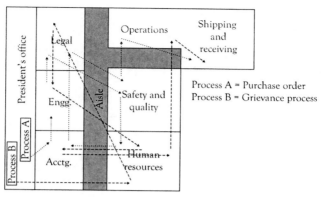

Figure 11.3 Administrative process flow

administrative personnel tend to be located in office buildings according to their function, the process paths in Figure 11.3 look much like production paths in a job shop: Work tends to be done in batches, travel time and distance are excessive, waiting time between processing steps is excessive, work-in-process tends to be high, and the lead time is long. Therefore, work cells can potentially be used in administrative processes to resolve these performance issues, especially where work is paper based rather than electronic. Relocating people on a permanent basis to a work cell dedicated to a limited scope of work may be difficult, however, especially in small organizations, because some departments might be small. In that case, staffing work cells on a part-time basis might effectively reduce lead time.

With more and more administrative work being handled electronically, the time to physically move paper forms from department to department is reduced, thus reducing some of the motivation for administrative work cells. However, significant wait time might still persist in electronic work-in-process, so that there still might be some benefit to cells or at least in developing a signaling device to indicate when work must be done (i.e., a visual tool).

The improvement made in the retail hiring process as discussed in Chapter 6 can be viewed as being conceptually identical to implementing a work cell. Figure 11.4 (which replicates Figure 6.1 here for convenience) shows the value stream map for the retail hiring process where an applicant needed to visit the store on three occasions in order to complete the application and interview process. Between steps in the process,

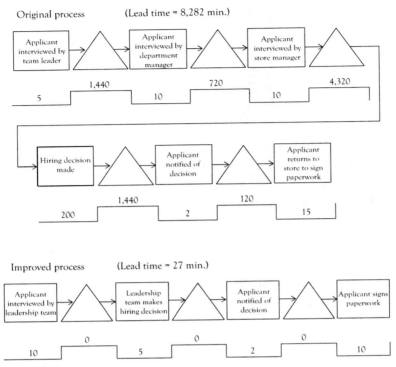

Figure 11.4 Retail hiring process

applicants would return home and wait until the next step, when they would return to the store. The lead time of this process was therefore very long, which posed a problem, particularly in the winter holiday season when the store needed to ramp up its sales associate workforce by 30 percent. Collocating the managers for the interview is much the same idea as collocating different types of machines in an area and greatly reduces transportation and waiting time.

Work cells might sometimes be beneficial in service processes as well. For example, a Harvard Business School Publishing case on United Services Automobile Association (USAA)[2] describes an insurance claims process where both complex and simple claims were handled in the same department as part of the same process. Complex claims required all 21 steps of the process, whereas simple claims required only a subset of those process steps. An argument can be made in this case for building a work cell to handle simple claims. Doing so would reduce the jumble due to mixed processing flows, reduce the transportation and waiting times between steps, and reduce the lead time. Reduced lead time fits with USAA's culture and strategy of offering exceptional service, and so a cell makes sense in this application, not only for increased efficiency but also for increased customer satisfaction through a more responsive claims process.

Final Comments and Further Study on Work Cells

Our explanation of work cells has emphasized reducing transportation time, making small batches feasible, reducing inventory, and reducing lead time. It is important to reiterate another benefit of cells, which is particularly important in a manufacturing environment. Specifically, collocating operations in a work cell also coordinates and synchronizes process steps because inventory between steps can be limited to a maximum level dictated in part by the space between the stations. This prevents a workstation from getting too far ahead of those before or after it. In other types of processes, work-in-process inventory between two workstations is often stored in a warehouse area, and managing the inventory level is accomplished with a computer program, which is usually less effective. In addition, more work-in-process inventory is needed in these cases to compensate for uncertainties in workstation scheduling and transportation between steps. Work cells also increase the probability that quality problems will be recognized immediately, which has a positive influence on quality. Limiting the inventory between process steps also limits the number of possible defective units between steps, which reduces rework cost. Lastly, one can argue that the quality of a repaired product is never up to par with a unit that was made properly on the first attempt, so the quality reaching the customer is improved as well.

With only 10 products, identifying parts with common processing paths was very simple and we could do it visually. This is not practical when a factory produces hundreds or thousands of parts. In that case, we might well need a computerized algorithm to help us determine which parts have similar processing sequences so that they can be processed together in a work cell. The logic of such an algorithm, however, is conceptually identical to the simple method described here.

In the utilization computations that we made in this chapter, we have ignored an important discussion of how high capacity utilization can be before problems ensue. This is a complex topic, and a full discussion is beyond the scope of this book. Note, however, that utilization must be kept at some margin below 100 percent to allow for changeover time and variability in production requirements. Day-to-day variations in demand and season-to-season demand variations require us to have some slack capacity so that we might idle the cell during slack times and respond to demand when it surges. Alternatively, the cell can be kept busy all year, in which case the cell would work ahead during slack times to accumulate inventory for the peak sales period. In some cases this is acceptable despite the cost of holding inventory and its other downsides; however, in some cases where demand is very erratic, where demand cannot be forecasted accurately, where the precise configuration of the products cannot be forecasted accurately, where products become obsolete, and where raw material costs are declining, building inventory by leveling the production schedule may not be a good idea.

We have also ignored in our discussion how the production sequence through the cell might be managed to reduce the effect of the work imbalance presented by product 3. This is a finer level of detail that the reader may investigate by looking at references that deal with work cells in a more comprehensive fashion.[3]

Exercises

1. In reference to work cells, verify the capacity utilization computations in this chapter where they are not explicitly shown.
2. Download the Excel spreadsheet from http://mason.wm.edu/faculty/bradley_j/LeanBook, and follow the instructions and see if you can find a good process to put in an administrative work cell.

CHAPTER 12

Reduce Changeover Time

Machines or people responsible for multiple tasks must occasionally switch from performing one task to the next. The time required to do so is called *changeover* or *setup time*. Examples where changeover time is required in manufacturing include the following:

1. Changing the design printed on aluminum cans in beverage can manufacturing
2. Changing the type of part produced by a metal-stamping press
3. Changing the part made in a plastic injection-molding machine
4. Changing the product being put into containers in beverage, personal product, and household cleaner filling operations
5. Changing the type of product being put into bags in pet food, snack food, and other food manufacturing processes or changing the size of the bag

Changing from one aluminum can design to another requires the old ink to be replaced with new ink and printing plates with the new design to be installed in place of the old plates. There may also be a period of time required either to calibrate the positioning of the design on the can or to adjust the color hues. Changing the type of part made by a stamping machine or an injection-molding machine requires that dies and molds be changed, respectively. Dies are large metal forms between which sheets of metal are pressed between the top and bottom dies such that the metal is stretched and bent to conform to the shape of the die. Stamping presses are like panini presses although, rather than being flat, the inside of the dies are contoured to the shape of a car door, a washing machine lid, or whatever part is being stamped. A stamping machine might also need to have different parts-handling devices installed to automatically remove parts from the press: Parts of different shapes need to be picked at different locations, possibly by different types of tooling. A stamping machine changeover might also require a different raw material; either the type or the shape of metal going into the process might change depending on the part being manufactured. A changeover in a filling operation might require that different bottles and different labels be loaded into a filling machine, as well as a switch in the type of material being supplied to the machine. Adjustments are also likely to be required to the controls of the machine to calibrate how much fluid is filled into the bottles. Changeover requirements for filling bags or boxes of dry goods are similar to the requirements for filling operations.

In summary, time is required to change a machine from one operation to another to replace equipment and tooling, switch the raw material being used, make changes to the programming or controls of the machine, and to calibrate the new process after changeover to ensure that it is creating a product that adheres to quality specifications. Although we have not described the changeovers in full detail, each of them requires time for these four types of activities.

Changeovers also occur in nonmanufacturing processes where people switch from performing one task to another. These changeover processes, like ones in manufacturing, may involve physical changes in the tools and equipment being used to perform a task, such as changing the computer application being used. In addition, changing from one task to another many times requires changing one's train of thought. Although switching mental gears might seem inconsequential, it is indeed a type of changeover time with the same effects as physically readjusting a process. Examples of changeover in nonmanufacturing situations include the following:

1. Hospital operating rooms must be cleaned and resupplied between surgeries.
2. Commercial aircraft must be unloaded (people and luggage), cleaned, resupplied, and reloaded before departing on the next flight.
3. Restaurants must be transitioned from breakfast, to lunch, to dinner operations.
4. Banquet and meeting rooms must be set up differently from one event to the next.

5. An administrative worker in a procurement department switches from processing purchase orders to working on supplier assessment, supplier certification, and supplier development activities.

The hospital, airline, restaurant, and meeting room changeover scenarios are in nonmanufacturing contexts, but they share critical similarities with manufacturing changeovers: The resources (operating rooms, planes, restaurants, and meeting rooms) cannot serve customers or clients while equipment is rearranged from one activity to the next and while different raw materials are delivered. Note that although the terminology *equipment* and *raw materials* might not be used in these scenarios, analogous entities do exist. For example, equipment in the operating room might be surgical devices that are changed according to the type of surgery and raw materials might be sutures, medicine, and medical instruments. Changeover time for administrative workers might involve the activities already mentioned: starting a different computer application, *switching mental gears*, or gathering different file folders. Thus the structure of these nonmanufacturing changeovers bears sufficient resemblance to changeovers in manufacturing for us to apply the changeover time reduction methodology that we discuss here, which was developed in manufacturing. To further demonstrate that point, we will discuss the application of changeover time reduction to an administrative process later in this chapter.

Effects of Changeover Time

During changeovers, the equipment involved in the process is unproductive: A stamping press cannot make parts while its old die is exchanged for a new die; a hospital operating room cannot be used until it is cleaned and restocked; an aircraft cannot be flown until new passengers are onboard, it is refueled, and luggage is loaded. So, one obvious effect of changeovers is that they idle equipment can represent a substantial investment. The potential return on investment is thus reduced. Indeed, very long changeover times might make it necessary to buy additional equipment. Besides idling equipment, changeover time consumes labor hours of those involved in making the changeover. The longer and less efficient a changeover is, the greater the number of labor hours required to make it. In addition, when machines must be calibrated after a changeover to ensure appropriate quality, costs are incurred for the material that is used for the first, substandard items that are thrown away.

Another less apparent cost of long changeover times is the need to have more inventory, which obviously requires a financial investment. In addition, we can infer from Little's law that the increased inventory caused by changeover times also increases process lead time. To understand conceptually why changeover times are related to inventory, consider the circumstance when a machine makes two parts, A and B, and changeover is required to change either from A to B or from B to A. Assume that both parts are required simultaneously by a downstream process and they are consumed continuously. One example is an automobile door fabrication process that feeds the assembly line. (In this case, part A represents left-hand doors and part B represents right-hand doors.) The assembly line continuously consumes right-hand and left-hand doors that are produced by one machine. Further assume that the door fabrication process cycles back and forth between part A and part B. (Even when these assumptions are not satisfied, the observation we make next is still true for different circumstances and scheduling algorithms.) Upon finishing a production batch of part A, the inventory of part A must be sufficient to last during (a) the changeover from part A to part B, (b) the production of part B, and (c) the changeover from part B back to part A. If inventory of part A is depleted before its production commences again, then the downstream production process will be shut down due to a material shortage. Observing the three buckets of time over which the subsistence of the downstream process depends on the stockpile of part A makes it clear that a greater stockpile of part A is needed as the two changeover times increase. Greater changeover times thus cause larger production batches and a larger average level of inventory.

We can determine how much inventory is made necessary by change-overs by using the algebraic variables, as shown in Table 12.1, from which we can derive a mathematical formula for the average inventory level. The variable n represents the number of different parts made on a particular machine; in the previous example, $n = 2$. The variable c represents the time required to changeover from one part to the next. The variable

Table 12.1 Changeover notation

Variable	Meaning	Notes
n	Number of parts produced by a machine or workstation.	This must be an integer value.
c	*Changeover time* in seconds, minutes, hours, and so forth.	
r	*Production rate*, or parts produced per second, minute, hour, or some other period of time.	Value can have a fractional part. Time units must match the time units used for changeover time.
d	*Demand or consumption rate*, or the number of parts consumed by the downstream process step per second, minute, hour, or some other period of time.	Value can have a fractional part. Time units must match the time units used for changeover time.

r represents the production rate of the machine in parts per measure of time and d represents the demand rate (or consumption rate) of each part by subsequent manufacturing operations. Note that all n parts are consumed by downstream processes at the same rate d. The Greek letter rho, ρ, is used in the equation to represent the percentage of time that the machine needs to be producing parts in order to keep up with demand: $\rho = nd/r$. The time not required for production is available for changeovers, maintenance, and, perhaps, idle time. When the machine repetitively cycles through the parts in the same sequence and all nonproductive time is dedicated to changeovers, the average number of units of inventory on hand, which we denote by I, can be calculated to be[1]

$$I = \frac{nc\rho(r-d)}{2(1-\rho)}.$$

Substituting the values for n, c, r, d, and ρ in the equation that are appropriate for a specific circumstance yields the inventory level I. From the equation it is clear that as the changeover time, c, increases, inventory increases proportionally. Furthermore, Little's law tells us that lead time increases proportionally with inventory. Hence, increased changeover time causes increases in both inventory and lead time.

Long changeover times also make it difficult to respond to customers who want quick turnaround on orders or who request last-minute changes to order quantities. For example, the total time, T, to cycle through the production of n parts is[2]

$$T = \frac{nc}{1-\rho}.$$

Unless excess inventories are somehow provided for in advance, increasing the momentary rate of supply must wait until a part is again in production, which on average is $T/2$. Thus longer changeover times cause a larger schedule cycle length, T, which causes a delay in responding to customers. In reality, changing the production rate r of a part, even temporarily, is much more complicated than implied by this discussion; however, the explanation is beyond the scope of this book. Another tack that could be taken if an immediate response to customers' change in demand was required would be to make an additional changeover to the part that had requirements increase. Again, although this turns out to be a much more complicated issue to analyze than it may seem, it is outside the scope of this book; but we can glean from the formula for cycle length that a greater number of changeovers increases the cycle length T, which implies that the supply of other parts would be delayed. An extra changeover could also cause the inventory of other parts to run out before they were produced next.

Shorter changeover times make the effect of an additional changeover less onerous: Reduced changeover times reduce inventory and allow faster response to customers. In addition, with shorter changeover times, it is easier for companies to leave some machine time unscheduled for the occasion when a customer has a rush order. If idle time in the quantity of u minutes is reserved in the schedule during each production cycle, then the average inventory level is

$$I = \frac{\rho(nc + u)(r - d)}{2(1 - \rho)}.$$

Thus reserving the time to respond to quick turnaround orders affects inventory levels and lead time in the same manner as changeover time.

It should be noted that all the equations presented so far assume that production comes off without a hitch and that the demand rate is steady at a known rate. When machines break down, workers are absent, and demand is uncertain, the equations need to be modified, and managing such a real-world system with these uncertainties is much more difficult than the perfect system described here. Among the effects of uncertainty is that inventory levels rise and the effects of changeover time are more significant than portrayed in these formulas. An in-depth analysis of this scenario, however, is outside the scope of this book.

Sequence-Dependent Changeover Times

In general, changeover times between any two parts made on a machine are not the same as we have assumed in deriving the formula for average inventory. We have used this assumption to make our explanation more easily understood. When changeover times are different depending on which part is finishing its run and on the next part to be produced or, in other words, when changeover time is dependent on the sequence of parts produced, then changeover times are said to be *sequence dependent*. Sequence-dependent changeover times do not change the basic observations that we have made, such as longer changeover times increasing the inventory level. However, the sequence in which parts are made must be carefully considered with sequence-dependent changeovers because the total changeover time and, subsequently, the inventory level can be significantly different depending on the sequence of production.

Changeover Terminology

The terms *internal changeover time* and *external changeover time* are used, respectively, to differentiate between the time required to perform changeover-related tasks during a changeover versus before or after a changeover. A central cause of changeovers lasting longer than necessary is that tasks are performed during the changeover (internal changeover time) that could be performed either before or after the changeover. Thus the first main task in reducing changeover time, as we will describe next, is to determine which tasks need not be performed while a machine is idled for changeover.

Steps to Reduce Changeover Time

The general steps to reduce changeover times are described in the highly regarded book *A Revolution in Manufacturing: The SMED System* written by Shigeo Shingo.[3] Indeed, Shingo is credited with developing the widely used methodology of reducing changeover time called single-minute exchange of dies (SMED). Shingo worked for Toyota in the auto manufacturing industry, and stamping dies was the first and foremost application of SMED in that company. The steps of SMED are the following:

1. Document the sequence of tasks used to implement a changeover noting the following data for each step of the current changeover procedure:
   a. Description of the task
   b. Time required for the task
   c. Classification of each task as internal or external.
2. Determine which activities done in internal changeover can be done external to changeover, and develop tactics to transform internal time to external time.
3. Reduce internal changeover time.
4. Reduce external changeover time.

The first step gives an overview of the tasks performed in a changeover, and by adding up the durations of all internal tasks, one can determine the total time required for changeover. All tasks made necessary by a changeover should be documented, whether the tasks are performed before, during, or after the machine is idled. Most importantly, however, this listing of the steps provides the classification of each task as being either internal or external. Using the terminology we introduced, this simply means whether a task is performed while the machine or operation is shut down for changeover (internal) or the task is done either before or after the operation is idled (external).

Once the internal tasks have been identified, the second step of the methodology is to determine which of these tasks can be done either before or after the changeover. Some tasks are easy to do externally. For example, a changeover worker brings his or her tools to the operation after the machine has been shut down for changeover—it is easy to decide to do this task before the machine is shut down. Why wait? Bringing tooling, jigs and fixtures for the next part to be produced can also be easily done before changeover commences. In other cases, changing a task from internal to external takes more effort or cost. For example, if an internal task in a changeover is to warm up molds for a plastic injection molding process after they have been installed in the production equipment, then transforming that step to an external one would require building or buying an offline system to warm up the molds before the operation was shut down for changeover. Fortunately, many changeover reduction efforts take little cost or effort to implement.

Once tasks originally done internally to changeover have been converted to external changeover operations, then the third step of the methodology is employed to further reduce changeover. Specifically, the remaining internal operations are streamlined and made more efficient. If remaining internal tasks are shortened, then so, too, is the duration over which the operation is idled, which is the changeover time.

The final step of SMED is to reduce the amount of time and effort required for the external changeover activities. Reducing external changeover time does not reduce the changeover time during which the machine is unproductive, but it does reduce the overall workload imposed on the workforce and thus increases overall efficiency. Benefits of this include minimizing the total staff needed to do changeovers and having less chance of needing a changeover worker in multiple places at the same time. The lack of availability of changeover personnel when a changeover is needed can, obviously, prolong a changeover.

The foregoing description of the steps of changeover reduction can be made more concrete by considering an example.

An Example: Reducing Operating
Room Changeover Time

We will consider the example of reducing the changeover time in a hospital operating room. To illustrate the SMED methodology more clearly, we will assume that only one worker performs all the changeover tasks. In this and many other situations, changeover activities might be performed by a team of people. We describe in the next section how our analysis would change when a team of people were involved. The analysis is hardly changed in that case, although illustration with one changeover operator is simpler to describe. This example might seem ripe with easily observable opportunities for improvement, almost to the degree that it is an unbelievable scenario. While this scenario may seem unrealistic, one would find that opportunities are just as obvious and plentiful when real-world changeovers are analyzed.

Completing step 1 would result in a table of data as shown in Figure 12.1. Excel is a good, readily accessible software package and, as shown in this figure, it can be used to catalog changeover steps and make the calculation of total changeover time easy. The total time for internal changeover in this case is 3 hours 5 minutes 43 seconds, starting when the

Changeover Analysis (As-Is Process)

Task Sequence	Task Description	Internal/External	Time	Task Time (mm:ss)
1	Gather cleaning supplies	E	9:42:00 AM	12:31
2	Put on coveralls	E	9:54:31 AM	02:42
3	Go to operating room	E	9:57:13 AM	07:02
4	Surgery ends		10:04:15 AM	00:00
5	Remove tools and waste from operating room	I	10:04:15 AM	10:51
6	Clean and sterilize operating room	I	10:15:06 AM	32:49
7	Go to Supply Room 1 and select surgical tools required for the next operation using pick list	I	10:47:55 AM	45:11
8	Go to Supply Room 2 and pick surgical materials from the shelves (sutures, tape, other consumable materials)	I	11:33:06 AM	09:51
9	Stock the operating room with surgical tools and disposable materials from supply rooms	I	11:42:57 AM	05:47
10	Rearrange operating room fixtures for next surgery (tables, lights, IV stands, monitoring devices, etc.)	I	11:48:44 AM	12:08
11	Dispose waste from cleaning	I	12:00:52 PM	05:20
12	Notify hospital operations control that operating room is ready	I	12:06:12 PM	00:45
13	Wait for nurses and doctors to arrive	I	12:06:57 PM	22:40
14	Doctors and nurses scrub and don operating gowns	I	12:29:37 PM	14:00
15	Doctors and nurses introduce each other; surgeon briefs participants on general and specific instructions for upcoming surgery	I	12:43:37 PM	07:29
16	Doctors and nurses go over presurgery checklist	I	12:51:06 PM	06:07
17	Patient is admitted to operating room	I	12:57:13 PM	01:25
18	Patient administered general anesthesia	I	12:58:38 PM	04:32
19	Wait for patient to lose consciousness	I	1:03:10 PM	06:48
20	Next surgery begins	I	1:09:58 PM	

Figure 12.1 Changeover data

operating room completes one surgery until when the next surgery begins (from 10:04:15 AM until 1:09:58 PM).

Step 2 of reducing changeover time is to determine which internal tasks can be done externally. Of the internal tasks from task 5 through task 19, tasks 5, 6, 9, 10, and 17 must be internally—that is, the prior surgery must definitely be complete before these tasks can be done. Performing these tasks before the prior surgery is completed would disrupt that surgery. Tasks 7, 8, 11, 13, 14, 15, and 16 could be accomplished either before the prior surgery is finished or at least concurrently with the cleaning and stocking tasks. Assuming that it is known what the next surgery will be, which is reasonable in nonemergency situations, supply room items (tasks 7 and 8) might be retrieved prior to the surgery based on the type of surgery to be performed next. Even if some consumables in the operating room were on a pull system and the usage of those items for the prior surgery was not yet known, the kanban levels could be set to withstand two surgeries' worth of demand. In that case, the current replenishment would be in response to two surgeries prior. We should scrutinize the timing of task 11 because it need not prolong the changeover. The waste might be taken to waste receptacles after the next surgery begins. So we would make this task external, but after rather than before the internal changeover tasks. If keeping the operating room busy (and generating revenue) is a priority, then task 13 could be eliminated and task 14 could be done concurrently with cleaning operations or before the previous surgery was completed so that neither task prolonged the changeover. Similarly, briefings and reviewing checklists (tasks 15 and 16) could be done concurrently with cleaning or before the previous surgery was completed. With those activities being transformed to external changeover tasks, the remaining internal changeover tasks, which, again, determine how long the operating room is unproductive, are as shown in Figure 12.2, which has been reduced to a little over 1 hour 15 minutes. Other tasks might potentially be made external to changeover, such as beginning the anesthesia process outside of the operating room, but we will be content for the moment in identifying the improvements observed thus far.

The next step of the changeover time reduction process is to make the remaining internal changeover tasks more efficient. Although we have not specified details about how the changeover tasks are done, here are

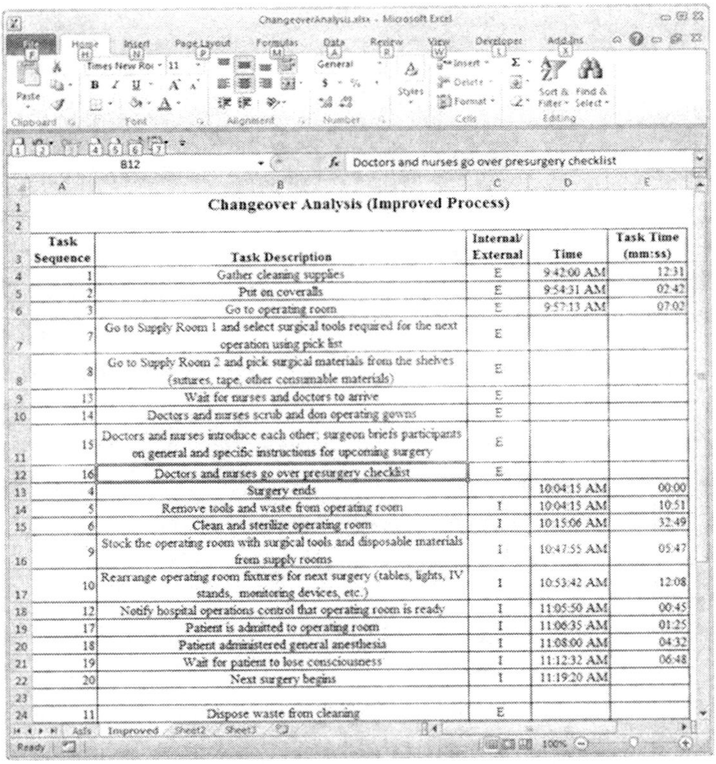

Task Sequence	Task Description	Internal/ External	Time	Task Time (mm:ss)
1	Gather cleaning supplies	E	9:42:00 AM	12:31
2	Put on coveralls	E	9:54:31 AM	02:42
3	Go to operating room	E	9:57:13 AM	07:02
7	Go to Supply Room 1 and select surgical tools required for the next operation using pick list	E		
8	Go to Supply Room 2 and pick surgical materials from the shelves (sutures, tape, other consumable materials)	E		
13	Wait for nurses and doctors to arrive	E		
14	Doctors and nurses scrub and don operating gowns	E		
15	Doctors and nurses introduce each other; surgeon briefs participants on general and specific instructions for upcoming surgery	E		
16	Doctors and nurses go over presurgery checklist	E		
4	Surgery ends	I	10:04:15 AM	00:00
5	Remove tools and waste from operating room	I	10:04:15 AM	10:51
6	Clean and sterilize operating room	I	10:15:06 AM	32:49
9	Stock the operating room with surgical tools and disposable materials from supply rooms	I	10:47:55 AM	05:47
10	Rearrange operating room fixtures for next surgery (tables, lights, IV stands, monitoring devices, etc.)	I	10:53:42 AM	12:08
12	Notify hospital operations control that operating room is ready	I	11:05:50 AM	00:45
17	Patient is admitted to operating room	I	11:06:35 AM	01:25
18	Patient administered general anesthesia	I	11:08:00 AM	04:32
19	Wait for patient to lose consciousness	I	11:12:32 AM	06:48
20	Next surgery begins	I	11:19:20 AM	
11	Dispose waste from cleaning	E		

Figure 12.2 Changeover data for improved changeover

some examples of how some health care processes have been improved in this regard:

1. Kits of presterilized tools can be procured that are customized for various surgical procedures. (For example, see Avid Medical at http://www. avidmedical.com.) This could reduce stocking time, since the tools need not be handled one at a time in the hospital given in the example.

2. The remaining internal tasks of removing waste and cleaning, sterilizing, and rearranging equipment in the operating room could be analyzed with tools already discussed, including a spaghetti diagram. More efficient work sequences might be found and more effective placement of (spare) equipment storage might be determined.

3. If many of the surgeries performed in the operating room were the same or similar, then perhaps visual controls could be used to place

equipment more quickly and unambiguously, such as having tape on the floor that indicates the location of various pieces of equipment. In the extreme case when an operating room was used for only one type of surgery, then the equipment need not be rearranged at all.

4. The remaining internal activities could be performed in parallel by multiple people rather than sequentially.

Finally, the efficiency of external time should be improved. If the selection of surgical tools (task 8) was made external to changeover by performing it before the changeover started, then one of the improvements noted would reduce external changeover time: Obtaining ready-made kits of surgical tools would reduce the time required for assembling surgical tools from the stock room. Alternatively, if the hospital did not outsource the selection of surgical tools, then it could analyze the layout of its storeroom to make assembling those kits more efficient. In addition, if cleaning supply storage could be moved closer to the operating room, then external changeover time would be reduced through the reduction in time required for task 1.

Changeovers with Multiple Workers

When multiple workers perform a changeover, create a sequence of tasks for each worker like those shown in Figures 11.2 and 11.3. Besides transforming internal changeover activities to external activities, one can consider reassigning tasks among the workers to those who might have idle time during the changeover to either take over a task performed by another worker or help another worker to reduce their task time and the total internal changeover time.

Use Videotapes for Changeover Analysis

It is difficult to observe a changeover and measure the time required for each activity as it occurs. If possible, create a video of the changeover. This will facilitate accurate timing because it allows a task to be viewed multiple times. Also, a videotape is useful to motivate the team working on the changeover to reduce changeover time because it causes anxiety when activities are obviously wasteful. For example, if a worker goes off camera for a half hour looking for tools during a changeover, it is difficult for anybody to refute that a problem exists or not to be motivated to fix the problem.

Another Application of the Changeover Time Reduction Methodology

The methodology presented here for reducing changeover time can also be used in other contexts where the issue is how to quickly start and finish a process. Sometimes these are processes that may only be performed intermittently, and little advance warning is given. For example, an engineering and design company might secure new business by responding to requests for quotations (RFQs). There may be no advance warning of when an RFQ is announced, and the time frame for submitting a response may be short. It is important to submit responses to RFQs by the stated deadline; not doing so would intuitively reduce the likelihood of winning the contract or, in most cases, would disqualify a bidder altogether. Bidding for the contract by responding to an RFQ requires that the bidding company provide many details about how they would provide the goods or services described in the RFQ document, including price and delivery timetable. In increasing the chances of an on-time submission, a company might instinctively entertain the question "What can we do in advance to reduce the time required to respond to an RFQ?" That question is essentially the same question as "How can we transform internal changeover time into external changeover time?" Many companies have ignored this challenge because they reason that no advance preparations can be made when the specific requirements of the next RFQ are not known and the required responses for each RFQ are unique.

It may seem impossible to prepare for an event where no two RFQs are likely to be identical. The specifications of the goods and services are likely to change from instance to instance, and companies might require different information. Nonetheless, one company has found, contrary to what many in the organization thought, that it can prepare in advance to a large degree for future events with unknown data requirements. What that company did was to study a number of RFQs to which they had responded, cataloging all the data requirements of each RFQ, and then checking for similarities among the RFQs. They found that 80 percent of the data in the RFQs was always required for every RFQ. Moreover, some of this data was unchanging, such as the name of the responding firm, its address, and contact information. Thus the company could construct a fill-in-the-blank form for a bulk of the information required by any RFQ, and the omission of one of those data fields was visually evident. Some of the blanks could even be filled in for some of the more stable data. This resolved many of the problems caused when each RFQ was looked on afresh and read to determine what information was required: Required data was often missed. Fewer omissions occurred with the new form. So even though each RFQ was unique in this situation, a standardized form solved a vast majority of the problems.

Many other business situations exist where activity must commence quickly, including the following:

1. *Unloading oceangoing ships at ports.* It is important to commence unloading as quickly as possible so ocean liner companies can keep their assets productive.
2. *Manufacturing plant retooling.* In the auto industry, for example, plant equipment must be changed on an infrequent basis (annually or less often) when a new vehicle is produced or when modifications are made to an existing vehicle. Again, less downtime is important here to keep assets productive and minimize the assets required to produce the same output.
3. *Helping new employees become productive.* New employees need to be productive as soon as possible. Reducing the time until computers, communications equipment, and passwords are issued to new employees allows them to contribute sooner.

Many other areas where quick changeover methodology can be applied exist similar to the three here. Therefore, it is wise to keep quick changeover in mind even when an operation is not the prototypical manufacturing scenario in which the quick changeover methodology was developed, in which a machine's tooling needs to be changed quickly in order to minimize inventory and increase responsiveness to customers.

Calibration Time

Changeovers in manufacturing often last much longer than required for the equipment and tooling to be changed. For example, new raw materials might not be delivered by the time the equipment is changed. This is an example of an activity that should be performed externally rather than internally. Another activity that extends changeover, which is ubiquitous in manufacturing, is the calibration of the equipment. This is an important type of activity to discuss in detail because it not only occurs often but also can prolong changeover for a considerable amount of time. In addition, calibration must be internal time: Equipment cannot be calibrated until it is set up for the next operation. Calibration manifests itself in different ways depending on the process. In a stamping press, calibration means making fine adjustments on the pressure that the stamping press exerts on different areas in a die to eliminate buckles and creases in the stamped metal parts. In aluminum can printing machines, where each of multiple printing pads prints a single color, calibration means adjusting each of the pads so that they print in the correct position relative to one another. Otherwise, words and images are blurred. In addition, color hues might need to be adjusted. In filling operations, calibration might mean adjusting the controls so that the proper amount is filled into containers. Most often, as is the case in these three examples, calibration activities are conducted in order to bring the product within quality specifications.

The root cause that often makes calibration necessary is that the process is not set up in precisely the same way every time a changeover occurs for a particular product. For example, if the die for a particular part could be placed in exactly the same spot every time, then one cause of unequal pressures on the metal being formed would be eliminated. (The moving part of a press, which is called the ram, may not be plumb, which could cause uneven pressure to be exerted at various points of the platen, thus causing variation in how the die performs depending on its location relative to the ram.) If the different printing pads for aluminum cans, each of which prints one color of ink, could be placed on the printing drum

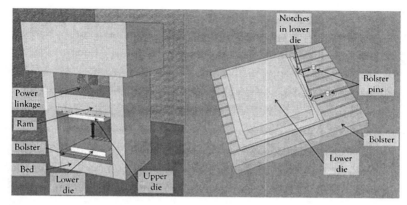

Figure 12.3 Stamping press and enlargement of die positioning

in exactly the correct relative position, then adjustments to the locations of the pads relative to one another would be unnecessary. Thus reducing calibration is often a matter of finding a way to ensure low variation in the placement of equipment during changeover and, more generally, making sure that all aspects of the process are set up consistently from changeover to changeover. In changing stamping dies, simple pins and notched dies locate dies precisely and consistently in the same position in the stamping press. Figure 12.3 shows how notches on the lower die can correct the horizontal position of the die as the notches engage the pins when the lower portion of the die is inserted into the press. The pins also stop the die in a consistent location front to back. Consistently arranging the process is critical in any process, thus underscoring previous discussions in this book about the importance of standardization in reducing variability and improving quality. In the case of changeover, standardization of equipment installation reduces changeover time.

Exercises

1. Chickin-Lickin is a fast-food restaurant where the breakfast menu differs substantially from the lunch menu. Currently, at one of Chickin-Lickin's retail outlets there is a nearly 50-minute period between breakfast and lunch when no food can be offered to customers because of the transition required between the breakfast

and lunch menus. The changeover task sequence followed by the worker who fries chicken (in a deep fryer) and subsequently assembles biscuits (during breakfast) and sandwiches (during lunch) is shown in Table 12.2 Can you make any suggestions to help the worker reduce this changeover time? By how much would you estimate your suggestions would reduce changeover time? Can a spaghetti diagram be used to advantage in this analysis? If the changeover time could be reduced, then the lag during which no food was offered could be shortened, thus improving customer satisfaction and offering the potential of increased revenue. A floor layout of the relevant parts of the restaurant is shown in Figure 12.4.[4]

2. Find an activity that you perform at work or at home that constitutes a changeover or otherwise needs to be done quickly when it is periodically performed. Apply the methodology presented in this chapter to reduce the changeover time.

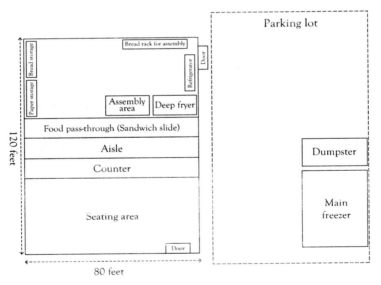

Figure 12.4 Floor layout of the Chickin-Lickin

Table 12.2 *Chickin-Lickin changeover*

	Changeover analysis (as-is process)			
Task sequence	Task description	Internal/ external	Start time	Task time (mm:ss)
1	Gather leftover chicken biscuits from sandwich slide, which serves the cash register area, and dispose in dumpster.	I	10:30:00 AM	05:20
2	Remove small chicken patties from refrigerator near deep fryer and return to the main freezer in parking lot.	I	10:35:20 AM	10:42
3	Return unused biscuits to bread storage area.	I	10:46:02 AM	02:02
4	Retrieve buns for sandwiches from the bread storage area and place in rack near the sandwich assembly area.	I	10:48:04 AM	01:42
5	Remove biscuit sandwich wrappers from assembly station, return them to paper goods storage area, and retrieve chicken sandwich wrappers from paper goods storage area.	I	10:49:46 AM	08:51
6	Get large chicken patties from main freezer in parking lot and stock in refrigerator near deep fryer.	I	10:58:37 AM	12:49
7	Put large chicken patties into deep fryer.	I	11:11:26 AM	05:11
8	Retrieve large cooked chicken patties and assemble, wrap, and place sandwiches in sandwich slide, which feeds cash register area.	I	11:16:37 AM	02:51
	Start lunch business.		11:19:28 AM	

PART III

Implementing Lean

CHAPTER 13

Successful Implementation of Lean

This chapter discusses some of the logistical and organizational considerations that must be negotiated for a Lean program to be successful, where the term *program* is intended to mean an effort within a company where many Lean projects are undertaken over a sustained period. Questions that must be considered in designing a Lean program include: How many Lean projects should be pursued simultaneously, which Lean projects should be pursued, how should management support Lean projects, how should Lean project teams be staffed, how should Lean projects be planned, and what are common roadblocks that are encountered in Lean programs? These questions are addressed in this chapter.

Employee Involvement and Lean Team Personnel

Lean projects are best done in teams for many reasons. First, constructing and improving the value stream map (VSM) requires knowledge of all steps of a process. The scope of Lean projects is usually large enough that no one person is familiar with all the process steps, thus multiple people are required to develop a comprehensive understanding of the entire process. Moreover, buy-in to process improvement solutions is required for successful implementation, and involvement in the team fosters that buy-in. In addition, besides people who are directly responsible for the operations in a process's steps, personnel from relevant support departments should be involved because their involvement during the project should encourage, first, buy-in and, second, support during the ensuing implementation phase. Finally, it is often a good idea to involve people from outside the process. Intuitively, people from similar processes in the same organization can share best practices across the organization.

In fact, including people from outside the process with no knowledge of the process to be improved can be a good, albeit unintuitive, idea. How so? People's familiarity with a process can cause them to be too wedded to the current process, which promotes continuing to do it the way they have been doing it. Team participants who are not so close to the process have a greater capability to think of ideas that are out of the box and groundbreaking.

Involving personnel from the entire process, from support functions (e.g., information technology, engineering, maintenance, human resources, etc.), from other similar processes, and from other plants has a benefit for highly siloed operations that is, perhaps, unexpected. While communication and coordination within departments may be fairly effective in many companies and organizations, coordination across departments is more difficult. Companies, especially those that operate within departmental silos, can expect opportunities for organizational development from Lean projects. In particular, having people on a Lean team from all departments involved in a process helps to break down barriers and animosity between departments that naturally build up over time among insular departments. People from different departments who work together on a Lean project sometimes develop personal relationships that dispel the negative notions held about other departments and make it more likely that those people will be able to work together in the future more effectively. Besides reducing interorganizational tensions, this benefit is particularly significant because processes naturally cut across departments and involve support groups. For processes to be executed well, all departments need to be focused on the processes in which they are involved rather than their department's self-interests.

Who should be on Lean teams? Many arguments point to involving workers on the lowest level of the organization who actually execute the process. First, any organization's hierarchy is likely to be a pyramid, with fewer higher level managers and many more workers on the lowest level. If Lean projects involve only managers, then the vast majority of an organization's human resources will not be leveraged in the Lean efforts. Making as much improvement as quickly as possible, therefore, requires involving lower level personnel. In addition, the old saying *Nobody knows a process like the person who stands within five feet of the machine all day* is true and implies that you should include workers if you really want the team to understand the process, which is a prerequisite for finding the greatest possible number of the best improvement opportunities. Further, employees who have not been involved in the process, or who have had representatives involved in the improvement process, are less likely to support the changes. Therefore, even if it was not a good idea otherwise, involving floor-level workers is essential to finding good improvements and getting them implemented. This is not to say that technical workers and managers should not be involved on a team. This can also be a good opportunity to build bridges across the levels of the organization.

The following is a true story that illustrates the importance of involving workers from all aspects of the process and, especially, involving lower level employees. A manufacturing company had an active and successful Lean program. One project that they pursued was a 5S project where one of the end results was an improved process layout within a work cell. Five days were allotted for the *kaizen* project to implement 5S. The team was justifiably proud of itself because it required only three days to clean, reorganize, and improve the flow in the work cell, which was approximately 40 feet by 80 feet. The new equipment layout reduced travel time and lead time of the process significantly and lent itself to ready identification of problems in the process because the entire process could be viewed from one vantage point. On the fourth day, the team returned to the work area to celebrate their early completion of the project. Much to their dismay, the entire work area had been rearranged back into the original configuration. What had happened? The second shift contract employees had not been invited to participate on the Lean team with the first shift permanent employees. When the second shift workers arrived to work on Wednesday night, they found an unfamiliar process layout, which they truly might not have understood. Possibly because they did not know how to operate the process under the new design, or perhaps in defiance for not being involved in the change, they took the time to put the process back into the layout with which they were familiar. Although frustrating, this experience was one that stuck with the team members, many of whom were likely to be more inclusive in subsequent projects.

The Project Charter

A document called a *project charter* is typically used by companies to define, propose, and plan Lean projects. This document might also be used to determine which projects a company will support in the short term. Another benefit of project charters is that filling them out forces a team to think through a project at a level of detail that increases its probability of achieving their goals and making a substantial contribution to an organization's improved business performance. Figure 13.1 shows a blank charter template and typical information required in a charter.[1] The charter's header section indicates key contacts and broad information about the project. The indication here of the product or service affected gives top management an idea of whether this project addresses the most important aspects of its business. A *champion* is a person who is at a relatively high level in the organization and whose business area will be addressed by the project. The identity of the champion indicates to top-level management that this project is supported by the champion, who is vouching for the importance of the project to the operations under his or her jurisdiction. The *business unit* indicated on the form would likely, therefore, be the champion's business unit. The *team leader* is responsible for managing the project if it should be approved. A team leader with a proven track record might enhance the chances that management would support that project. That said, new team leaders should be developed on an ongoing basis. The project *facilitator* is a person with expertise in Lean. He or she provides guidance for the team regarding which Lean tools should be applied in a project, as well as how these tools should be applied. This person is also likely to facilitate constructive conversation in team meetings.

Lean Project Charter

Product or Service Impacted		Team Leader	
Business Unit		Team Leader Phone Number	
Champion		Email for Team Leader	
Facilitator			

Figure 13.1a Lean project charter template

Element	Description	Specifications				
		Metrics	Current	Goal	% Improvement	Units
1. Process	Name of process to be improved.					
2. Project description	What practical problem will be solved? What is the project's purpose?					
3. Objective	What metrics will be improved, what is the current performance for those metrics, and how much improvement is targeted? Provide specifics on how metrics are computed.	Metric 1				
		Metric 2				
		Metric 3				
4. Process scope	Which process steps will be considered in this project? What is the first step, and what is the last step?					
5. Business case	Why is it important? Why is it critical to business success? What is the justification?					
6. Benefit to internal and external customers	How will internal or external customers benefit from this project? How does improvement in the metrics that you have selected help them improve their performance?					
7. Team members	Names and roles of team members.					
8. Schedule	Project start					
	Project charter approved					
	Current state VSM					
	Future state VSM					
	Project completion					
9. Support required	What resources, people, and departments are required?					

Figure 13.1b Lean project charter template

The body of the document gives the details about the project in terms of nine elements. In order to describe these elements more concretely, we will give examples of how they might be specified for the five processes shown in Table 13.1. Some of these processes have been described elsewhere in this book, so the reader who has progressed linearly through the book will find these processes to be familiar. For those who have used this book as a reference, the chapters that relate to these processes will be cited. In the context of manufacturing, we will consider the job shop setting used in the chapter on work cells (Chapter 11) and, in particular, a product family manufactured in that job shop, which is a group of parts that require common processing. In the realm of sales and marketing, we will consider the process that a company uses to respond to a request for quotation (RFQ), such as was discussed in Chapters 2, 5, and 12. In administration, we will consider the process that creates invoices that are submitted to customers for payment, as was discussed in Chapter 2. In a service industry, we will consider baggage handling at an airport, which is an allied process to the Jetway management process that was briefly discussed in Chapter 1. In health care, we will consider the process of delivering medications to patients in a hospital. For an in-depth consideration of such a process, Harvard Business School Publishing has published an excellent case, which is titled *Deaconess-Glover (A)*.[2]

The *process* element of the project charter describes the process within the business unit identified in the header section that will be addressed. The process names that are specified in the second column of Table 13.1 might be appropriate responses for this element on the project charter form, except that we would want to be more specific in the manufacturing example. For our illustration, let us consider a manufacturing process for

Table 13.1 Process examples

Process context	Process
Manufacturing	Manufacture of a product
Sales and marketing	Response to RFQ
Administration	Issuing of invoices
Service	Handling baggage
Health care	Medicine delivery in a hospital

mePads, which are relatively small and thin handheld computing devices consisting of an internal circuit board, a screen, and a case. The current layout of the mePad factory is similar to the job shop layout described in Chapter 11 with three production departments: circuit board assembly, final assembly, and packaging. MePads are produced in batches, 1,000 to a batch. Circuit boards for 1,000 units are assembled and stacked on a pallet before being transported to final assembly. After those 1,000 circuit boards are assembled together with screens and cases into a finished unit, they are, again, loaded on a pallet of 1,000 units, and then transported to the packaging department. The packaging department puts the finished units in boxes, along with manuals, and then puts them into racks in the warehouse. With this backdrop, the process name that might be entered on the project charter is *mePad production process.*

The *project description* element describes the problem that will be solved by the project. In the case of our five projects, this element might be stated as shown in Table 13.2.

If the process description is well stated, then it should be relatively easy to identify the metrics that are listed as part of the *objectives* element on the project charter. In fact, the project descriptions in Table 13.2 are so clear in our case that we can easily identify the appropriate metrics that should be targeted with the projects, as made explicit in Table 13.3. If the metrics are not so clear from the process description, then perhaps the description can be improved. Lead time is clearly a metric that if approved would help resolve the issues identified in the process description for the first four projects. In fact, the mePad manufacturing process description implies two lead times: overall process lead time and time from when customers place orders to when the orders are shipped (see Table 13.3). The focus of Lean is lead time reduction, and so it is clear that the Lean methodology is an appropriate avenue to resolve the issues identified in these four projects. Furthermore, the other nonlead-time metrics listed for the first four projects involve quality improvements, which also tend to occur with Lean projects. Management should be looking for this congruence between a project's goals and the Lean methodology when it approves Lean projects.

The congruence between Lean and project goals is not so apparent in the case of the health care project. The metrics that fall out of

Table 13.2 Project charter project description

Process	Project description
Manufacture of mePads	The investment in in-process and finished goods inventory needs to be reduced because it represents more working capital than can be financed. Also, when finished goods inventory is depleted, the response time to customer orders is very slow, thus reducing customer satisfaction and goodwill. Thus responsiveness to customers must be improved.
Response to RFQ	The time to respond to RFQs is too long. A higher percentage of responses need to be submitted on time to improve the win rate.
Issuing of invoices	Invoices take too long to be created and sent to customers. This needs to be reduced in order to reduce accounts payable and increase the cash account.
Baggage handling	The time to get baggage from planes to the terminal sorting system needs to be reduced in order to facilitate closer connection times and reduce the number of bags that do not make their connections. Also, misrouted bags cause customers to temporarily lose their bags. These errors need to be reduced. Besides reduced customer satisfaction, misrouted and late baggage that does not make it to the customer's final destination incurs charges for special delivery.
Medicine delivery in a hospital	The number of errors in filling prescriptions needs to be reduced, as does the number of prescription changes. A prescription change occurs when medications have already been pulled from the pharmacy's inventory and staged when a physician changes the prescription. Filling the new prescription is time-consuming, and the old medication needs to be either restocked or thrown out, causing wasted material or additional labor hours.

the process description for that project (see Table 13.3), increased frequency of medication delivery and reduction in prescription changes, a measure of efficiency and a measure of wasted labor hours, may not be so clearly related to Lean, at least to the novice. Hopefully, the management has some knowledge of Lean or asks the right questions of the project participants to realize that increased frequency of fulfillment is synonymous with reduced batch sizes and reduced setup times. Furthermore, the lead time of the fulfillment process must be reduced so that fulfillment can be performed more frequently. In addition, if the lead time of the fulfillment process is reduced, then it could be delayed until

Table 13.3 Project charter process metrics

Process	Metrics
Manufacture of mePads	1. Process lead time 2. Average time to ship customers' orders
Response to RFQ	1. Lead time to respond to an RFQ 2. Average number of errors made on an RFQ
Issuing of invoices	1. Lead time to create an invoice 2. Errors made on invoices
Baggage handling	1. Lead time to get luggage from plane to terminal baggage system 2. Percentage of bags misrouted 3. Average cost per bag for special delivery
Medicine delivery in a hospital	1. Frequency of medication fulfillment 2. Percentage of prescriptions changed after already being fulfilled 3. Average hours per patient spent restocking medications 4. Dollars of waste for medications thrown out

closer to when the medications were needed. Postponing the selection of medications in that way allows a greater percentage of the doctors' revised prescriptions to be taken into account, and thus the percentage of prescriptions that needed to be replaced would be reduced, as would the associated waste of throwing medications away and the additional labor hours required for rework. Finally, Lean usually uncovers opportunities for improving efficiency. Thus, although not as apparent from the process description, Lean is an appropriate tool for this health care project mainly because reducing lead time is required to improve the metrics for this project. Because reducing lead time is so important to this project, it could also be listed as one of the project metrics.

Besides lead time to respond to an RFQ, another metric was added to the sales and marketing project—namely, the average number of errors on an RFQ. Although not explicitly mentioned in the project description, this might be an important metric to include because we do not want to decrease lead time if we are going to sacrifice accuracy. Additionally, fewer errors should support the stated goal of a higher win rate, and including this metric puts a focus on a facet of performance on which we can expect Lean to deliver. This metric also reminds us to look for quality improvements as we analyze the process. Similarly, in the administrative process, reducing errors is important because invoices with errors will result in the customers having extra time to submit their payments, which would result in a longer lead time to be paid (as the terms of payment are typically extended when invoices are in error).

In the baggage-handling process, reducing the lead time from plane to terminal will reduce the number of bags that do not make close connections and, furthermore, allow closer connections, which increases the number of feasible flight combinations and perhaps customer satisfaction due to a greater selection of feasible combinations of flight legs. Again, a measure of quality (percentage of bags misrouted) is important in this process because it is not sufficient for bags to be placed in any plane: They need to be in the correct plane in order for them to arrive with customers at the final destination. Including this quality metric, again, heightens team members' attention to potential causes of misrouted bags. Including the average cost paid for special delivery of late bags is perhaps redundant with the percentage of bags misrouted. However, using metrics that are measured in dollars is often effective in convincing people that the process is worthy of the resources that would be dedicated to it in a Lean project.

Because Lean can often result in process lead times being reduced by 90 percent or more, managers who advise Lean teams and who approve projects often look for teams to target lead time reductions, and improvements in other metrics, by 50 percent or more. The idea is to have the Lean teams realize that significant improvements are possible and to strive for them.

The next element in the project charter is *process scope*, which defines the size of the process that the project will address. In Lean projects it is best to think of defining process scope by listing the first step and the last step of the process that will be addressed. The scope of a project must be carefully selected for the project (a) to be feasible in a reasonable amount of time and (b) to yield a significantly improved process. If the scope is too small (i.e., too few process steps), then there are fewer opportunities for improvement and a greater probability that any suggested changes will conflict with other process steps not considered within the project scope. A small scope also reduces the advantages discussed previously of having a project that crosses departmental boundaries. Examples of how the scopes for our five projects might be stated are shown in Table 13.4.

Table 13.4 *Project charter process scope*

Process	Scope
Manufacture of mePads	From start of circuit board assembly to the time when goods are put away in the warehouse
Response to RFQ	From announcement of an RFQ opportunity until the submission of RFQ
Issuing of invoices	From the completion of service to issuance of invoice
Baggage handling	From the plane landing on the runway to bags being inducted into terminal sorting system
Medicine delivery in a hospital	From medication picking in the hospital pharmacy until delivery of medications in hospital wards

One scope that is illustrative is the baggage-handling process. One might argue that this project is about what the baggage handlers do to get bags off the plane and how they interact with the baggage-handling system. One might further argue that what the pilots and ground control do to get the plane to the gate sooner or later is beyond the control of the baggage handlers. Defining a larger scope, however, has advantages in this case. If it is not deemed important for the plane to get to the gate as soon as possible, this is time lost that makes it more difficult for the bags to get to their next destination. Including the steps required to get the plane to the gate would motivate taking a closer look at these preliminary steps, which do matter to the ultimate goal of this project. Also, including people outside the realm of the baggage handlers would expose more problems and opportunities for improvement. Having a wider scope and more interdepartmental interaction also has advantages as mentioned previously in terms of organizational development. One could even argue that the scope of the baggage-handling project should be expanded beyond what is listed in Table 13.4. Transferring baggage is not complete until the bags make it onto their next flight or arrive at the baggage carousel. Hence, a greater number of process steps could, and possibly should, be included, such as the sorting process itself and moving the bags to the outgoing planes.

Similarly, the scope of the RFQ process could have begun when work begins on an RFQ response. However, defining the scope as it is in Table 13.4 makes it clear that the clock starts ticking when an RFQ is announced, and it is important to detect RFQ opportunities as soon as possible to start work on the responses as soon as possible. In other words, we have enlarged the process scope from what it might have otherwise been.

The next element, *business case*, is a short statement of why a project is important to the organization. Although this may be apparent from the metrics and problem statement, this may still be a reasonable element to require of project teams. This is an opportunity to express how a project relates to the organization's strategy and top-level metrics. For example, Table 13.5 lists how this element might be completed in the case of the five projects we are considering.

Table 13.5 Project charter business case

Process	Business case
Manufacture of mePads	Quick delivery of mePads is expected by our customers and part of our company's value proposition. Slow delivery reduces customer satisfaction and goodwill, which are critical to customer retention. Additionally, reducing inventory is needed to improve the company's capital structure.
Response to RFQ	Responding to RFQs is the main source of generating revenue, and late RFQ responses will reduce the company's revenue potential.
Issuing of invoices	Delay in issuing invoices increases the amount of uncollected revenue, which in turn increases the company's working capital needs. Reducing the required working capital reduces the cost of working capital, not only because less money will need to be borrowed but also because our lenders will give us lower interest rates if we improve our capital structure.
Baggage handling	Bags arriving at the wrong destination or not making connections severely reduces customer satisfaction and repeat business. In addition, great cost is incurred to deliver late baggage through special delivery services. Thus, this project has benefits in both increasing revenue and decreasing cost, which implies increased profit.
Medicine delivery in a hospital	Medication errors are a leading cause of patient deaths in hospitals. Additionally, increasing medication replenishment frequency will reduce labor and material cost of out-dated prescriptions, as well as ensure that recently revised prescriptions are delivered to patients in a more prompt fashion, thus supporting patient well-being and recovery.

The sixth element, *benefit to internal and external customers*, specifies the customers who will benefit from the project and how they will benefit. External customers are people, companies, and institutions outside the company or organization undertaking the project. Sometimes external customers are considered people outside the facility undertaking the project but still within the same company. Internal customers are people and departments within the organization undertaking the project. Table 13.6 shows possible responses for this element for the five projects.

The seventh and eighth elements of the project charter, *team members* and *schedule*, simply list the team members (and their departments) and the proposed schedule for the project. Management who critique this proposal might check that the team is sufficiently interdepartmental and involves all relevant parties. The schedule should be reviewed to ensure it is not so short as to be unfeasible and not too long as to lose focus. Finally, the ninth element, *support required*, lists the support functions, departments, and resources that are required to successfully complete the project. Management might check here to see if any department or resources are listed that are not represented on the project team. If a critical resource is not represented on the team, then perhaps expanding the team should be considered for the reasons previously discussed.

Table 13.6 Project charter internal and external customer benefits

Process	Customer benefits
Manufacture of mePads	Retail customers will receive more prompt delivery; internal financial department will improve performance.
Response to RFQ	Clients who have issued the RFQs will receive more prompt and accurate responses; internally, top management will see greater revenue.
Issuing of invoices	Customers will receive more accurate invoices and, although more prompt invoicing implies they will be paying sooner, there will be less inconvenience, labor hours, and cost associated with sorting out invoices for services provided that are in error.
Baggage handling	Customers will enjoy fewer lost bags; internal financial performance will be improved.
Medicine delivery in a hospital	Patients will receive more accurate and prompt delivery of medications with better health outcomes; internal costs will be reduced.

Support might include departments such as maintenance, engineering, information technology, human resources, and so forth.

The project charter in Figure 13.1 should be considered malleable. The data fields and terminology used can and should be adapted to a particular organization's needs. For example, different organizations might have different titles for those involved in their Lean effort or have different roles altogether.

Kaizen Events

Process improvements can be made more quickly if a concerted effort can be dedicated to improvement projects. Allowing team members two to five days away from their day-to-day jobs allows focused effort on a project that might otherwise take months, if it could ever be accomplished at all. These focused events are often called *kaizen events*. Of course, this places a burden on a company or organization who must either find replacement personnel or have somehow worked ahead to relieve the burden of day-to-day deliverables. In manufacturing operations, production areas must be shut down when a *kaizen* event focuses on rearranging production flow through a work area. Alternatively, these projects can be pursued in periods of slack demand or activity.

Some examples of activities addressed during *kaizen* events are the following:

1. Constructing a VSM
2. Reducing changeover time
3. Improving work area design
4. Implementing 5S
5. Designing a kanban replenishment system

Notice that the first item on the list can be distinguished from the remaining items on the list in that it involves the highest level tool within Lean, which is the VSM, whereas the other topics are lower level tools in a sense that will be made clear shortly.

The creation of a VSM results in an understanding of the current state of the process, as well as its deficiencies. Thus the result of value stream mapping is the identification of waste and its causes, and a typical deliverable from a value stream mapping *kaizen* event is a list of places in the process where waste exists and the Lean tools that can be applied to reduce those sources of waste. That list would typically be prioritized in terms of which sources of waste have the greatest impact on lead time and the other metrics for the project. Alternatively, opportunities for improvement might also be prioritized, putting those with the biggest bang for the buck at the top of the list—that is, priority would go to projects that returned the greatest improvement in metrics for the effort expended. The remaining four types of *kaizen* events listed would address the wastes that were identified in a value stream mapping *kaizen* event. Thus we call the VSM a top-level Lean tool and the tools used in the other *kaizen* events lower level tools because their use follows from the creation of the VSM.

Selecting the Right Projects

Companies with an active Lean program must decide which of the proposed projects will be supported because it is often the case that there are more candidate projects than can be sponsored by the company at any one time. Any company can support only a limited number of projects at one time because of the resources required to pursue them. Actually, even if the number of candidate projects is fewer than the number that can be supported, then the information in this chapter should still be used to make sure that all those candidate projects are important and the team has done adequate investigation and planning to make the success of the project likely.

The project charter contains information that can be used to judge which projects should be supported. Of course, if any project is not immediately supported, it can either be put in the queue for later implementation or, if the project charter is not yet satisfactory, the team can be directed to further develop their project proposal. In general, these criteria can be used to select the best project prospects:

1. Importance of the process to the overall organization
2. Importance of the project goals and metrics to the business

3. Magnitude of improvement possible
4. Feasibility and resource requirements of the project
5. How well the project has been planned and whether Lean is the appropriate improvement methodology

Of course, there may not be candidate projects that score highly in all these categories, and in that case, trade-offs among the criteria must be made. Feasibility of a project might have many connotations such as:

1. Will the parties involved cooperate?
2. Is data available for the project?
3. Are the required Lean tools the simplest ones to use or the most difficult and time-consuming?
4. Can a Lean expert see that this project is likely to end in successful improvements to the process?

One exception might be made to the criteria in the case of a company that is just embarking on a Lean program. In that case, early success is important to convince people in the organization that Lean is viable and to help train people in Lean. In that case, some companies early on in their Lean program focus on the feasibility of the project and whether it is likely to improve a process, regardless of how much it may improve. One aspect of projects to focus on here is which and how many Lean tools are likely to be required for a project, whether they are the simplest of the Lean tools, and whether the team members have already been trained in those tools.

Organizational Structure to Support Lean

This section describes a hierarchy of roles that medium-sized to large firms employ to support their Lean efforts, as displayed in Table 13.7. A successful company need not copy this managerial format exactly. However, even though all the positions described here might not be needed, the roles served by each might need to be served by someone. In smaller companies, it may be appropriate to have fewer positions filled with people who play multiple roles.

Table 13.7 Roles in Lean

Position title	Roles
Plant or facility steering committee	1. Reviews and approves project charters 2. Selects projects from candidate projects 3. Allocates resources among potential projects
Champion	1. High-level manager who supports a particular project and vouches for its worth
Project leader	1. Leader of the project team responsible for team progress
Project facilitator	1. Expert in Lean who facilitates constructive team interaction and provides support in implementing Lean tools

If a company pursues too many projects at one time, it risks not meeting day-to-day deliverables because workers and managers on project teams are often relieved of day-to-day responsibilities to do their Lean project (see the description of *kaizen* events earlier in this chapter). In the interest of allocating the scarce human resources to pursue Lean projects, the steering committee is responsible for selecting which candidate projects offer the greatest potential improvement and the greatest probability that the potential improvements will be attained. The remaining roles of champion, project leader, and project facilitator were described earlier in this chapter when project charters were discussed.

Roadblocks

Getting Out of Firefighting Mode

The typical mode of operation for many companies and organizations is manifest in the need to respond to a plethora of crises on a daily basis. (Does this describe where you work?) This is particularly true for organizations that have not yet defined their processes, standardized them, and used Lean to improve them. For these organizations, it is difficult to divert resources from the continual firefighting and crisis management to do a Lean project. This is possibly the biggest hurdle in getting started with Lean. Controlled, stable processes are needed to make people available to thoughtfully improve processes with Lean, but how does an organization attain process stability when it cannot ignore daily crises? Getting started is thus a difficult task, and the early going may be slow because it is difficult to dedicate resources to Lean.

Coping with Improved Worker Efficiency

Lean focuses on reducing lead time, and as we have discussed, many other metrics improve concurrently, one of which is worker efficiency. In other words, fewer worker hours are required after a Lean project to produce the same output. This creates another issue that often arises as Lean projects begin. If an organization's business volume remains constant, then a company will have extra workers due to Lean. Several alternatives for dealing with this situation exist, including (a) increasing business volume to absorb the workers, (b) reducing the workforce level through attrition, and (c) laying off the excess workers. Of these three approaches, the best alternative is the first, where workers do not lose their jobs and management improves the company's bottom line. Increasing business volume is not always easy to do, however, particularly in economic downturns. In that case, a company might resort to one of the other two alternatives. It might be obvious that the third option is rife with issues. We have argued that Lean is most effective when the lowest level of workers are involved in Lean projects. What happens when a team of workers completes a successful project and then the workforce is rewarded with layoffs? The answer to that rhetorical question is that you have most likely ended your Lean program and eliminated any sort of effort to improve processes. Even the second option can be met with cynicism from the workforce. For example, in the 1980s and 1990s General Motors (GM) formed a jobs bank by negotiation with the United Auto Workers, whereby workers whose jobs had been reduced due to efficiency improvements would be guaranteed a job. Redundant workers were removed from the work floor and put on other make-work projects until attrition opened up a spot for them back on the production floor. Conceived as an innovative solution to the second option, the jobs bank was not effective in gaining widespread worker support for productivity improvements due to the organizational climate and the relationship between the union and management. Thus the second alternative was difficult for GM to implement.

Telling the Truth About Performance

A necessary situation for Lean to be successful is that an organization must be able to admit that its operations are not as good as they could be. In other words, an organization must be honest in calculating and reporting its metrics. This practice may be difficult for some organizations, and there are a number of possible root causes for this. One root cause is when workers and management are penalized whenever metrics do not match up with expectations or mistakes are found. If workers are yelled at, chastised, disciplined, or otherwise penalized for mistakes, then a manager should not expect their metrics to reflect reality. Workers and supervision will find ways to avoid delivering bad news by doing things like taking quality measurements after inspection and repair or, where latitude exists, defining a metric in the most favorable way possible. In organizations like this, the picture communicated to management grows increasingly rosy as it percolates to the top of the organization. Management, consequently, is pleased with the metrics reported while the bottom line performance of the company (such as profit) languishes. Conversely, Lean only succeeds when all errors, inefficiencies, and shortcomings can be acknowledged. If you do not know you have a problem, then you will not be able to fix it. In order for an organization to be honest with itself and measure its performance accurately, the culture must be one where shortcomings can be safely reported and not immediately penalized. It is important to remember Deming's philosophy that 85 percent of errors are due not to lazy workers but to faulty processes, which are predominantly management's responsibility. If one subscribes to this philosophy, then workers should not immediately be blamed for mistakes, but rather the mistakes should be taken as indications of a less-than-perfect process. Furthermore, the most stringent metrics—that is, those that reveal the greatest number of improvement possibilities—will result in the greatest improvement and should be used. So rather than glossing over errors and inefficiencies, an organization should want to reveal as many issues as possible.

Misaligned Incentives

Another barrier that is frequently encountered is improper incentives that prohibit the lean flow of goods through a process. Realignment of misaligned incentives is a necessary condition for the success of Lean projects. One example of this is where piece-rate incentive pay systems are used. Using a kanban system together with piece-rate systems is difficult because ceasing production when kanban production cards are depleted affects workers' pay immediately and directly: Workers can be expected to rebel against such production controls or otherwise to continue producing goods because of their individual incentives. Piece-rate systems or other efficiency-based bonus systems (e.g., gainsharing or goal sharing systems) also run contrary to Lean when employees are empowered to schedule work through their own work stations. Such bonus systems can motivate employees to prioritize the parts that generate the greatest bonus rather than those parts that are actually most needed. This misalignment occurs when the *standard* rates for parts are not equitable. Standard rates might be in the form of some number of parts per hour that employees can reasonably produce. If employees produce at a greater rate, then a bonus is paid. Such standards can never be set across many parts such that equivalent effort is required to earn equivalent pay. The standards for some parts will be more easily attained and those parts will be made first.

Still, in other circumstances, employees' behavior can influence overtime. In one operation, weekend overtime would be scheduled in one of the process steps if the inventory waiting to be processed there was greater than a predetermined threshold level, regardless of whether the parts were needed or not. Employees at the preceding step were conditioned to push parts as fast as possible toward the step where overtime might be scheduled and, as one might presume, that incentive motivated workers at the step where overtime might be scheduled to work more slowly than might otherwise be possible. When a kanban system was implemented, a maximum inventory of one unit was set preceding the workstation in question. The workers, unfortunately, had been conditioned to slow down when little inventory was waiting to be processed. Thus, one unit of inventory was viewed as a signal to stop production rather than to process it. Production ground to a halt and the kanban system was abandoned.

CHAPTER 14

Conclusions and Summary

What is Lean about? Lean is about reducing the lead time of a process. Applying Lean requires that we find the waste in the process, where waste is those activities that increase lead time but do not add value to a product or service. The seven deadly categories of waste guide us toward identifying it. The Lean methodology can be summarized by these steps:

1. Define the metrics that are important for improving the target process.
2. Construct a value stream map (VSM) of the current process.
3. Find waste and brainstorm process improvements.
4. Construct a VSM of the future process reflecting the proposed improvements.
5. Prioritize the improvements and implement them, possibly using *kaizen* events for improvements needing additional planning or work to implement.
6. Verify that the process has improved according to the hypothesis expressed in the future state VSM.
7. Go back to step 2 and repeat.

It is obvious that reducing lead time increases the responsiveness of a process. In addition, we have seen that reduced lead time always generates other benefits. Inventory or work-in-process is always reduced and other benefits are also realized, which depend on the process, including increased productivity and efficiency, improved quality, fewer errors, increased customer satisfaction, improved cash flow, and many others.

Philosophically, we can view the Toyota Production System and Lean as a fundamental shift in how we think about manufacturing processes. From the Industrial Revolution throughout much of the 20th century, manufacturing managers predominantly paid attention to keeping machines and people busy, focusing on measures such as capacity utilization and utilization of workers' time. Lean, conversely, focuses on steady utilization of the products and services flowing through a process: If value is not being added to a part, then it is simply unproductive inventory requiring an investment but getting no closer to yielding a return. So one might look at the traditional approach to manufacturing as keeping investments in machines and people busy while Lean focuses on keeping the goods flowing through the process busy. A naïve approach to choosing between these two philosophies would revolve around the cost of machines and people versus goods: One might think that, obviously, whichever represents the greatest investment is the most important to keep busy. However, further reflection on the goals of manufacturing might suggest that business success involves producing goods in sufficient quantity to meet customers' delivery and quality expectations without producing any more goods than necessary and using any more of other resources than necessary. In financial terms, this means maximizing revenue, minimizing cost, and minimizing investment. Lean clearly helps on-time delivery and reduces inventory cost, but what about minimizing consumption of other resources? We have seen that applying Lean can also increase worker efficiency so that the same output can be achieved with fewer workers and labor cost is reduced. Lean can also reduce the amount of equipment and building space needed. Many factories make this point apparent by roping off the floor space freed up by Lean with yellow tape. The people and equipment formerly in this space are no longer needed, and the floor space is available for expanded output. So for the traditional mind-set, keeping machines and people as busy as possible sounds attractive, but not if the people are not doing anything to benefit the customer (wasted motion) or the machines are making product that is not needed in the near term (overproduction, excess inventory). Blindly keeping resources busy, then, can be detrimental to profitability. One of the benefits of Lean is that it helps us decrease inventory by keeping machines busy with the right goods, which are those that downstream processes can consume and what customers want (e.g., using a kanban system). Furthermore, Lean helps us expand the capacity of people and machines: Worker efficiency increases as processes are simplified and streamlined, and machine capacity is expanded by reducing changeover time. Thus Lean can minimize the investment made by a company. We have also seen in this book many examples where revenue is enhanced by Lean. Operating a business according to the principles of Lean, therefore, trumps the traditional manufacturing mind-set because it simultaneously maximizes revenue, minimizes cost, and minimizes investment. Although the foregoing argument is grounded in a manufacturing context, this book has entertained processes in many nonmanufacturing contexts and demonstrated the analogous benefits of Lean in those contexts.

Another conceptual observation about Lean is that it is a data-driven improvement methodology. Lean is data driven because the VSM is based on actual data from the process, on which our ideas for improvement are based. Other Lean efforts rely on data as well, such as reducing changeover time and constructing a work cell. Lean is not about using our intuition to improve a process and trusting that our ideas, without any supporting data or analysis, will improve a process. This is important because we do not always (perhaps rarely) have a good idea about how processes are actually performed until we go out and observe them. Hence, acting on intuition, at best, would not likely address the best opportunities for improvement and, at worst, might not result in improvements at all. It is important to take time to understand the process before we can improve it. Think about Taiichi Ohno's idea about standing in a circle (see Chapter 4). This is, indeed, the scientific method, which is to develop improvement hypotheses based on data, test the proposed changes to see if improvement has resulted, and use the changed process if improvement has indeed occurred. Until a better way to execute a process is proven with data, the process is executed according to the old definition. Thus the scientific method, as applied to business processes, requires the standardization of how processes are executed.

The definition on which we should standardize includes the VSM. We have argued that any improvements we find might not be improvements tomorrow if the process has changed, and our future state VSM will yield no benefit because we cannot ensure that we will execute the process that way. We have also discussed standardizing on the details of a process using Standard Work documents, which should reflect the best method found to date. The process should be executed according to the VSM and Standard Work documents until a data-driven approach identifies an improved process. Theoretically, process improvement never ends. We can always revisit a process and find improvements.

I hope this book has clearly explained the philosophies of Lean, as well as how to apply Lean tools that are generally applicable and the most frequently used. This is not a comprehensive book on every philosophy and tool having to do with Lean. Instead, it is a quick-start manual. Other books and materials that have been referenced throughout this book provide clues on where to find more in-depth coverage of particular topics if it is needed. It is also useful to identify someone who has experience with Lean to help you or your company get started. While the concepts of Lean are straightforward, leaning on the expertise of others can accelerate the effectiveness of a Lean program and help ensure that early endeavors are successful, which will have great bearing on whether a Lean program is successful in the long term.

One way to solidify the concepts in this book is to perform a Lean project for an organization. This book can be used in a course that involves applying Lean in a company setting. Alternatively, consider analyzing one or more of the cases found in Chapter 16. They offer an opportunity to test if a reader has understood the foregoing material. Moreover, although reading material may breed familiarity, truly understanding a topic at a deeper level requires that the concepts be applied. Applying Lean in a project setting is, therefore, a requirement for truly understanding Lean and, certainly, the only way to experience firsthand how effective it can be.

Exercise

1. Read *The Goal*, by E. M. Goldratt.[1] For an opportunity to comprehensively apply the methods discussed in this book, answer the following questions:

    a. Describe the components of the Drum-Buffer-Rope method used in *The Goal* to control the release of work onto the plant floor. Describe how the Drum-Buffer-Rope could be considered a pull system and, in that regard, analogous to a kanban system. Describe the similarities and differences of that pull system with the more common version described in this book.

    b. Describe the methods used in *The Goal* to improve the plant's performance that are consistent with Lean methods as described in this book.

PART IV

Practice

CHAPTER 15

Exercises

Improving processes with Lean is a skill and, like any other skill, Lean requires practice and experience to understand its principles deeply, to apply its concepts appropriately, and to successfully navigate the barriers one will encounter. It is not unlike an apprenticeship where knowledge is acquired with initial training and then skills are honed and mastered through considerable practice. The Lean learning curve takes longer than one might ideally hope because the gestation of projects is typical long: Projects are often tackled while individuals on the team are still performing regular job duties and the data required to understand the process and pinpoint causes of waste may need to be collected. Where data already exist it may require information technology (IT) support personnel to extract it from data sources. The latter can take time because priority is usually highest for those IT tasks that support daily operations than for projects whose delay will not compromise short-term operating requirements.

The goal of this chapter is to provide exercises that can be read quickly and do not require comprehensive data analysis. Thus, readers can gain experience quickly through repetition, thus enabling a steeper learning curve than if experience relied solely on executing projects with long gestation periods. These exercises are designed to train an apprentice to quickly identify the type of waste present, determine the root cause of the waste, and determine the most appropriate Lean tool to mitigate the root cause. While multiple tools might be applied in any of these scenarios, some tools are more appropriate and, often, a single tool most effectively addresses the waste at hand.

Before presenting the scenarios we first present a table that provides a partial summary of the foregoing material in this book and which may be used as a reference with the exercises. It is not comprehensive, but it does serve as a road map for resolution of some frequently observed wastes.

Table 15.1 lists in its first column various types of wasteful activities that are frequently observed in processes. The second column classifies the waste using the seven categories discussed previously. The next column describes common root causes of the waste: Root causes will sometimes be different from those listed in the table but the root causes in the table, nonetheless, are often the culprits. The fourth column lists the category of tool that resolves the root cause. The fifth and last column gives specific examples of what tools might be used to provide the *functionality* described in the previous column.

For each of the scenarios in the subsections of this chapter, perform the following tasks:

1. Identify and classify the waste(s) that you observe in the scenario.
2. Perform a 5-Whys analysis, as necessary, to identify the root cause of the waste.
3. Identify the type of Lean tool required to reduce the waste and make specific recommendations of what tools you would use and how you would apply them.

This sequence follows the sequence of columns in Table 15.1.

Scenario 1: A Bottling Process

A soft drink bottler had a filling line where the main operation was to fill 12-ounce bottles. The line was used to fill multiple products, and so it needed to be changed over from time to time. While the soft drink syrup and carbonated water were delivered via pipes to the filling machine, the process was also fed with glass bottles and cartons in which the filled bottles were placed in quantities of 24 bottles for each carton. The empty bottles and cartons were delivered from their own respective storage areas via conveyor belts. See Figure 15.1 for a floor layout of the operation. The bottling line personnel complained that the operators feeding the line with cartons and bottles never got the correct quantities loaded to finish the desired production quantity. Furthermore, the filling operators complained that when the bottle feeders (and the carton feeders also) needed to add more bottles (cartons) to complete the end of the filling

Table 15.1 Roadmap for waste elimination

Observation	Type of waste	Root cause(s)	Appropriate type of Lean tool	Specific tool examples
Administrative and Service Processes				
Paperwork waiting to be processed at a step in an administrative process	Waiting	• Downstream worker unaware that work has arrived	• Visual systems	• Visual signal that work is waiting
		• Downstream worker currently overloaded	• Synchronize	• Kanban system
		• Downstream worker currently busy processing another type of work units	• Synchronize if wait is inappropriately long • Reduce changeover time	• Kanban system to make amount of WIP of each work unit type visually apparent to signal appropriate priorities • Changeover time reduction
Some tasks in a downstream step in an administrative or service process do not require the prior step to be completed	Waiting	• Poor process design	• Simplify and streamline	• Break downstream step into multiple steps and perform tasks of downstream step that are not sequence dependent in parallel with prior tasks
Manufacturing Processes				
Inventory between manufacturing processing steps	Inventory	• Downstream worker unaware that work has arrived	• Visual systems	• Visual signal that work is waiting

(Continued)

Table 15.1 Roadmap for waste elimination (Continued)

Observation	Type of waste	Root cause(s)	Appropriate type of Lean tool	Specific tool examples
		• Downstream worker currently overloaded	• Synchronize	• Kanban system • Possibly reduce batch size and changeover time at upstream step
		• Large delivery batch sizes due to long changeover times or distant preceding process step	• Reduce changeover time • Collocate to reduce transportation distance; specialized tooling for changeover reduction	• Changeover time reduction • Work cell
		• Downstream worker currently busy processing another type of work units	• Synchronize if wait is inappropriately long • Reduce changeover time	• Kanban system to make amount of WIP of each work unit type visually apparent to signal appropriate priorities • Changeover time reduction
Production being accomplished in large batch sizes	Inventory Waiting Overproduction	• Large changeover time	• Changeover time reduction • Collocate process steps	• Changeover time reduction • Work cells, product flow process layout
		• High utilization of workstation resources	• Changeover time reduction	• Changeover time reduction
		• Remote location of sequential process steps	• Collocate process steps	• Work cells

Parts that can be configured in many ways being built in advance of orders and then needing to be reworked because forecasted configurations do not match customer demand. New defects may be introduced in the rework operation	Waiting Defects	• Long production lead time	• Any Lean tool may be appropriate depending on the analysis of the process • Reduce process lead time
Damaged parts needing to be repaired or parts with obsolete engineering release needing to be reworked	Defects	• Parts or products produced too far in advance—lead time too long • Excessive handling	• Any Lean tool may be appropriate depending on the analysis of the process in order to reduce the need to forecast • Reduce process lead time
Lost parts or products needing to be remanufactured	Defects	• Parts produced too far in advance	• Many Lean tools might be appropriate including changeover time reduction or other methods to reduce lead time of manufacture • Reduce process lead time • Reduce changeover time
Needing to handle material multiple times because the storage capacity of the next processing step is depleted. Goods might be stored in secondary WIP storage locations and then reintroduced into the process flow	Inventory Errors Wasted motion Transportation	• Large batch sizes	• Synchronize • Collocate steps • Work cells • Changeover time reduction

(Continued)

Table 15.1 Roadmap for waste elimination (Continued)

Observation	Type of waste	Root cause(s)	Appropriate type of Lean tool	Specific tool examples
		All Processes		
Workers searching for materials, tools, supplies, or other needed items	Wasted motion	• Lack of standardization or poor 5S	• Standardize • Simplify and streamline	• 5S • Shadow boards • Visual signals and signs for dedicated location of materials, tools, etc. (tape or paint, on floor and walls).
Workers performing little value-added work but walking excessively between points where value-added work is done		• Poor work area or tooling design	• Simplify and streamline	• 5S • Delivery of smaller batches of material to reduce footprint of work area • Kitted parts delivery • Spaghetti diagram analysis • Redesign of operation layout or tooling and equipment
Excess transportation	Transportation	• Large distance between successive process steps	• Collocate	• Work cells or other layout improvement
Customers needing to enter or recite same information multiple times	Wasted motion (effort)	• Redundant data gathering built into process • Poor process design	• Simplify and streamline	• 5S process to know what information is asked at each step and make information gathered at one step available at all process steps • Interoperability of all process systems

Customers making errors when supply information for orders or customer support	Defects	• Difficult for customers to know what data is required • Poor process design	• Mistake-proof • Simplify and streamline	• Visual signals of what data and format are required • Mistake proofing data entry
Support personnel not knowing history of previous contacts or other information that could improve speed and effectiveness of a support intervention	Wasted motion (Effort)	• Poor process design	• Simplify and streamline	• 5S process to know what information might have been gathered previously and make all data available at all process steps • Interoperability of all process systems
Each request for products or services is initiated from scratch where the configuration of each request is unique	Overprocessing Waiting	• Unrecognized commonality of some characteristics of the products or goods	• Standardization	• Recognize common characteristics of overall unique products and services and preprocess by having common information precompiled and components having common part characteristics premanufactured • Changeover reduction • Common components

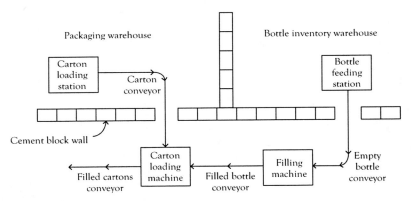

Figure 15.1 Bottling process floor layout

run for the current product, it would take too long. Their allegation was that the bottle feeders would have already put away the cartons for the current product and would already be preparing to feed the cartons for the next product and that retrieving the cartons that had just been restocked to the storage shelves took too long. Basically, a changeover was needed at the feeding operations back to the materials for the prior product. Conversely, if the bottle feeders and carton feeders put too much inventory on the line, either it would need to be thrown away at the next changeover or considerable effort would be necessary to retrieve the material and place it back into storage. Consequently, a project was initiated to reduce the changeover time at the bottle and carton feeder operations to be able to quickly reverse a set-up when the materials on the feeding conveyors were discovered to be insufficient to finish a production run.

Subsequent investigation revealed that one source of uncertainty was that bottles and cartons would be damaged and thrown away during the filling process. The losses were not being communicated to the carton and bottle feeders, and it was difficult for these operators to observe the material losses because the bottle and carton feeding operations were separated from the filling operation by cement block walls. Thus, even if the filling, carton feeding, and bottle feeding operations had planned on the same production quantity for a particular product, an insufficient quantity of materials might be loaded onto the feeding conveyors because carton feeders and bottle feeders weren't aware of the losses. Still further investigation revealed that the production quantity almost always exceeded the published production schedule. Interviews of the filling operators suggested that production runs were lengthened because of the desire to use complete batches of flavor syrup and to ensure an extra buffer above and beyond the desired production quantity, just in case. These deviations to the plan were not communicated to the operators that fed materials to the filling machine.

Scenario 2: A Distribution Center Conveyor System

A consultant was called in to assess a newly constructed and highly-automated distribution center that was not attaining its target throughput rate. Among other analyses, the consultant was looking for the bottleneck that restricted the facility's output rate.

In one part of the operation, the consultant noticed two identical conveyors between which a weighing station was located (see Figure 15.2). The two conveyors were identical, particularly in their mechanical attributes that caused their speed (in feet/minute), when they were running, to be identical. The weighing station would receive a carton of goods from the incoming conveyor and process each carton's weight before ejecting it to the outgoing conveyor. A momentary pause on the scale caused the spacing of the cartons on the outgoing conveyor (i.e., the distance between cartons) to be greater than on the incoming conveyor.

The consultant wondered if this part of the distribution conveyor system be a bottleneck and, if so, how could she prove it?

Scenario 3: A Landscaping Contractor Receivables Process

A landscaping company had a reputation for creating innovative designs and executing those designs expediently with quality craftsmanship.

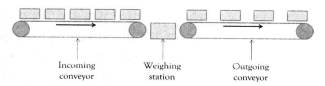

Figure 15.2 Conveyors and weighing station schematic

The company, however, was concerned with cash flow, which was important to minimize its borrowing from the bank and to be able to pay its employees every Friday as the employees expected. The company, therefore, decided to map out the process steps that led to receiving payments from customers.

Multiple payments were received for each job, the first one being at the point in time when the customer accepted the proposed work plan and signed the contract. Another payment would be made when the work commenced, which might be a few weeks after contract signing depending on the work backlog. The final payment would be made when the work was complete. The first payment would either be received by the landscape architect when the plans were approved by the client, if the client had their checkbook or if the receptionist was still in the office and able to take the client's credit card number. Otherwise, the receptionist would need to be instructed to call the client for the first payment, which might be paid by credit card over the phone or with a check when the client had an occasion to stop by the office. The receptionist would call for the second payment when the work supervisor indicated to her that work had commenced on the job. Most often this communication was verbal when the supervisor had a free moment and the receptionist was also available. The final payment would be received when the supervisor returned the contract documentation package to the receptionist for filing. Typically, the supervisor would place the file on the right back corner of the receptionist's (cluttered) desk. When the receptionist had time and noticed the files she would call the clients to request payment. Upon investigation of contracts where delays had been experienced in making calls to clients, it was determined that the files either had been moved or covered up, or the receptionist just hadn't noticed that they were there.

Scenario 4: Wiring Harness Manufacturing

A particular defense contractor produced wiring harnesses for planes and ships. Wiring harnesses are bundles of wires, each wire of a specified length with preattached connectors. These greatly simplified the assembly of defense articles compared with the alternative procedure of stringing many single wires individually in what were many times confined spaces of planes and ships: Wiring harnesses allow many wires to be installed at once and quickly connected to mating wiring harnesses. Producing a wiring harness requires that wires with different colors of insulation be cut in the proper lengths, then laid out in the proper orientation to one another, and, finally, to have the connectors installed.

Having wires of precisely the right length is critical: Harnesses that are too short cannot be connected to their mating harnesses, and harnesses that are too long sometimes cannot be installed because there is no room for the excess wire. This contractor, therefore, purchased a computer-controlled machine for measuring and cutting wires. The machine could cut wire from only a single spool at a time with a particular color of insulation. The machine was very expensive, but management was quite pleased with it because of its accuracy and because it was very fast. Because changing spools of wire was somewhat time consuming, it was general practice to load a spool and consume it in its entirety to avoid change-overs. The workers would look at the forecasted production, sometimes months in advance, to determine what lengths of wire of a particular color would be needed down in the future. Wires that were immediately needed went to the layout step. Those wires not needed for a while were put into storage after being labeled with the work order number for which they would be used as well as the length of the wires.

The cutting process step with the new machine was much faster than the layout process step and so a significant inventory of cut wire was maintained. The accountants were eager to justify the new machine based on its productivity and so they checked on its percentage utilization every day. One day the accountants found the machine idle. The workers' supervisors' explanation that the workers had run out of spools of wire and there was enough wire cut to supply layout for months into the future was not met with the accountants' approval. An emergency purchase of wire was made and expedited to the plant so that the new machine could be put back into productive service for the afternoon shift. This was a fortunate event because later on that day an engineering revision was issued calling for the length of a wiring harness to be increased. Since some of the wires already cut were now too short, some of this incoming wire could be used to replace those lengths. The remainder of the wire would be cut to lengths for planes that the company hoped to win the bid on, but the outcome of that contract competition would not be known for months yet.

Scenario 5: Hospital Medication Fulfillment Process

A hospital maintained its inventory of medications in a single, central location on the ground floor of the hospital. The operation had been scrutinized by industrial engineers and other process design experts to make it as efficient as possible in terms of the number of hours required of pharmacists to pick medicines from inventory. Efficiency was accomplished by having the third-shift pharmacy workers pick all the medications that were needed by all hospital patients over the course of the next day. At 6:00 AM all the medications were delivered in carts to each of the hospital wards, which had compartments for each of the patients in that ward.

The pharmacy on the first shift had many fewer workers whose responsibility was to handle circumstances where patients' prescriptions or doses had changed, or to fulfill the medication needed for newly admitted patients. These needs were usually acute and so it was not unusual for a nurse to walk to the pharmacy to retrieve the needed medicine or, otherwise, for a pharmacist to walk to the wards where the medications were needed. Subsequently, or simultaneously with these activities, it was a nurse's responsibility to identify medications that were included in previous delivery that were no longer needed. It was against hospital policy to restock these medications for fear of putting a medication back in the wrong container and to avoid contamination. These medications were, therefore, thrown out.

Scenario 6: A Refrigerated Goods Picking Process

Some foods sold by a company, who sold mainly through Internet sales, were refrigerated or frozen. These perishable goods needed to be maintained within a specified temperature range at all times. They were shipped to customers as parcels in which food was kept cold by using ice packs and packing the items inside of Styrofoam containers.

The picking process was laid out as shown in Figure 15.3. The refrigerated and frozen items were picked first, before nonrefrigerated items, because of the locations of the cooler units. The refrigerated goods were kept closer to the picking conveyor while the freezer was farther away. An insulated rolling bin was kept near the picking conveyor in which was kept the ice packs for shipping. The person who packed the refrigerated

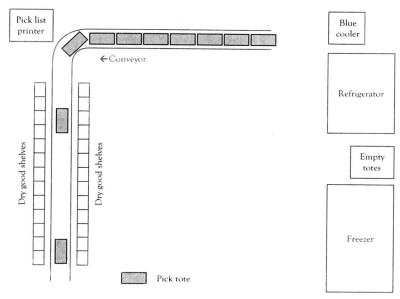

Figure 15.3 Refrigerated goods picking area layout

items first needed to pick up the next picking list from the printer. Then she would retrieve an empty tote, into which she would place all the items she picked. After placing an empty tote on the line, she would travel to the refrigerator and freezer as necessary to pick items for an order. A typical path she would follow for an order is shown as a spaghetti diagram in Figure 15.4.

This operator would most often process orders faster than the subsequent pickers who would pick nonrefrigerated items. Thus, the conveyor passing through her portion of the picking process would almost always be full. The conveyor was not mechanically driven and so periodically she would walk up and down her portion of the conveyor to push more totes toward the subsequent operators when they needed them.

Scenario 7: Allergy Testing

A common test to identify allergies in patients is to give patients hundreds of shots that place a possible allergen slightly below the outer layer of skin. An allergen that caused a reaction, which could be along a continuum from a slight redness to a severe rash, indicated a possible allergy. Giving the shots in a prescribed pattern was, obviously, a requirement

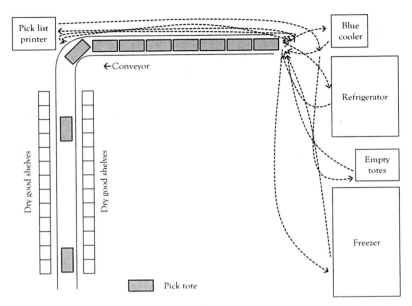

Figure 15.4 Spaghetti diagram for picking one order

because reactions, when they occurred, needed to be associated with a particular allergen. Even when no reaction occurred a small red dot was sometimes visible that indicated where a shot had been placed, but not always. Problems interpreting the test results sometimes occurred when a particular spot of redness could not be identified as being in a particular row or column of the shot pattern grid because the locations of the non-reactive shots could not be identified. Associating a particular reaction with an allergen was made more difficult because reactions took time to manifest themselves, which necessitated being able to recall the location of each shot.

In addition, research results recently suggested that the distance of one shot from another is important in allergy testing because of cross-allergic effects, and if two shots were too close, then a spot of redness might be associated with the incorrect allergen.

Scenario 8: A Distribution Center Picking Process

One Lean project focused on a fairly typical distribution center picking process. *Pickers* would retrieve empty pallets upon which to place the items they picked from the shelves and other storage locations. The operators would transport the pallets from one picking location to the next using either a fork lift truck or a pallet jack. A student intern was studying the process as a precursor to constructing a value stream map. Two of the more startling observations he made were as follows:

1. While the average total time to pick a pallet of goods was 15 minutes, on average 17 minutes were consumed by the task of finding an empty pallet. In an interview, the picker told the intern that no one location provided a guaranteed supply of empty pallets so they needed to hunt for pallets throughout the distribution center to see which process might have recently freed up a pallet.

2. The full pallets would be loaded on outgoing truck trailers on the shipping dock, which had 42 truck dock doors. The pickers dropped off the pallets wherever there was space available in the vicinity of the truck dock and often, it seemed to the intern, the picker would leave the pallet at the nearest location to wherever they picked the last item on their pick list.

The intern wanted to reduce the lead time of completing the execution of a pick list, but they also wanted to improve the quality of the process if possible. In distribution activities, percentage of on-time deliveries is one measure of quality. It turned out that the on-time delivery performance of goods picked in this process was poor despite the supervisor in charge of the pickers claiming that nearly 100 percent of pick lists were completed on time. If that was indeed true, it was hypothesized that some pallets were not being loaded onto trucks as early as they could be.

Scenario 9: Producing Industrial Tanks

A heavy rolling machine was used to roll very thick steel plates into cylindrical shapes, which would subsequently have the seam welded to create a tank. These tanks were used for industrial refrigeration systems as well as other applications where gases needed to be held under pressure. The curvature in the steel plate was caused by passing the steel through two rollers, the differential diameters of which would cause the plate to curve. Different tank diameters were achieved by having different sets of rollers: A different set was required for each tank diameter.

The steel plates that were formed in this process were cut with a computer numerical controlled (CNC) cutting machine prior to being delivered to the rolling machine. The cutting process always took longer than the rolling operation. Once the prepared sheets were delivered to the rolling press, the rolling press operators would look at the work order accompanying the plates and determine which set of rollers were required. After having retrieved the rollers, which were sometimes difficult to locate, the rolling machine would undergo a changeover and the steel plate would be made into a cylinder.

Scenario 10: Insurance Claims Process

An insurance company needed to reduce its cost of operations, which motivated each department in the company to analyze its cost structure. Wages were the largest component of the Claims Department budget and so its manager decided to determine what waste there might be in employees' daily work practices. Thus, she required the employees in her department to document the tasks that they worked on each day and record how long each task took. A startling result was that workers spent 50 percent of their time contacting either the clients who had submitted the claims or co-workers to get additional information that was required for them to process claims. Customers who were making the claims sometimes did not seem to understand what data was required in particular fields on forms or sometimes left the data fields blank. In other cases, workers in the Claims Department were responsible for performing analyses or making judgments about various aspects of the claim that were needed in subsequent steps of the process. These data were, however, sometimes seemingly not included in the file as it progressed through the process, they could not be located within the file, or the annotations did not contain all the details required later in the process. When this happened workers would need to contact co-workers who had already worked on a particular file. Sometimes it was difficult for the co-workers to remember the details about individual cases because it had been so long since they had worked on that claim. In other cases, the co-worker with the needed information was busy on a phone call or absent from work so that more delay was introduced into the process.

Scenario 11: Metal Automobile Parts Manufacturing

One manufacturing plant performed three steps of a process that resulted in fabricated metal parts for automobiles. The first step was to make *blanks* from rolls of steel: Blanks were flat pieces of steel with the rough outline of a metal part. The blanks were given their contours in the second stamping step. In the third and final step, multiple stamped parts were assembled together using various welding technologies to create completed metal assemblies. It was not unusual in this process that the quantity of parts shown in the computer to be in inventory did not match the quantity that could actually be found on the production floor. In some instances, the computer indicated that a sufficient number of blanks were available to produce a particular batch quantity of stampings, but the stamping operation would need to be shut down before the desired quantity was produced because no more blanks could be found. Two things might happen in this case: Either the stamping operation would be changed over to produce another part or the stamping operation would be idled while the blanking process underwent an emergency set-up to produce more blanks. In the former case, the press might essentially be forced into an additional set-up because it would need to resume production of the part whose run was interrupted when more blanks were available. Subsequent investigation revealed that sometimes blanks were in inventory but could simply not be found. In other situations, the parts were never found. Parts could be lost in a number of ways including when defective parts were scrapped. In this case, paperwork was required so that adjustments could be made to the inventory status in the computer system. Sometimes, perhaps, that paperwork was not filled out or its information was not entered into the computer. In order to cope with material losses, which were well recognized to be a common event, managers would extend stamping and assembly runs as long as possible to protect against the inevitable overstatement of inventory levels in the computer. While there were informally understood locations for each particular part, alternative storage locations were found when the space in the standard locations was exhausted.

One dimension of plant performance was inventory levels and a considerable amount of time was spent by production and material managers walking the plant to count inventory in hopes of reconciling it with the figures in the computer system. The unexpected locations for the excess quantities complicated this task.

The blanking, stamping, and assembly steps for a particular finished part were never run simultaneously. Blanks were always run in advance of the stamping being made and the quantities were determined by a production schedule. Similarly the various stampings were made in advance of the parts being assembled. Drivers would put the blanks and stamping into inventory and then retrieve them when they were needed. One rationale for this asynchronous approach was to protect against the effects of downtime: If all machines worked on a part synchronously, then downtime at one machine would idle the other downstream machines. Also, the blanking, stamping, and assembly equipment did not run at the same rate.

Scenario 12: Business School Rankings Applications Process

Business schools submit applications every three years to a prestigious business publication that is used by that publication to rank business schools. A particular business school was frustrated that the required fields in the application would change every three years. Even worse, some of the definitions of particular data fields evolved during the period when schools were completing the documentation. The applications had a strict deadline and so the evolving specifications, short time window, and the need to collect information from all departments of the schools created significant anxiety. A particular school, call it BusSchool, would start compiling information as soon as the current application requirements were announced: They did it no sooner than this because the data requirements would change from the last application. The current year's data submission requirements would be studied and each field would be assigned to a particular department through a variety of means including phone calls and e-mail messages. The data responses were collected by a coordinator who received responses in various formats including e-mail messages, phone voicemail messages, and e-mail attachments which might be either Microsoft Word or Excel files. Still other information was transmitted in hard copy.

Given the short time window between when the data requirements were announced and when the applications were due, BusSchool decided that Lean and its focus on lead time would be the perfect methodology to relieve some of their frustration with this process. One of the studies that was done was a comparison of the data requirements and how they changed over time. That study revealed that, while the data requirements for two successive applications were never identical, only some data requirements changed from one application to the next. Roughly 85 percent of the data fields remained constant from one application to the next. The types of data fields that tended not to change included point of contact information for the school, the names and contact information for deans and associate deans, the school mission, demographics of the current student body, GMAT scores, career placement data, the courses contained in the curriculum, and so forth.

Scenario 13: Supermarket Chain Pharmacist Hiring Process

A chain of supermarkets maintained an onsite pharmacy in each of its stores. These pharmacy units produced substantial profits although they exposed the supermarket to significant liability if mistakes were made in filling prescriptions, for example, if the wrong medication was filled, if the wrong dose was provided, or if the required paperwork for controlled substances was not properly administered and maintained. It was therefore, critical, that the supermarket hired the most competent pharmacists.

Multiple constituencies had input into the pharmacy hiring process. The manager of each store pharmacy unit wanted to ensure that new hires could work constructively in a group setting. Each store manager also wanted input into these additions to their teams. In addition, the supermarket chain had regional human resource (HR) managers who would give final approval for those candidates who had already been approved by both the local pharmacy and store managers.

The hiring process had embedded in it multiple interviews:

1. Local stores would advertise in multiple channels when a pharmacist position was open.
2. Candidates would visit the stores to fill out and submit their written job applications.
3. The local pharmacy manager would review applications and then call in a *batch* of candidates whose applications looked promising for an interview when a critical number of applications had been received.
4. The local pharmacy manager would typically disqualify about 25 percent of the candidates based on these interviews, at which point they would pass the applications onto the local store manager.
5. The local store manager would call the applicants in for interviews. The local manager would rarely disqualify a candidate based on hiring criteria for the store in general, which were distinct from the qualifications being evaluated by the pharmacy manager.
6. When they found a convenient time to meet, the pharmacy manager and the local store manager would rank the candidates and pass their top five candidates to the regional HR manager for evaluation.
7. The regional HR manager would schedule interviews as soon as possible, and the candidates would drive to the regional office for an interview. Some regions were large and so this drive could be as much as 90 minutes, one way, for a candidate. The regional manager almost never disqualified the top choices of the local management, although many candidates would cancel their interviews because they claimed they had secured employment elsewhere.

The entire cycle from when a candidate submitted an application to when they would have an interview with the regional HR manager on average was six weeks. Sometimes, the regional manager would request additional candidates from the local store because all of the candidates claimed to already have found a job. Based on these observations, the managers hypothesized that they were losing many of the best candidates, possibly because their process took too long. And if any candidate was still available after six weeks they possibly were hiring the worst candidates, which put their pharmacy operations at risk.

CHAPTER 16

Case Studies

This chapter contains four cases. With each of these, perform the same steps that would be performed if you were working on a Lean project in an organization:

1. Determine the metrics that should be included in a project charter for improvement of the process described in each case.
2. Draw a value stream map (VSM), and then calculate these quantities:
   a. Lead time for each process step
   b. Total process lead time
   c. Total value-added time
   d. Total nonvalue-added time
   e. Value-added ratio (VAR)
3. Find the waste in the process.
4. Devise improvements to reduce the waste and improve the metrics determined in the first step.
5. Draw the VSM of the process as if the improvements in the previous step had been made.
6. Create a list, in order of priority, of the improvements identified and how they should be addressed (i.e., which Lean tools would be appropriate?).

One of the cases also lists additional questions that direct a reader toward problems and possible solutions for that particular context.

The lead time of all steps might not be clear in some instances. In those cases, make reasonable assumptions. Remember that value stream mapping can be considered a rough tool to point us in the right direction, and even with some error in lead time measurements, the VSM often points us toward the same improvements.

Garth's Gardens

Garth's Gardens is a premier landscaping service and garden store in Richmond, Virginia. The company is owned by Garth Gardenia, and it sells plants and landscaping materials from its garden store to walk-in customers. In addition, Garth employs landscape designers and construction workers who design and install landscaping for residential and commercial clients. Garth was particularly concerned with ensuring continued business in landscape design and installation because this was the source of significant revenue, as projects brought in $50,000 of revenue on average. Being a reasonably small company, Garth could not afford poor performance in this part of his operation because the loss of even one project would severely impact on his profits: $50,000 was not an inconsequential portion of Garth's revenues. Moreover, many of the landscape designers and construction workers were on salary and thus represented fixed costs that needed to be covered regardless of business volume.

Although Garth advertised in the Yellow Pages and in mailings, he realized that most of his business came from repeat customers and friends and acquaintances of current customers who were particularly impressed with the visual appeal of a project that Garth's company had previously completed. Besides the aesthetic attraction of Garth's work, word of mouth from former clients was important—although a project might look beautiful, people were often quick to communicate any problems experienced with the project. Thus every aspect of interaction with the customer needed to go smoothly. The most common perception of a customer's experience with a construction project is that once a contractor has the job, it was often difficult to get the contractor to finish the job in a timely manner. Often, clients felt as though they were in competition with other jobs that the contractor had on his or her plate and that they were given low priority. Garth was particularly sensitive to this and did not want his clients to relate such experiences to other potential clients.

Garth's obtained landscaping projects through phone calls from potential clients who would call to ask for quotations. Some of these people were former clients of Garth's, some had heard of Garth's through word of mouth from former clients, and others might have found Garth's Gardens in the telephone book. Garth was particularly concerned with being prompt in responding to queries from potential clients about landscape design because he realized the popular conception that contractors had little regard for getting jobs done on time and being slow to respond might cement in potential clients' heads that Garth's company was nothing but a typical contractor in that regard. Accordingly, if another contractor was quicker to respond, they might steal the business from Garth. Thus Garth was interested in reducing the amount of time it took to respond to customers' requests for proposals and price quotations on landscaping designs and installations. A faster response to potential customers' inquiries would communicate a sense of competence and professionalism to the customer that would translate into winning a higher percentage of the projects for which they submitted quotations to the clients. Garth was also interested in developing a relationship with the client during this process: Even if Garth's did not win the contract in a particular instance, then perhaps making a favorable impression could translate into business at a later time. Moreover, Garth felt that it was important to visit customers at their house or place of business because, first, Garth felt that interaction on the customers' site rather than in a conference room at Garth's store better facilitated the building of relationships and, second, this gave Garth's representatives better information about a customer's yard and thus Garth's representatives could give the client better advice on potential alternatives for achieving the customer's landscaping goals. In addition, this allowed Garth's to determine up-selling opportunities— that is, opportunities to suggest to the client future projects that Garth's might perform.

Because this process of developing new business is so critical to the financial success of Garth's operations, and because reducing the time to prepare and develop quotes for customers was one of the important metrics in the process, Garth's managers decided to improve this business development process using the Lean methodology. The two most prominent employees involved in the generation of a quotation for any particular client were the client administrator (CA) and one of several sales associates (SAs) that Garth employed. The CA worked full time in the Garth's Gardens office building and, among her many tasks, received the initial calls from clients who wanted Garth's to give them a quote on a particular project. During that initial call from the client, the CA would record the client's contact information and general details about the type of project in which the client was interested. That call would usually take about five minutes. The CA would batch the client requests, and approximately every 24 hours, she would determine which SA would receive each client request based on the type of project the client was considering. (The requests would, therefore, average 12 hours before they were passed on.) The CA felt that it took her less time to determine which SA should receive each request, and she did a better job when she could set a block of time aside to "get her mind into the job." She could make the assignment decision for each client request in about five minutes. Batching, or delaying the handling of customer requests, also allowed the CA, in her opinion, to comfortably handle her other tasks without needing to multitask. Each potential client's name, contact information, and a brief description of their project were put into the assigned SA's inbox after the CA had made the assignments.

Often, the SAs would not be at Garth's retail site but rather on-site with clients reviewing potential business. For this reason, the paperwork that the CA filled out with the client's information would remain in the SA's inbox, on average, for 12 hours. Also, while clients were believed to be of great importance, the organization was not sensitized to handling the potential leads in an ASAP fashion.

Once the SAs got to their inbox, it obviously did not take them long to retrieve the paperwork (five minutes or less). Once each client's request was retrieved, it would take on average 12 hours to contact the client: Some of this was due to telephone tag, but much of it was just being sidetracked by other tasks, such as working on other clients' requests. Once contact was made with the client, it took about one day (1,440 minutes) before the SA met with the client. This wait time was due partially to the SA's schedule and partially to the availability of the client.

The meeting with the client usually took about one hour, and the SA would make notes about the project during that meeting so that he or she could accurately estimate the cost of labor and materials. The SA would also take this opportunity to suggest alternative ways to accomplish the client's goals. Sometimes, what the customers conceived as an initial design concept was not the most effective, economical, or aesthetic approach to the project. This is where the expertise of Garth's could in many cases offer the client a better way to do the project that was both more satisfactory to the client and, sometimes, more economical.

Usually, about one day after the meeting with the client, the SA would sit down to prepare a handwritten version of the quotation for the client based on the notes that he or she had taken the day before. This took about 60 minutes. SAs were not always on-site at the Garth's retail store when they prepared these quotations, so it would take some time (on average about four hours) before the SA would get back to Garth's to put the drafts into the CA's inbox.

The CA tended to batch the typing of the electronic version of the quotations from the SAs' handwritten notes. For this reason and also because of being interrupted by other tasks, it would take about 12 hours before the CA got around to typing a quotation. It took on average 1,440 minutes (one day) to finish typing the quotations for two reasons: (1) Several quotations had usually piled up before the CA started working on another batch, and (2) the SA's handwriting could sometimes not be read by the CA, in which case the CA would need to contact the responsible SA and resolve the issue. Contacting the SAs in the field was not always easy because they were often meeting with clients.

After the CA typed the quotations, she would put them in the inboxes for the responsible SA, who after about a 12-hour delay would review it for accuracy. Again, the delay was largely due to the fact that the SAs spent most of their time in the field and sometimes were absent from the office for a reasonably long period.

After reviewing the typed quotation and noting required revisions, the SA would put the marked-up copy in the CA's inbox. Changes were sometimes due to the SA having had more time to think about how to approach the project and the bidding of it, and sometimes it was because the CA had misinterpreted what the SA had written. Getting the marked-up copy out of the inbox took the CA little time. The time to revise the report in the computer was usually short. The CA tended to do these corrections right away, since they were easier than interpreting the SA's notes when the first draft was typed.

At that point the CA indicated in the computer system that a quotation was finalized, and she would print out a hard copy. Since the SA most often had left the office by then to see other clients, that hard copy would remain in the SA's inbox until he or she returned to the office, which would usually be in about one day (1,440 minutes). Upon retrieving the revised proposal from their inbox, SAs would again make an appointment with the client to deliver the proposal. It, again, took on average a day to get in touch with a client, and then another day, on average, before the meeting would take place due to the availability of the SA and the client. Finally, delivering the quotation in person to the client and explaining it took the SAs about an hour. A summary of the process steps is shown in Table 16.1.

Table 16.1 Garth's Garden quoting process

Process steps for developing a landscaping proposal		
Step number	Description	Responsibility
1	CA receives call from client	CA
2	CA assigns projects to SAs	CA
3	CA distributes hard copies of client contact information to SA's inbox	CA
4	SA retrieves the client information from his or her inbox	SA
5	SA contacts the client to arrange an appointment	SA
6	SA visits the client site	SA
7	SA prepares handwritten draft of proposal	SA
8	SA turns draft of proposal into CA's inbox	SA
9	CA retrieves drafts from her inbox	CA
10	CA types drafts	CA
11	CA places drafts in the SA's inbox	CA
12	SA reviews the draft and makes corrections	SA
13	SA puts revised draft in CA's inbox	SA
14	CA revises draft in computer and prints it out	CA
15	CA puts revised draft in SA's inbox	CA
16	SA retrieves revised draft	SA
17	SA schedules appointment with client	SA
18	SA visits client and delivers proposal	SA

Il Negozio Internet Prosciutto Sales

Il Negozio is an Internet retailer of fine Italian foods with offices in Williamsburg, Virginia. Its sales were almost solely through the Internet, and one of its featured products was dry-cured hams from central and northern Italy. Although it sold lesser grades of prosciutto, its most expensive sold at a retail price of $100 per pound. Whole legs of prosciutto weighed between 10 and 15 pounds, so purchasing an entire ham could cost a customer as much as $1,500. Although some wholesale clients' sales volumes could justify a purchase in such a quantity, most of Il Negozio's clients were individuals who wanted, and could only afford, a much smaller portion of prosciutto. Smaller, vacuum-packed portions of prosciutto were easy to ship via UPS in Styrofoam boxes with a dry ice block to protect the perishable prosciutto.

Il Negozio had enjoyed rapid growth, as many people of Italian descent who lived in the United States discovered its products. In addition, Italian food was popular with those who traveled to Italy on vacation or who otherwise found out by word of mouth about the unique, high-quality foods offered by Il Negozio.

Il Negozio offered ham for sale in multiple packaging options. A customer could buy a full ham leg, but most customers wanted a smaller quantity of ham, and so Il Negozio offered four-ounce and eight-ounce packages of presliced ham. Il Negozio bought prosciutto directly from producers in Italy, and because the producers would only ship in large quantities, Il Negozio was required to purchase full hams rather than partial hams or prepackaged slices. Preslicing prosciutto in Italy also presented quality concerns due to the perishability of the product. Il Negozio therefore needed to have the full hams sliced and packaged after it received the hams in order to sell ham in quantities other than full legs.

It was currently necessary for Il Negozio to outsource the slicing of ham to another company, mostly because ham could be sliced only at a facility that was approved for the processing of food by the federal Food and Drug Administration (FDA). Il Negozio currently had neither that certification nor a facility for slicing. The slicing subcontractor was located in Virginia Beach, Virginia, approximately a two-hour drive from Williamsburg. Given the congestion on Interstate 64 that connected Williamsburg and

Virginia Beach, the trip could take much longer if the tunnels in the Hampton Roads area were backed up, which they often were.

It was important to quickly receive, slice, and record the inventory as available for shipment in the computerized inventory system because the prosciutto was available for purchase on the Internet site only after the entire process was completed. If Il Negozio ran out of ham before the process was completed for the next batch of ham to be sliced, then the Internet site would show that the product was out of stock. Thus, although Il Negozio physically owned the ham, if it was still in the slicing process, Il Negozio's website might show the ham as out of stock, thus causing customers either to be dissatisfied or to shop elsewhere for ham. The importance of quickly getting ham sliced and into inventory was increased because ham represented such a large investment: Unless the ham was ready to sell, it represented a significant investment from which Il Negozio could get no financial return.

Il Negozio received ham with other products in refrigerated containers. The first step in the process was to unload the containers. Typically Il Negozio received 20-foot-long refrigerated containers (or *reefers*, as they are known in the logistics business) that contained many items besides the hams. Unloading the reefer took about four hours, of which 20 minutes were for the ham.

After the hams and other items were unloaded from the container, Dana, the warehouse supervisor, would notify Kevin, who worked in an upstairs office, when the shipment arrived. Typically, Dana could let Kevin know that the container was unloaded within 20 minutes of the crew finishing, although sometimes emergencies came up that delayed her from alerting Kevin. When Kevin became aware that a shipment of ham had been received, he would then create a work order in the computer system, which was the official authorization needed to allow the ham to be shipped out to Il Negozio's slicing subcontractor in Virginia Beach.

Once the work order was created, Kevin would need to contact Dana (downstairs) to tell her that it was okay to proceed with the next step, which was to weigh the ham, add the weight onto the work order record in the computer system, and then pack the hams onto a pallet. Sometimes Kevin would find it difficult to contact Dana if she was busy or on the phone, and sometimes he would get sidetracked by other tasks so that he was not able to immediately get in touch with Dana after he created the electronic work order. Due to these types of delays, it would typically take four hours before Dana started with the process of weighing the hams, which took 80 minutes. This time also included the time required to enter the information into the computer and load the hams onto a pallet. After this step was completed, the paperwork had to be printed to accompany the order to the subcontractor; so Dana would contact Kevin (upstairs) who would print out the paperwork. Making contact with Kevin was usually fairly quick at this point in the process, taking only five minutes. Printing the paperwork took approximately 15 minutes.

Unless it was near the end of the work shift, one of Dana's crew would then drive the hams to the subcontractor in Virginia Beach, which took two hours. When researching this process, Kevin and Dana found that the subcontractor waited 10 hours, on average, before starting to slice the ham. It was unclear to Kevin and Dana why this delay occurred.

Once the slicing step commenced, it took approximately four days (5,760 minutes) for the subcontractor to finish slicing and packaging the typical shipment of ham (the time required depended on the size of the shipment). Kevin and Dana had done a little research about this step to uncover some of the details of how slicing and packaging were done. This step was influenced by FDA regulations regarding the safe handling of perishable food products. Those regulations stipulated that the ham could only be out of refrigeration for a limited period of time, and the slicing and packaging machines were not in a refrigerated area. Because only one operator was assigned to the slicing and packaging operation, he or she would slice a certain quantity of ham and then stop the slicing process in order to vacuum pack what was just sliced. Then the operator would return the finished product to refrigerated storage. The size of the batch of ham that could be sliced needed to be small enough such that the total elapsed time of slicing and packaging the ham was less than the maximum time allowed by the FDA for the ham to be out of refrigeration. Thus this step was slowed down because one worker was operating two workstations, as well as performing all the material handling.

After completion of the slicing and packaging operation, the subcontractor then needed to count the packages of ham, weigh the ham, and finally pack it into boxes. This process took approximately two hours, but often there was a large time lag before this step of the process commenced; it was not clear to Kevin and Dana why this was the case but they guessed that it was because the subcontractor did not put a priority on their order versus other operations that the subcontractor performed. Weighing the ham at each step of the process is important because the ham is valuable and prone to theft. The Italian hams are so cherished that every part of the ham is used. Il Negozio required that the subcontractor return even the fat that they trimmed from the ham because Il Negozio could sell this to customers who used it to season the recipes they cooked.

After the order was boxed and ready to go, it would take the subcontractor approximately six hours before they got around to calling Il Negozio to let them know that the order was complete and to arrange for a delivery time. That call took only five minutes. The subcontractor's truck would then leave the facility between 12 and 24 hours later, and the drive from Virginia Beach to Williamsburg would take about two hours. Upon arriving back at Il Negozio with the ham, it would take the driver about 10 minutes to find Dana to let her know that the truck had arrived and was ready for unloading. Unloading the truck and getting the ham into refrigerated storage took approximately one hour.

After about four hours, the packages of ham would be counted and weighed one more time by Dana or one of her crew. This took about 90 minutes. After being delayed on average by 15 minutes for other tasks and interruptions, Dana would take about 15 minutes to fill out a receiving report that verified the count of ham packages and the total weight. The next time Dana went upstairs to the offices, she would take the receiving report with her and hand it to Kevin or put it in Kevin's inbox if he was away from his desk. Kevin had authorization to enter this data into the computer, while Dana did not. Kevin would take about 90 minutes to get around to this task, and then after another five minutes on average for interruptions, Kevin would update another computer system that made the ham available online for Internet shoppers to purchase.

A Supply Chain for Automobile Doors

Figure 16.1 shows the supply chain for automobile doors. The general steps of the process are the following:

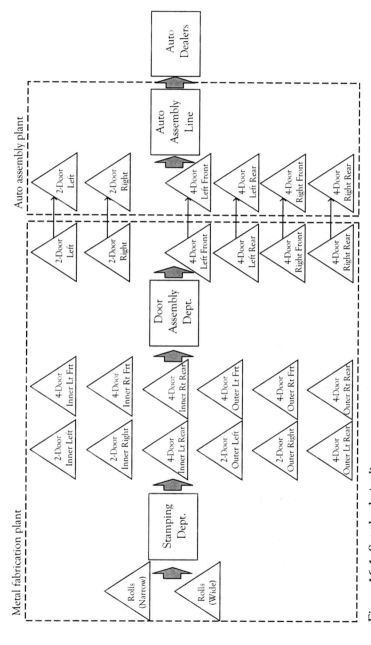

Figure 16.1 Supply chain diagram

1. Steel parts are stamped out of coils of steel.
2. The steel parts are welded together to make door assemblies.
3. The door assemblies are installed on automobiles.

The first two steps are performed in what was called the *metal fabrication plant*. Within that plant, parts were stamped in the *stamping department* and they were welded together in the *door assembly department*. The third step occurred in the assembly plant.

The assembly plant produces both two-door and four-door vehicles. Thus the auto assembly plant requires six different types of doors:

1. Two door, left
2. Two door, right
3. Four door, left front
4. Four door, left rear
5. Four door, right front
6. Four door, right rear

Both the metal fabrication plant and the assembly plant operated exactly the same number of days each year (on exactly the same days) and the same hours per day. Specifically, both plants worked 220 days per year and .16 hours per day.

The following paragraphs describe the supply chain structure and management decision policies in each supply chain link:

- *Steel manufacturer.* This plant supplies two types of rolls of steel to the metal fabrication plant (the next link in the supply chain), one of narrow width (0.9 meters wide) and one wider roll (1.4 meters wide). Both types of steel are 1.3 millimeters thick. The first roll is used to stamp inner door panels, and the second type of roll is used for outer door panels in the metal fabrication plant. The wide rolls weigh 25 tons and the narrow rolls weigh 15 tons. During the previous year, 5,000 wide rolls were used and 10,000 narrow rolls were used. Production rates at the assembly plant this year and next year were anticipated to require steel at this same rate.

- *Transportation from steel manufacturer to metal fabrication plant.*
  The current policy was to load trucks with either two large rolls
  or three small rolls on a truckload. Weight restrictions limited
  trucks to carry no more than 55 tons of steel. Furthermore, the
  truck had the capability of hauling no more than three rolls at a
  time due to the length of the trailer bed. (Any combination of
  three rolls was possible because the rolls were the same diameter
  although different widths.) The fixed cost for each truck
  delivery was $800 and the variable cost per ton was $0.50.

The following five steps are all within the metal fabrication plant,
which stamps metal parts for doors and then produces an assembled door
by welding one inner panel together with one outer panel:

- *Incoming raw materials inventory of roll steel.* Rolls of steel were
  stored here when they were received from the steel plant.
- *Stamping department.* The schedule for stamping parts was
  the same order as indicated by the triangles after the stamping
  department in Figure 16.1, which represent work-in-process
  inventory: First, the parts in the first column were produced,
  from top to bottom, then the parts in the second column,
  and then the same sequence was repeated again. (This is called
  a cyclic schedule.) One press line was used for producing all
  these parts, although other press lines were capable of producing these parts as well. Changing the dies in the presses from
  those required for one part to those dies required to produce
  the next part in the sequence required four hours (i.e., this
  was changeover time). This department produced panels
  (either inner or outer panels) at a rate of 400 per hour. Each
  wide roll of steel yielded 150 outer panels and each narrow
  roll of steel yielded 75 inner panels.
- *Inventory of stamped inner and outer panels.* The inner and
  outer panels were stored here once they were stamped. Those
  inventories are designated in Figure 16.1 by the triangles.
- *Door assembly department.* The assembly of each of the six
  styles of doors required two parts, an inner panel and an outer

panel. The operation cycled among the six parts listed in Figure 16.1 following the sequence from top to bottom, and then it repeated. Changeover time is required to change the operation from the production of one part to another, which takes four hours. This operation produces doors at a rate of 200 per hour. Each batch of doors is completed before it is transported to the subsequent inventory step.

- *Inventory of assembled doors.* Finished doors were stored here until it was time to ship them to the assembly plant. This inventory is designated by triangles in Figure 16.1.

The following two steps were within the auto assembly plant:

- *Incoming raw materials inventory of assembled doors.* Doors were stored here when they were received from the metal fabrication plant until needed at the assembly line.
- *Auto assembly line.* The assembly line produced cars at a rate of 60 per hour, and on average over a month, 50 percent of the cars were two-door models and 50 percent of the cars were four-door models. The percentages of two-door models and four-door models varied considerably, however, from hour to hour and shift to shift. It was very difficult to forecast how many two-door models and how many four-door models would be made even an hour in advance: The auto assembly plant was notorious for continually changing the schedule. The schedulers claimed that they needed such flexibility to respond to dealers' last-minute orders. Such responsiveness, they claimed, was a competitive advantage for the company versus other auto manufacturers.

Additional Questions

1. Suggest a revised shipping policy (quantity of each type of roll of steel that should be shipped in a truckload) that could both reduce annual trucking cost from the steel plant to the metal fabrication plant and also reduce the average inventory level of raw materials at the metal fabrication plant.

2. How much time is required to go through the cyclic schedule for the stamping department in the metal fabrication plant as described in the case?

3. How much time is required to go through the cyclic schedule for the door assembly department in the metal fabrication plant?

4. It has often been observed that the inventory between the stamping department and the door assembly department in the metal fabrication plant is out of some part that is currently needed in the door assembly department while there are large inventories of other parts. Suggest changes that could be made in the stamping department schedule, changeover times, or equipment investment to reduce this lack of coordination or, in other words, reduce excess coordination inventory, and describe conceptually how your suggestion would increase synchronization between the two departments.

5. An engineer visited a Toyota assembly plant and saw a different method for assembling the inner panel with the outer panel. Rather than a big machine that required a setup, it was a flexible machine that could make two-door and four-door doors in any sequence, and it was small and simple enough that it could be placed right beside the assembly line in the assembly plant. The machine could produce doors at a rate of 95 doors per hour, so that one machine on each side of the assembly line would have sufficient capacity. What are the advantages and disadvantages of acquiring this equipment?

6. Suppose that the door assembly department intended to schedule their production for each shift to be exactly the quantities of two-door doors and four-door doors that the assembly plant had used the previous shift, thus implementing a pull system (a work shift is eight hours long). Also under this proposal, the inventory after the door assembly department would be eliminated so that door assemblies made by the door assembly department would be immediately shipped to the assembly plant. How would the door assembly department operation need to be improved, and what change in management of the inventory between the stamping department and the door assembly department would be required to accommodate a varying schedule in the door assembly department? Why?

Alvin's Auto Parts

Alvin owned and operated an auto parts store in Williamsburg, Virginia, which was associated with the Regional Automotive Parts Association (RAPA). All parts sold at Alvin's were supplied by RAPA. Upon entering Alvin's store, one might first be struck by the peculiar ambiance of the store, which was in stark contrast to the national car parts retail chains that have sprung up over the past two or three decades. Instead of a sparkling clean retail space, Alvin's store was dimly lit and one might suspect that it had been a long time since the store had received a thorough cleaning: The parts racks seemed to be covered with a thin coat of grease or machine oil, and greasy fingerprints were visible on some boxes. This was a place where somebody who prided themselves on being called a grease monkey would feel comfortable hanging out on one of the stools at the counter that were upholstered in a shiny vinyl with RAPA's logo. Some of the upholstery was ripped, perhaps by tools carried in customers' pockets. While not a sparkling environment, one of Alvin's competitive advantages was that he did not mind placing special orders for customers, and customers found doing business with Alvin advantageous when they were trying to track down hard-to-find parts. It was probably true that Alvin's willingness to special order parts was one aspect of his business that helped him to secure repeat customers, who after purchasing a part via a special order would then return to purchase other, more common parts from Alvin. Alvin had reluctantly agreed to let some local college students help him with his special order process. Alvin really did not see that much wrong with it, but he liked to help support the local school, so he agreed to the project. In discussions with the students, who were taking a course in Lean, Alvin agreed that reducing the time to get special order parts would be an advantage to his customers and satisfy them to a greater extent, but he did not see much reason to investigate the special order process: He had been fulfilling special orders for 25 years now and he did not think there could be many opportunities for improvement here. After all, what did these kids know about auto parts? In any case, although he did not see much point, he relented to answering questions about this process and letting the students observe it.

The Special Order Process

The process for fulfilling a special order started when the customer came into the store and, perhaps, after finding out that the particular part they were searching for was not stocked on an ongoing basis, Alvin (or whoever was at the counter) would handwrite the customer's order on the closest scrap of paper. The sales associate (SA) would ask the customer for their name and phone number and, after consulting the catalogs, would write down the part number, supplier, and retail price on the scrap of paper. It would take between 2 and 15 minutes to write down the order information depending on how difficult it was to locate the part in the catalogs. After taking a special order, it would be placed on the corkboard immediately, which was located 25 feet from the sales counter, unless another customer was waiting at the sales counter to be served, in which case the order slip would be taken to the corkboard at a later time. It took about 15 minutes, on average, for the special orders to find their way to the corkboard.

Customers would often inquire about an estimated delivery time. Alvin did not have electronic access to the RAPA distribution center inventory, and so he always quoted one week from the upcoming Thursday as the delivery date, although he knew sometimes it would take longer if the distribution center was out of stock.

Although replenishment occurred daily from RAPA for parts that were stocked by Alvin on an ongoing basis, Alvin would place special orders only once a week, on Thursdays, because of the time involved. Every Thursday morning, Alvin would accumulate the special order slips from the corkboard and place an order with RAPA. Actually, it was probably more accurate to say that Alvin would start accumulating orders on Thursday morning. While there were approximately 10 special orders per week, it would take Alvin four hours, on average, to put the orders together because he also needed to staff the sales counter on Thursday mornings besides placing special orders. In addition, the special orders from the past week would arrive on Thursdays, and so Alvin worked with the newly arrived merchandise over the course of the morning, which is discussed later. The inventory levels for the items that Alvin always stocked were recorded in the point-of-sale (POS) computer system. Every time an item was sold, the inventory quantity recorded in the computer system would be adjusted downward accordingly. Inventory was replenished using a reorder point method: When inventory decreased to a specified threshold level, then a certain quantity (which was established in the computer system) would . be ordered automatically from the RAPA distribution center. Alvin's POS system, which was supplied as part of his agreement with RAPA, was tied electronically to RAPA's computer system and these orders were placed automatically. The automatic orders generally were received two days after they were placed, unless the RAPA distribution center was out of stock. Special orders were handled differently, however. Alvin would accumulate all the information from special order slips from the past week by writing that information, by hand, on an 8.5-by-11-inch piece of paper before faxing it to RAPA. The list of all the parts would take about an hour to put together, if Alvin worked on it without interruption. However, interruptions usually caused this task to take most of the workday. Alvin would generally fax the special order list to RAPA before he left work on Thursday, which was usually around 7:00 PM

Special orders took one week to arrive, coming in on the following Thursday. The RAPA delivery truck would arrive at the truck dock door on Thursday and drop off a pallet of goods, or however many pallets were required in total by the regular and special orders combined. The next step was for Alvin (or one of his associates) to receive the goods, which meant that he needed to enter the item number and quantity of each item received into the computer system. This step was important because it resulted in correctly updated inventory levels in the POS computer system. This process could be done either by using the paper packing slip, if you trusted that document to correctly reflect the quantities actually received, or by manually scanning each item on the pallets with a bar code reader and entering the quantity of each item as confirmed by a manual count. Alvin preferred the latter method to ensure accurate inventory levels and to make sure that he received what RAPA would later bill him for. This task would commence when it occurred to Alvin that the time was right—that is, when he remembered that it needed to be done and counter business was slack. About four hours generally lapsed before the receiving step started. Receiving both regular and special orders, which was done simultaneously, typically took about two hours. Alvin needed to handle both types of items at the same time because the special and regular orders were not separated on their own pallets.

After entering the merchandise into the POS computer system, Alvin would identify the items that were special orders so that he could set them aside. To do this, he took the packing slip, which came with the shipment, and compared each item on it with the handwritten order slips on the corkboard. Alvin took approximately an hour and a half to do this reconciliation, after which he would rummage through the pallets to find the special order items so that he could put them on his shelving unit for special orders. Alvin did not do this right away for several reasons. He did not like to sort through the pallets of items because he routinely would miss the special order items and need to go back though the pallets multiple times. So he procrastinated before starting on this step. Also, he would be interrupted by customers while he was searching for the special order items, which would delay him. Alvin estimated that he would wait approximately eight hours on average before he started searching for special order items and that it took him three hours to complete that task. He thought he could find all the special order items in about 1.5 hours if he was not interrupted, but he felt that he needed to give customers at the sales desk priority attention.

After the special order items were found, they would be stacked on the floor besides the recently received pallets. Once they were all identified, they would be placed on the shelving unit for special orders. Alvin would assign one of his associates this task. (Alvin did not like doing this step because it involved carrying parts by hand about 50 feet to the shelving unit, and as Alvin was getting on in years, he could not afford to have his back go out on him.) This would take about 15 minutes, but it did not usually happen right away because it might take Alvin a little while to remember that it needed to be done and all the SAs might be needed at the counter.

Next, Alvin or one of his SAs would call the customers whose orders had arrived. This would be accomplished by pulling the paper order slips down from the corkboard as the incoming items were being reconciled with the packing slip. Then that stack of order slips would be placed by the telephone until such time as somebody could make the calls. Ordinarily, about 8 to 12 hours would pass before somebody got to that job. It would be a different person who made the calls each week, and Alvin would designate that person when business at the counter lightened up and he remembered that somebody needed to do it.

Each call took about two minutes. Then the slips would go back onto the corkboard. Sometimes customers' phone numbers had not been recorded or were apparently not recorded properly, since some calls ended up in wrong numbers or to phone numbers that were out of service. Even when phone numbers were recorded, they were sometimes difficult to read because of sloppy handwriting.

When a customer would arrive to pick up their order, they would inform the SA at the sales counter, who would then go to the corkboard to look for an order slip with that customer's last name on it. More than occasionally, the order slip would be difficult to locate due to poor hand-writing, in which case the SA would return to the sales counter to ver-ify the customer's last name and perhaps ask them what part they had ordered. Upon verifying the last name and finding the order slip, or if the order slip could not be found, the SA would start looking for the item on the shelves for special orders. If the order slip was found immediately, then locating the part could take as little as four minutes. However, locat-ing the part could take as much as a half hour. Sometimes the part was difficult to find and sometimes the part had already been sold and it took the SA a while to conclude that the part was not on the shelf.

Customers might call to inquire about the status of their order before the part had arrived. Many times this was due to the part not arriving in the quoted amount of time. Some customers were very impatient and called often. Finding a customer's order status involved searching the orders on the corkboard and the shelves. This could take as much as 15 minutes per inquiry.

Further Investigation

The student team learned the information about the special order process discussed thus far in the case by observing Alvin and asking him the basic questions about lead time and cycle time that they would need to construct a VSM. As the students began to construct the VSM, questions naturally occurred to them that they had not thought to ask before.

In subsequent interviews with Alvin and learning about the process by standing in a circle and studying it for long periods of time, here are some other data that the students collected.

Observations from Standing in a Circle

1. On two occasions team members observed customers coming in to pick up their parts. After spending 5 to 10 minutes looking for the parts, Alvin and one other SA announced to the customers that they could not find the parts and that they must have already been sold. One customer asked why their part would have been sold within one day of when it arrived and why the store had not held on to the part at least one day. Alvin said that if customers wanted the store to keep a special order part, then they need to pay for it up front and notify the salesperson that the part should be held for them. Otherwise, the policy was to sell the part to the first customer who asked for it.

2. Although Alvin had said that approximately 10 special orders were placed a week, the students observed on three different occasions, at different times of the week and on different weeks, approximately 30 special order slips on the corkboard.

3. Observations of the order slips on the corkboard revealed that not all slips contained all the information that Alvin would collect if he were taking the order. For some reason, some information was missing on some orders.

4. Observations of the order slips on the corkboard raised questions about the legibility of handwriting on many of the slips. Legibility caused problems that have already been mentioned, as well as difficulty reconciling the received parts with the handwritten part numbers on the order slips.

5. The organization of the corkboard and the order slips did not lend itself to easily identifying how far a particular order had progressed in the process. For example, it was difficult to determine whether an order was yet to be placed with the RAPA distribution center, had been ordered from the RAPA distribution center, had been received, or had already been delivered to the customer.

Answers to Questions Asked of Alvin

The student team asked the following questions, and received the corresponding answers:

Q. Why do you place orders once per week? Would RAPA object to a greater number of special orders per week and fewer items per order?

A. We have always placed special orders once per week. I have never asked RAPA if they would process more than one list of special orders per week, but I can only imagine they would not be too pleased about it. Now that I think about it, special orders are a hassle for me to handle. For example, I would need to compile the special order list and fax it multiple times per week if I ordered more than once per week. Then I would need to reconcile orders more than once a week, and I dread that process.

Q. Why do you fax orders to RAPA?

A. We've always done it that way. They told me once that special orders needed to be either faxed or phoned in.

Q. When did they tell you that?

A. I can't recall exactly. I think it was in the late 1970s.

Q. We've looked at the shelf where you keep the special order items that have arrived. We were wondering what your method was for determining where a particular item would be placed on the shelf. Can you describe the thought process you go through?

A. Sure. Some parts are heavy. I want to place them neither too high nor too low. Otherwise, it hurts my back to take them off the shelf. I have one of my associates put them on the shelf, so that isn't a problem. Besides that, I look for a place that will accommodate the particular size of package that the part comes in.

Q. How do you locate a particular item on the special order shelf when a customer comes to pick it up? We were expecting to see some sort of documentation on each item, like a tag or label, but we saw nothing.

A. I look through the items on the rack looking for the one with the matching part number.

Q. You said that you ordered, on average, approximately 10 special orders per week, but we saw about 30 order slips on the corkboard. Can you explain that?

A. Hmm … I never thought about that. I'm not sure, but it may have to do with the fact that some people take a while to come in and get their parts. Does that make sense?

Q. Does the RAPA distribution center need nearly an entire week to process special orders?

A. Of course. We have always done it this way. Distribution centers are very complex operations, and I wouldn't even think of asking the RAPA people of doing this operation faster. I'm sure there is some reason why it takes them that long to process orders but, after all, I don't know how distribution centers are run, so I wouldn't want to be presumptuous and even ask them that question. Have you ever driven by the RAPA distribution center on Interstate 95? It's a huge place, over one million square feet. It's no wonder it takes a week.

Q. Have you ever received any complaints from customers about the special order process?

A. Only one that I can think of. Sometimes customers come in on the Thursday that I quote as the delivery date and ask for their part. Sometimes we have it, but we haven't yet found the part and put it on the shelf with the customer's name on it. In that case the customer needs to come back to the store again, and the second trip doesn't make them happy, especially since the part was really in the store. Sometimes we haven't actually received the part because the distribution center is out of stock and I wouldn't be able to find it even if I took the time to look through the items on the pallet that comes in on Thursday.

Q. Does any part of this process annoy you in any way?

A. Well, some customers insist on calling to see if their part has arrived. These calls take at least 15 minutes, since we do not have a good way to easily identify whether the part has not been ordered, if it has been ordered and was out of stock at the distribution center, if it has been ordered and is on its way, or if it is in the store. The status of orders is tough to determine. Some customers call many times.

APPENDIX

The Effect of Variation on Kanban Systems

This appendix demonstrates the effect of variation in replenishment times and material consumption rates on the number of kanban cards required to sustain production and, therefore, on the maximum amount of inventory needed at the point of use and its resupply. The demonstration is provided by a spreadsheet model, which simulates the dynamics of a kanban replenishment system with varying degrees of uncertainty. The spreadsheet allows for a hands-on experience that helps to develop intuition about kanban dynamics. While our intent is primarily to illustrate the effect of uncertainty, this model could also be used to estimate the cards required in an actual process. The spreadsheet model can be downloaded from the website http://mason.wm.edu/faculty/bradley_j/LeanBook/ and its file name is KanbanSimulation.xlsm.

Spreadsheet Model Overview

Many or, perhaps, most readers will be concerned with the model for purposes of illustration rather than as a decision tool, and so the structure of the spreadsheet model and instructions for its use in experimentation are described first without delving into the details of its construction. In a subsequent section, a more detailed description is provided for those interested in adapting the model as a decision tool. In that section, we provide a detailed description of the model's construction and sufficient detail about the formulae and the Visual Basic for Applications (VBA) programming used in the model such that a reader with the requisite spreadsheet and programming skills could either construct a similar model for their particular application or adapt the current model.

The model simulates a one-card kanban system that is used to replenish parts to a workstation in an assembly process from a supermarket inventory area. The operator at that workstation removes the kanban card from a carton of parts before the first part is removed from the new carton and places the kanban card in a card holder that is affixed to the material rack (see Figure A.1). Various methods can be used to collect these cards, but we assume that the same material handler who delivers parts also picks up the cards: At each instance when the material handler delivers cartons to the workstation they also pick up the unattached kanban cards from the card holder that signal the material requirements for the next delivery. The time that elapses between subsequent replenishment visits would vary depending, in part, on how many cartons of parts were needed for the workstation on which we are focusing. It is likely, however, that this material handler would also be replenishing a number of other parts for other workstations in the vicinity. If the workstation analyzed in our model is one of many workstations served by this material handler, then it is reasonably accurate to assume that the varying times between replenishment deliveries are (statistically) independent of the number of cartons needed on each run for our workstation because it is a small portion of the load that is being replenished.

The consumption rate of parts might also vary over time, especially in systems where multiple products are made, due to the varying mix of products being produced. Unpredictable downtime and other factors can also cause the consumption rate to vary.

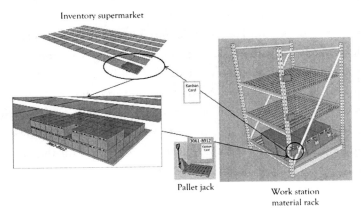

Inventory supermarket

Pallet jack

Work station
material rack

Figure A.1 One-card kanban replenishment process

The model replicates variation in replenishment response time and the material consumption rate by generating numbers that vary with a certain mean and standard deviation and, more specifically, whose variation is described by a particular probability distribution. We use the normal distribution in this analysis. While this distribution might likely be inappropriate for most circumstances, it is easy to use in a demonstration, it illustrates the principles of interest, and it is easy to substitute other distributions to adapt the model if it were to be used as a decision tool.

Spreadsheet Model Description

The various regions of the spreadsheet model that implement different facets of the analysis are designated by different colors. While the color coding is apparent upon opening the spreadsheet, it is not rendered in the screenshot of the model in Figure A.2. Thus, this text will refer to the spreadsheet contents by row and column with parenthetical cues regarding the spreadsheet color coding. The parameters that describe the variation in consumption and replenishment times are shown in the cells in Columns A and B, Rows 1 through 6 (blue color coding). The area where the consumption and replenishment of parts are simulated is shown in Columns A through K, Row 9 and below (yellow color coding). This area is divided into three parts. Part 1 models the consumption of parts and Part 2 models replenishment, that is, when the unattached kanban

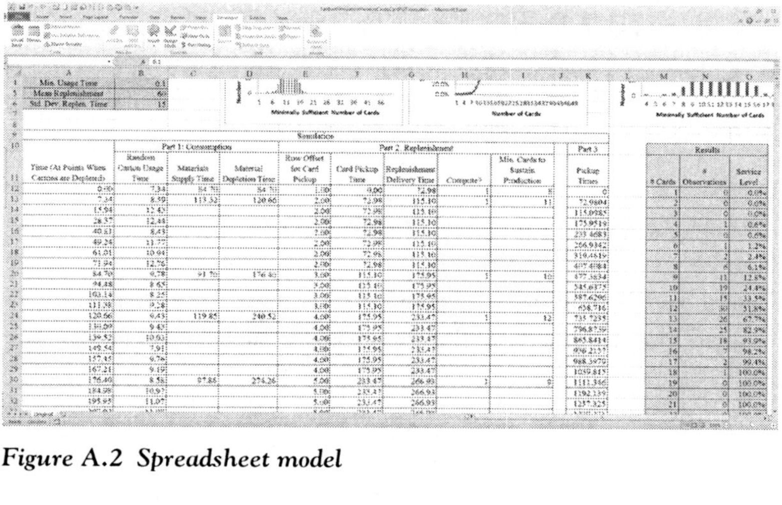

Figure A.2 Spreadsheet model

cards are returned to the workstation attached to a fresh carton. Part 3 generates the times when the material driver arrives at the workstation with parts deliveries. Each row in Parts 1 and 2 of this region contains data corresponds to a particular carton of parts being opened and its associated card being removed and placed in the card holder. Column A shows how much time has elapsed since the beginning of the simulation at each point in time when a new carton of parts is opened. Part 3 contains the varying delivery times, but the values in each row in Part 3 correspond neither to the points in time shown in Column A nor to the data about the cartons being opened in each row of data in Parts 1 and 2: This is a separate stream of data that interact with Parts 1 and 2 to determine the earliest time when an unattached kanban card is returned with a fresh, unopened carton. The results of the simulation analysis are shown in Columns M through O (green color coding) and are described later.

In the material consumption portion of the worksheet (Part 1), numbers varying with the mean (average) and standard deviation specified by the parameters in the upper left corner of the spreadsheet are generated in Column B. Each row in Part 1 and Part 2 corresponds to a point in time when a card is removed from a fresh carton of parts as it is opened. For example, in Row 12 in Figure A.2 a carton is opened at the beginning of the simulation (Column A shows that no time has elapsed) and the parts in that carton last 7.34 minutes before running out. Thus, Column A in the next row below shows an elapsed time of 7.34 minutes when the next carton of parts is opened.

Replenishment activity is reflected in Columns E through I (Part 2), and Column F shows the time when the card associated with each row is picked up for subsequent replacement with a fresh carton of parts: This is the time of the earliest visit from the material handler subsequent to a card being removed from a carton of goods. Calculating this time entails choosing the smallest time from Column K that is equal or greater than the time when each card is detached from its carton, as designated in Column A. This is the first opportunity for the material handler to retrieve the unattached kanban card. The replenishment time in Column G when a fresh carton is returned in response to each card is simply the time of the material handler's next visit after having retrieved an unattached card, which also comes from Column K: This is the time of the next visit subsequent to the times shown for card pickup in Column F.

The construction of the model hinges on one simple observation: At each instant of time when a kanban card is removed from a carton, the production process does not run out of parts if the operation has a sufficient quantity of material to last until the replenishment is received in response to that card. For example, if there are 21 minutes of parts already at the workstation when a kanban card is removed from a new carton and 60 minutes of parts that will be delivered by the material handler in their next visit, then the material handler must return in 81 minutes or less with the new carton in response to the unattached kanban card or the workstation will run out of material.

To determine the minimum number of kanban cards required to sustain production, we focus on the card that is removed from the first carton of parts that is opened after a visit from the material handler. That card will be returned with a fresh carton of parts two visits hence from the current time. Between the point when that card is removed from its carton until it is returned with a replenished carton the operation has some number of cartons on the rack plus it will receive a number of cartons in the next replenishment equal to the number of cards that were just picked up. The sum of those two quantities of cards equals the total number of kanban cards in the system. In order for the workstation's parts requirements to be satisfied without running out, the number of kanban cards (number of cartons of supply) needs to sustain production until the second visit hence. When the *Compute* button is clicked on the spreadsheet model (located in Column C near the top of the worksheet), values are computed in Column I for the minimal number of cards required for each row that corresponds to the first card removed after each visit of the material handler. A VBA program computes the smallest integer value (in Column I) such that the amount of time the workstation is sustained with that many cartons of material (summing materials supply times from Column B using OFFSET() and SUM() functions) as shown in Column C is sufficient until replenishment arrives. The materials supply time is added to the current time (Column A), which determines the material depletion time in Column D: This time must be later than the second subsequent visit from the material handler (in Column G). The VBA program is used to iteratively add 1 to the values in Column I, starting with 1, until the material will last until replenishment arrives. Clicking the button labeled *Compute* initiates the VBA program, which generates new random consumption and replenishment times (Columns B and K) and then calculates the minimal number of cards for each row. In this way the replenishment and consumption activities interact and the effect of the varying and uncertain consumption and replenishment times is computed. The number of cards in each instance varies because the usage rate and the interarrival times of the material handler vary.

Note: It is most convenient to make the calculation of the number of kanban cards required using as a reference the time when the first card is removed subsequent to a material handler's visit. The same calculation could be made at any point in time when a card is removed, even if it was not the first card, but we also would need to add to the required cards the number of cards that were already removed and waiting in the card holder for replenishment. Thus, we would obtain the same result regardless of our point of reference for the analysis: as we moved down each row we would compute one fewer card in Column I but we would need to consider that there would be one more card in the card holder awaiting pickup.

The results are summarized by computing in Column N a frequency histogram of the number of material handler replenishment visits when each possible number of cards or cartons was required to sustain production (green color coding). The service level in Column O is the percentage of instances, for each number of kanban cards one might use, when the material handler arrives at the workstation with replenishment to find that stock was sufficient to sustain the production process. The service level for any number of cards in the kanban system is the number of instances where that many, or fewer, cards were required to sustain production divided by the total number of material handler arrivals observed. Simply put, it is the cumulative probability distribution of the results data. The frequency histogram data are shown graphically at the top of the worksheet.

Analysis Using the Spreadsheet Model

The results for the number of kanban cards providing 95 percent service level and the maximum number of cards required over the simulation (100 percent service level) as 1,000 cartons of parts are consumed are shown in Table A.1. In this experiment, the average replenishment time was 60 minutes and the average carton consumption time was

Table A.1 Effect of replenishment and consumption variation on number of kanban cards

(95* SL, Max)	Consumption standard deviation			
Replenishment Time standard deviation	0	1	2	3
0	11, 11	13, 13	13, 14	14, 15
3	13, 13	13, 13	13, 14	14, 15
6	13, 15	14, 15	14, 16	14, 16
9	14, 15	14, 16	14, 16	15, 17
12	15, 17	15, 17	15, 17	15, 18
15	15, 18	16, 18	16, 19	16, 19

10 minutes. The standard deviations of those times varied according to the data shown in Table A.1. Clearly, as the standard deviation of either consumption or replenishment interarrival times increases, more cards and more inventory are required at the material rack and in replenishment in total. The number of cards required for a 95 percent service level increased by almost 50 percent from the situation with no variation to the situation with maximum variation. Over that same range of variation, the maximum number of cards increased by almost 100 percent.

The table also shows that low variation in both replenishment and consumption is required for low inventory levels. Starting from the cell in Table A.1 where there is no variation, an increase in either type of variation causes inventory levels to jump precipitously. Thus, for a system to be lean, all forms of variation must be driven out of the system. Much has been said about how level scheduling is necessary for using a kanban replenishment system. Less is said about the necessity of a reliable replenishment system. If the replenishment intervals have wild variation then level scheduling is ineffective.

The implications here are not only more inventory in the system due to variation, which has a financial cost, but also more space is needed in the assembly process to store materials. This causes more walking time (which is nonvalue-added) and causes the assembly process to be larger, which causes increased investment in larger buildings and racks.

Readers may experiment with this spreadsheet by choosing other averages and standard deviations for replenishment lead times and consumption rates.

Detailed Description of Spreadsheet Formulae and Programming

We discuss in this section the more technical spreadsheet formulae and VBA programming used in the kanban analysis worksheet. A logical description of how these two pieces of the analysis interact requires that we discuss the spreadsheet formulas and the VBA programming code in an integrated manner rather than describing one and then the other.

We do not describe how to draw random numbers from probability distributions here, but a user interested in modifying the spreadsheet will need to be familiar with that technique, which is described in many references including Law and Kelton.[1] The kanban model uses the inverse normal distribution (NORMINV()) along with the mean and standard deviation of case usage time from the parameter region of the worksheet (blue color coding) to generate the varying times in Column B. Similarly, the varying arrival times of the material handler, in Column K, are generated with NORMINV() also: Each arrival time is a varying normal random variable added to the last arrival time. (The time that passes between each of the material handler's successive visits to the workstation are called interarrival times.) New instances of these two streams of varying quantities are generated when the worksheet is recalculated, either by pressing F9 or through the VBA code when the *Compute* button is clicked. In this case, clicking F9 will make the analysis invalid because many of the calculations that require the VBA code need to be refreshed also.

The VBA code can be observed by first enabling the *Developer* Ribbon by clicking on *File*, then *Options*, and then checking the box indicated in Figure A.3 (which depicts Excel 2010 although Excel 2013 is similar). Clicking on *Visual Basic* icon on the Developer Ribbon (see Figure A.4) makes the VBA programming code visible (see Figure A.5). The first thing this code does is recalculate the worksheet using the Me.Calculate statement and, in so doing, it generates new case usage and material handler interarrival times. Once the varying case usage and interarrival times are

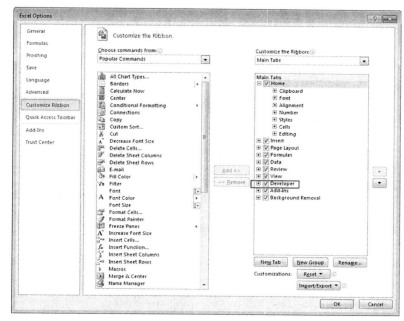

Figure A.3 Enabling Developer Ribbon

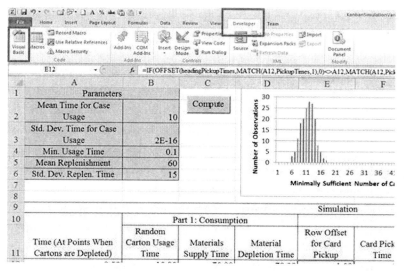

Figure A.4 Accessing the VBA programming code

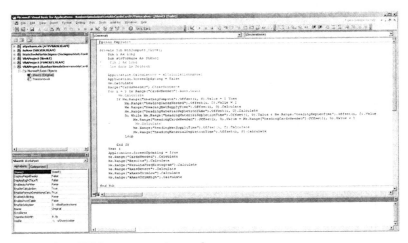

Figure A.5 *VBA programming code*

generated, the contents of Column I where the number of required kanban cards will be computed are cleared using the Range("CardsNeeded"). ClearContents statement: Range names are used liberally in the workbook to make the VBA code robust to changes in the spreadsheet. With new case usage times having been generated, it is known at what times each carton is opened (Column A). Then, using the MATCH() function in Column E the time can be computed in Column F when the material handler will pick up each card, which is the earliest visit after a carton is opened. Subsequent replenishment comes at the next visit, which is the time specified in Column G, which again uses the offset computed in Column E plus 1. The first card removed after each visit, which are the reference points for our analysis as previously described, are identified in Column H using IF() statements. Cells in that column containing a value of 1 indicate to the VBA code that the minimum number of cards that would keep the workstation from running out of material given the particular case usage and arrival times should be computed for that row. The VBA code uses a Do-While loop nested within a For-Next loop to increment the values in Column I until the material depletion time in Column D is at least as great as when the material handler arrives with replenishment. The For-Next loop causes this computation to be made in each row. A number of Range.Calculate statements at the end of the VBA Code refresh the frequency histogram data and the graphs.

This formulation has two implicit assumptions:

- The description of the system being replenished by a single material handler prevents the occurrence of replenishment crossover where the replenishment pursuant to a kanban card picked up at a later time arrives before the replenishment in response to a kanban card that was picked up at an earlier time. The analysis would need to be revised if the replenishment process allowed replenishment deliveries to cross over, which would be beneficial to operation resulting in reduced inventory requirements.
- In computing the minimum number of cards required to maintain operations at each replenishment event, the analysis ignores the effect if the workstation were to run out of inventory, which would be the case if the number of cards provided a service level less than 100 percent. If the workstation were allowed to be depleted of inventory, the analysis would need to be modified to accommodate that situation. This could be accomplished by modifying the analysis for a specific, constant number of cards in the system.

Notes

Chapter 2

1. Stretch wrap machines wrap plastic film, much like the plastic wrap used in kitchens, around loose boxes and the pallet on which they are placed so the pallet and the boxes can be handled as a unit. In prior years, banding iron was used for this purpose.
2. Womack and Jones (1996).
3. Pisowicz (2003).
4. Wysocki (2004).
5. Weed (2010).
6. Crosby (1980).

Chapter 4

1. Finney (2006).
2. Blossom (2011).
3. See http://mason.wm.edu/faculty/bradley_j/LeanBook for Excel value stream map icons
4. See http://mason.wm.edu/faculty/bradley_j/LeanBook for PowerPoint value stream map icons
5. Nakane and Hall (2002); Liker (2004).
6. Spear and Kenagy (2005).
7. Rosenthal (2007).
8. BP (British Petroleum) (2010).
9. Spear and Kenagy (2005).

Chapter 5

1. Sluti (1995).
2. Garvin and March (1990).
3. Gawande (2009).
4. Spear and Bowen (1999).
5. Gross (1996).

Chapter 7

1. Templates for Standard Work are provided electronically at http://mason.wm.edu/faculty/bradley_j/LeanBook

Chapter 8

1. P. Blossom, personal communication, March 21, 2011.

Chapter 9

1. Garvin and March (1990).
2. Many spelling variants can be found for poka yoke.

Chapter 10

1. Monden (1998).
2. Goldratt (2004).

Chapter 11

1. The term utilization can be defined in many ways, and a straightforward definition is used here to facilitate exposition. For example, utilization can be defined as the percentage of available hours that are used, and how available hours are computed might vary substantially from case to case. Available hours might exclude time for maintenance and changeovers or other activities that are considered essential but nonproductive. Utilization might also be calculated by scheduled hours rather than total available hours; here, scheduled hours might be only those hours where a workstation is scheduled for production.
2. Heskett and Hallowell (1993).
3. Hyer and Wemmerlöv (2002); Monden (1998).

Chapter 12

1. See Bradley and Conway (2003) for a derivation of this result.
2. See Bradley and Conway (2003) for a derivation of this result.
3. Shingo (1985).
4. The data for this exercise are available at http://mason.wm.edu/faculty/bradley_j/LeanBook

Chapter 13

1. An electronic version of this charter is available at http://mason.wm.edu/faculty/bradley_j/LeanBook
2. Spear and Kenagy (2005).

Chapter 14

1. Goldratt (2004).

Appendix

1. Law and Kelton (1991).

References

Blossom, P. February 12, 2011. "Eliminating Waste." http://leanpracticecoach. com

BP (British Petroleum). September 8, 2010. Deepwater Horizon: Accident Investigation Report. http://www.washingtonpost.com/wp-srv/politics/ documents/Deepwater_Horizon_Accident_Investigation_Report_ Executive_summary.pdf

Bradley, J.R., and R.W. Conway. 2003. "Managing Cyclic Inventories." *Production and Operations Management* 12, no. 4, pp. 464–79.

Crosby, P.B. 1980. *Quality Is Free: The Art of Making Quality Certain*. New York: Signet.

Finney, P.B. 2006. "Loading an Airliner Is Rocket Science." *The New York Times*, November 14. http://www.nytimes.com/2006/11/14/business/14boarding. html?pagewanted=all

Garvin, D.A., and A. March. February 28, 1990. *A Note on Quality: The Views of Deming, Juran, and Crosby* (Harvard Business School Background Note No. 9-687-011). Cambridge, MA: Harvard Business School Publishing.

Gawande, A. 2009. *The Checklist Manifesto*. New York: Metropolitan Books.

Goldratt, E.M. 2004. *The Goal: A Process of Ongoing Improvement*. 3rd rev. ed. Great Barrington, MA: North River Press.

Gross, D. 1996. *Greatest Business Stories of All Time*. Hoboken, NJ: Wiley.

Heskett, J.L., and R. Hallowell. August 5, 1993. *USAA: Business Process Review for the Great Lakes Region* (HBS Case No. 9-694-024). Cambridge, MA: Harvard Business School Publishing.

Hyer, N., and U. Wemmerlöv. 2002. *Reorganizing the Factory: Competing through Cellular Manufacturing*. Portland, OR: Productivity Press.

Law, A.M., and W.D. Kelton. 1991. *Simulation Modeling and Analysis*. 2nd ed. New York: McGraw-Hill.

Liker, J.K. 2004. *The Toyota Way: 14 Management Principles from the World's Greatest Manufacturer*. New York: McGraw-Hill.

Monden, Y. 1998. *Toyota Production System: An Integrated Approach to Just-In-Time*. Norcross, GA: Institute of Industrial Engineers.

Nakane, J., and R.W. Hall. 2002. "Ohno's Method." *Target* 18, no. 1, pp. 6–15.

Pisowicz, V. February, 2003. "Why Can't We Eliminate Waste in the ASC at West Penn?" PRHI Executive Summary. http://www.prhi.org/docs/ February_2003.pdf

Rosenthal, M. July 9, 2007. "The Chalk Circle." http://theleanthinker.com/2007/07/09/the-chalk-circle/

Shingo, S. 1985. *A Revolution in Manufacturing: The SMED System*. Cambridge, MA: Productivity Press.

Sluti, D.G. 1995. "Common Cause or Special Cause?" In *Games and Exercises for Operations Management: Hands-on Learning Activities For Basic Concepts and Tools*, eds. J.N. Heineke and L.C. Meile, 187–9. Upper Saddle River, NJ: Prentice Hall.

Spear, S., and H.K. Bowen. 1999. "Decoding the DNA of the Toyota Production System." *Harvard Business Review* 77, no. 5, pp. 96–106.

Spear, S.J., and J. Kenagy. August 25, 2005. *Deaconess-Glover Hospital (A)* (HBS Case No. 9-601-022). Cambridge, MA: Harvard Business School Publishing.

Weed, J. 2010. "Factory Finesse, at the Hospital." *The New York Times*, July 11, http://query.nytimes.com/gst/fullpage.html?res=9E06E6DB173BF932A25754C0A9669D8B63

Womack, J.P., and D.T. Jones. 1996. "Beyond Toyota: How to Root Out Waste and Pursue Perfection." *Harvard Business Review* 74, no. 5, pp. 140–58.

Wysocki, B., Jr. April 9, 2004. "'Industrial Strength': To Fix Health Care, Hospitals Take Tips From Factory Floor—Adopting Toyota Techniques Can Cut Costs, Wait Times; Ferreting Out an Infection—What's Paul O'Neill Been Up to?" *The Wall Street Journal* p. A1.

Index

OTHER TITLES IN OUR SUPPLY AND OPERATIONS MANAGEMENT COLLECTION

Johnny Rungtusanatham, The Ohio State University, Editor

- *Global Supply Chain Management* by Matt Drake
- *Managing Commodity Price Risk: A Supply Chain Perspective* by George A. Zsidisin and Janet Hartley
- *Improving Business Performance With Lean* by James Bradley
- *RFID for the Supply Chain and Operations Professional* by Pamela Zelbst and Victor Sower
- *Insightful Quality: Beyond Continuous Improvement* by Victor Sower and Frank Fair
- *Sustainability Delivered: Designing Socially and Environmentally Responsible Supply Chains* by Madeleine Pullman and Margaret Sauter
- *Sustainable Operations and Closed-Loop Supply Chains* by Gilvan Souza
- *Mapping Workflows and Managing Knowledge: Capturing Formal and Tacit Knowledge to Improve Performance* by John Kmetz
- *Supply Chain Planning: Practical Frameworks for Superior Performance* by Matthew Liberatore and Tan Miller
- *Understanding the Dynamics of the Value Chain* by William Presutti and John Mawhinney
- *An Introduction to Supply Chain Management: A Global Supply Chain Support Perspective* by Edmund Prater and Kim Whitehead
- *Sourcing to Support the Green Initiative* by Lisa Ellram and Wendy Tate
- *Designing Supply Chains for New Product Development* by Antonio Arreola-Risa and Barry Keys
- *Metric Dashboards for Operations and Supply Chain Excellence* by Jaideep Motwani and Rob Ptacek
- *Statistical Process Control for Managers* by Victor E. Sower
- *Supply Chain Information Technology, Second Edition* by David L. Olson
- *Supply Chain Risk Management: Tools for Analysis, Second Edition* by David L. Olson
- *International Operations: How Multiple International Environments Impact Productivity and Location Decisions* by Harm-Jan Steenhuis
- *Better Business Decisions Using Cost Modeling, Second Edition* by Victor Sower and Christopher Sower

Announcing the Business Expert Press Digital Library

Concise e-books business students need for classroom and research

This book can also be purchased in an e-book collection by your library as

- a one-time purchase,
- that is owned forever,
- allows for simultaneous readers,
- has no restrictions on printing, and
- can be downloaded as PDFs from within the library community.

Our digital library collections are a great solution to beat the rising cost of textbooks. E-books can be loaded into their course management systems or onto students' e-book readers.
The **Business Expert Press** digital libraries are very affordable, with no obligation to buy in future years. For more information, please visit **www.businessexpertpress.com/librarians**. To set up a trial in the United States, please email **sales@businessexpertpress.com**.